BEGGING QUESTIONS

Other related titles from
The Policy Press include:

New poverty series edited by David Gordon
Studies in poverty, inequality and social exclusion

Tackling inequalities: Where are we now and what can be done?
Christina Pantazis and David Gordon
Paperback   ISBN 1 86134 146 6   £15.99 tbc

The widening gap: Health inequalities and policy in Britain
Mary Shaw, Daniel Dorling, David Gordon and George Davey Smith
Paperback   ISBN 1 86134 142 3   £14.99 tbc

Inequalities in health: The evidence
The evidence presented to the Independent Inquiry into Inequalities in
Health, chaired by Sir Donald Acheson
Edited by David Gordon, Mary Shaw, Daniel Dorling and
George Davey Smith
Paperback   ISBN 1 86134 174 1   £16.99 tbc

Not mad, bad or young enough: Helping young homeless people with mental
health problems
Lynn Watson
Paperback ISBN 1 86134 145 8 £11.95

Homelessness: Exploring the new terrain
Edited by Patricia Kennett and Alex Marsh
Paperback   ISBN 1 86134 150 4   £18.99
Hardback   ISBN 1 86134 167 9   £45.00

Home Sweet Home?: The impact of poor housing on health
Alex Marsh, David Gordon, Christina Pantazis and Pauline Heslop
Paperback   ISBN 1 86134 176 8   £16.99

All the above titles are available from
Biblios Publishers' Distribution Services Ltd
Star Road, Partridge Green, West Sussex RH13 8LD, UK
Telephone +44 (0)1403 710851, Fax +44 (0)1403 711143

BEGGING QUESTIONS

Street-level economic activity and social policy failure

Edited by Hartley Dean

First published in Great Britain in 1999 by

The Policy Press
University of Bristol
34 Tyndall's Park Road
Bristol BS8 1PY
UK

Tel +44 (01)117 954 6800
Fax +44 (0)117 973 7308
e-mail tpp@bristol.ac.uk
http://www.bristol.ac.uk/Publications/TPP

British Library Cataloguing in Publication Data
A catalogue record for this book is available from the British Library

ISBN 1 86134 155 5

Hartley Dean is Professor of Social Policy at the University of Luton.

Photograph used on front cover kindly supplied by Jacky Chapman/Format Photographers.

Cover design by Qube Design Associates, Bristol.

Printed and bound in Great Britain by Hobbs the Printers Ltd, Southampton.

Contents

Acknowledgements

This book stems from a national day workshop, entitled 'Begging and street-level economic activity', sponsored by the Social Policy Association, and held in September 1998 at the University of Luton. Some of the chapters were first presented as papers in the course of the workshop. Others had been prepared beforehand or were commissioned as responses to themes which emerged during discussion. The purpose of the workshop was to stimulate the development of a research agenda. While this book is a tangible outcome of that process, it is no more than a first step. The contributors to this volume, though bringing a range of different perspectives and emphases to the themes I outline in the introduction, succeed in demonstrating the complexity of begging and street-level economic activity as subjects for research, and the considerable scope for further investigation.

I should like to thank the following: all the contributors for generating what I believe to be a stimulating set of papers; the Social Policy Association and the University of Luton for supporting the original workshop; my colleagues, Tony Fitzpatrick and Svetlana Sidorenko-Stephenson for reading and helpfully commenting on a penultimate working draft of the book; and The Policy Press and Dawn Pudney for accepting and efficiently preparing the book for publication. As editor I am more than prepared to accept responsibility for the limitations of the book as a whole. I acknowledge that this is not the last word on begging as a social policy issue, nor was it ever intended to be. My hope, nonetheless, is that the book will play a part in prompting debate, in promoting more extensive research, and in developing a more comprehensive analysis.

Hartley Dean

List of contributors

Michael Adler	Professor of Social Policy at the University of Edinburgh
Bob Coles	Senior Lecturer in Social Policy at the University of York
Gary Craig	Professor of Social Policy at the University of Lincoln and Humberside
Hartley Dean	Professor of Social Policy at the University of Luton
Angus Erskine	Senior Lecturer in Social Policy at the University of Stirling
Keir Gale	Community Development Worker with Luton Borough Council
Joe Hermer	Research Student at the University of Oxford
Roger Hopkins Burke	Lecturer in Criminal Justice Studies at the Scarman Centre for the Study of Public Order, University of Leicester
Jane Jones	Research Student at the University of Wales Bangor
Bill Jordan	Professor of Social Policy at the Universities of Exeter and Huddersfield
Ian McIntosh	Lecturer in Sociology at the University of Stirling
Margaret Melrose	Researcher at the University of Luton
Andrew Travers	Lecturer in Sociology at the University of Exeter
Julia Wardhaugh	Senior Lecturer in Sociology at the University of Wales Bangor

ONE

Introduction

Hartley Dean

The subject of begging and the activities of those who get their living (or a part of it) on the street have been neglected by social policy. They have been observed by historians, human geographers, sociologists and criminologists; they have been expounded upon by politicians and journalists; yet first and foremost begging is – or rather ought to be – a primary concern of social policy. This is for two reasons. First, social policy as a substantive phenomenon in the industrial capitalist era had its very origins as a response to begging. The institutions and techniques that emerged and developed to constitute the modern welfare state entailed the organisation of alms-giving and the regulation of provision for human need. Second, social policy as a critical academic discipline ought to be more alive than any other to the issues raised by what the European Foundation on Social Quality (1997) has called "the growing number of beggars, tramps and homeless in the cities of Europe". Though the evidence has been largely anecdotal, recent changes in British social security, housing and mental health provision would appear to have exacerbated the extent of begging. Certainly, the persistence of begging may be construed as an indictment of the failures of social policy in the Western world. Though begging tends to be intimately linked to street-homelessness, it is necessary to address the phenomenon more generally – together, for example, with busking, *Big Issue* selling[1] and unlicensed street trading – as a distinctive form of informal economic activity that reflects fundamental changes in the economic environment and in the role of the welfare state.

If one so much as scratches the surface of begging as a distinctive phenomenon, it reveals a seam of symbolic meanings and moral conundrums that is as perplexing as it is rich (the pun, were it intended, would be deeply ironic). This is demonstrated in the pages that follow. Before outlining the structure within which the diverse chapters which make up this book have been arranged, it is therefore important to draw out certain key themes which tend to criss-cross the different approaches which have been adopted by the contributors. The themes cannot each be neatly ascribed to particular chapters, but tend, to varying degrees, to permeate several or even all chapters.

The historical legacy and the social phenomenon

Begging is not a new, but an ancient practice. As such it is associated with all kinds of tradition, myth and imagery. I have argued elsewhere (Dean, 1991) that one way to understand the development of the modern welfare state is in terms of a transition "from begging bowl to social wage" (p 37). In place of indiscriminate alms-giving in the medieval era, industrial societies developed more or less elaborate social security systems. Whereas once the relief of destitution was dependent upon the distribution of largesse conspicuously donated by the rich in response to the entreaties of the anonymous poor, modernity required that such largesse be garnered anonymously through taxes, and distributed by way of an administrative process which conspicuously documents each recipient. The transition has involved a relational inversion: social redistribution is no longer associated with the gaze of the multitudinous poor upon the spectacle of their masters' riches, so much as the gaze of the state upon its multitudinous administrative subjects. In the process, as Ignatieff (1984) has observed, where once there was face-to-face contact between donor and recipient, now the giving of gifts to meet the needs of others is achieved through the machinery of the state. One of the recurring themes in this book relates to *the significance of the face-to-face contact* that is entailed between the beggar and the passer-by.

Associated with the transition from begging bowl to social wage (Dean, 1991), there have been other transitions: a transition from corporal to pecuniary sanctions and from repression to 'discipline' – in the sense that Foucault (1977) has accorded to that term. As early as 1349 in England the Statute of Labourers had sought to ensure that "valiant beggars ... may be compelled to labour for their necessary living" (cited in de Schweinitz, 1961) and in the course of the next 200 years increasingly violent and spectacular physical punishments were visited upon vagrants and beggars. The advent of the Elizabethan and later the Victorian Poor Laws portended the introduction of less violent – though no less coercive – means for the control of vagrancy and begging. At the root of these more sophisticated regulatory approaches, both in Britain and across Western Europe, was a *preoccupation with the classification of beggars* in particular, and the poor in general. To the extent that such a preoccupation survives to the present day, this constitutes the second of the themes to recur in some of the chapters which follow.

Classification is the necessary precursor to regulation. The point about Martin Luther's celebrated injunction – that "every town and village should know their own paupers ... and assist [only] them" (*Liber Vagatorum* ['The Book of Beggars'], 1528) – is that knowledge is power. The distinction to be made between deserving and undeserving classes of supplicant was fundamental to the operation of the Poor Laws and remains so, in countless subtle ways, in modern social security systems. It is a distinction that at various times between the 16th and 19th centuries informed the process of licensing, certification or 'badging' of certain beggars (a practice of which the authorisation or 'badging' of contemporary *Big Issue* vendors is strongly redolent). It is the same distinction that informed decisions about which paupers were to be incarcerated in the workhouse and which might be permitted 'out relief'. From such distinctions criteria have developed affecting the terms on which specific kinds of entitlement to social security benefits may be enjoyed. The process of classification is more than an administrative device; it has far reaching disciplinary consequences for supplicants and for non-supplicants alike.

Thus another of the recurring themes of the book relates to *the stigma that is associated with begging*. The voices of contemporary beggars are heard in some of the chapters and attest to this. More widely, however, it would seem that begging as a means of survival has been constituted as an activity that is beyond the pale of acceptability. Recent research among low-income families asked what approaches they might adopt to maximise income when money was short (Kempson et al, 1994). In the 'hierarchy' of favoured approaches this revealed, obtaining better paid (and legitimate) employment was regarded as the best solution, while petty crime was cited as a last resort: "begging was so unacceptable that it did not appear on the list at all" (Kempson et al, 1994, p 275). As an economic activity, begging is so tainted by its long association with punishment, regulation and suspicion that in the popular imagination it may be perceived to be even 'worse' than other forms of criminal behaviour.

Other voices to be heard in parts of the book are those not of beggars, but of the passers-by from whom beggars solicit money. The recurring theme here relates to *the judgements required of the passer-by*. At its simplest, the dilemma any of us face when confronted by a beggar is whether to give money or not, yet beneath this dilemma lies the necessity for the kind of classificatory judgements that had supposedly been colonised by social administrators: is the supplicant deserving or undeserving, genuine or fraudulent? Judgements about beggars and other people in the street are fashioned, blighted or distorted by an array of factors. In popular and political discourse alike there is a tendency to conflate with begging other activities which occur on the street, some of which are not economic in nature at all, such as rough sleeping or street drinking. The passer-by makes judgements (or, often involuntarily, forms impressions) about whether the people they pass are innocuous or threatening, passive or aggressive. The traditional 'tramp' described by Orwell (1933) may be seen as relatively unthreatening, while for some people the young rough sleeper may be construed as potentially dangerous merely by his or her presence in a public place. Begging and the imagery and assumptions which surround it are but one of the elements implicated in the deeply ambiguous symbolism that surrounds our awareness of the space that is 'the street'.

The economic conjuncture and the policy dilemma

The first of the other range of themes that will emerge relates to the suggestion (or the fear) that begging and street-level economic activity are back on the agenda precisely because *the welfare state is being eroded or fundamentally reconstituted*. In the last quarter of the 20th century social welfare has plainly been 'unsettled' (Hughes and Lewis, 1998). In the 1970s, it has been claimed, the welfare state confronted a 'crisis' (for example, Mishra, 1984), and while some argue it has weathered that crisis reasonably well (for example, LeGrand, 1990), others say it has been transformed, restructured, reconstructed, dismantled or even ended (for a summary, see Powell and Hewitt, 1998). However academics may choose to interpret the fate of the welfare state, it is plain from the language of politicians that the welfare machinery is being 'reformed'. Bill Clinton, for example, promised that his reforms in the United States signalled "the end of welfare as we know it" (Waldfogel, 1997), while in the United Kingdom New Labour promises to 'rebuild' the welfare state so as to promote "opportunity not dependence" (DSS, 1998). Significantly, the language of contemporary welfare reform is concerned not so much with poverty as with social exclusion (Levitas, 1996; Dean with Melrose, 1999) and beggars are likely at best to be understood as victims of the latter rather than the former. Whatever the connections might be, the current moral panic over begging coincides with a political process of welfare reform and an ideological realignment which, though concerned to ensure social cohesion, is clearly tolerant of social inequality.

Intimately associated with that political process are global economic trends. Although the concept of globalisation has been contested (Hirst and Thompson, 1996), it is clear that the ascendancy of international capitalism has changed the nature of the world we inhabit. Sociologists variously argue that we are living through an age of late-modernity (Giddens, 1990), post-modernity (Lyotard, 1984), the consumer society (Bauman, 1988), or the risk society (Beck, 1992). Another recurrent theme of this book, therefore, is the possibility that the apparent rise in street-level economic activity is to be understood as part of *the fall-out from economic globalisation and growing inequality*.

Certainly, the beggar is as powerful a symbol in the 'globalised', post-modern world as he or she was in the pre-modern world. The most sweeping expression of that symbolism has been provided by Bauman (1998) who, in seeking to characterise the way in which time and space have been restructured in the process of globalisation, speaks of the schism between two worlds: the world symbolised by the 'tourist', representing the cosmopolitan elite that may move effortlessly across geographical and electronic boundaries; and the world symbolised by the 'vagabond' or beggar, representing the socially excluded that are bound to an immobile and monotonous street existence. Evocative though this is, it is only partly to the point. The rise in begging as a global phenomenon is, in some instances, associated not with some state of stasis into which the poor descend, but with highly dynamic processes of disruption or displacement in time and space: the sheer speed at which communities have become impoverished, for example, in some post-Communist countries; and, in other parts of the world, economically driven migration patterns by which individuals or entire communities become detached from self-sustaining social networks. In the face of the scale of the transformations entailed, there is a considerable danger – from which the contributors to this volume are by no means immune – of overgeneralising both from concepts that are too specific, and evidence that is too limited.

In this wider context, begging is to be understood as just one of a range of informal economic activities by which those driven to the margins of society may get by. Another important theme recurring in several chapters concerns *the place of begging in the spectrum of informal economic activity*. Begging itself is to be distinguished, for example, from busking, pavement art and *Big Issue* selling because no entertainment, service or goods are provided in return for the money that is solicited. In practice, however, the distinction may be tenuous. Historically, to avoid prosecution for begging, people have resorted to token forms of entertainment (tuneless renditions on penny whistles or harmonicas, or even the parading of unusual hats or religious icons) or trading (the sale of matchboxes or bunches of heather) (for example, Ribton-Turner, 1987). While various chapters will address the legal status of begging, it is not always easy to distinguish begging from 'conning', an activity employing a degree of criminal deception. Equally, the line between so-called 'aggressive begging' and robbery is dependent on subjective judgements regarding the degree of violence or the implicit nature of the threat which may accompany a demand for money. At quite a different level it is clearly possible to distinguish begging from the activities of authorised charity collectors, but it can be difficult to distinguish it from more spontaneous appeals (on behalf of striking workers, for example), or from such 'innocent' activities as children's 'trick-or-treating' and carol singing (at Halloween and Christmas respectively), or hitch-hiking by penniless students[2].

However it may be defined, begging plainly is distinguishable from other kinds of "alternative career" (Craine, 1997), which might include casual employment in the informal economy, unlicensed street trading, prostitution drug-dealing, shop-lifting or burglary. Nonetheless, begging – while probably the least favoured of these alternative careers and one that is perhaps seldom engaged in to the exclusion of others – has certain features in common with them: *begging entails both its own economic rationality and a high degree of risk*. This is another powerfully recurring theme of the book. Begging is an economic activity. It may not resemble employment, but it is a sort of 'work' and it entails a money transaction. This is recognised, not only by those who beg, but in the public notices that adorn, for example, some London tube stations, warning that '*professional* beggars operate in the vicinity' (emphasis added). As a 'profession', however, begging is extremely hazardous. There is ample evidence (for example, Fooks and Pantazis, 1999) that people who beg risk violence and predation, not only from passers-by, but from others who get their living on the street.

The immediate dilemma for policy makers is whether beggars require *control* (to regulate their economic enterprise) or *protection* (from the risks they run on the street). This reflects, on the one hand, the dilemma faced by passers-by in their face-to-face confrontations with beggars, and the dilemmas of beggars themselves when they 'elect' to engage in an activity that is both reviled and dangerous. Beyond the immediate dilemma, however, is the question of how the changing nature of social policy intervention will be able effectively to accommodate the needs of those who are drawn or forced into begging and street-level economic activity.

Outline of the book

The book is in three main sections. Part I addresses the historical, political and social context of contemporary begging. Part II relates directly to recent research involving beggars themselves. Part III discusses issues concerning public attitudes towards and the governance of begging. The sections are in no sense water-tight and, as I have already indicated, there are themes and theoretical concerns that cross the boundaries between the sections.

Part I begins with a chapter by myself and Keir Gale that discusses the political context of contemporary begging and the ways in which begging may be understood in relation to theories of citizenship. This discussion is important for understanding how it is that social policy might engage with begging and street-level economic activity at a conceptual level, as well as explaining the sense in which the beggar may be regarded as an emblem of a failing social policy. This is followed by a chapter by Angus Erskine and Ian McIntosh, which helps to locate begging as an historical phenomenon. The chapter demonstrates that key aspects of the way in which begging is perceived and socially constructed exhibit a certain degree of continuity, especially with regard to the contradictions and ambivalences which surround our understanding of begging. Moving from an historical to international context, the next chapter by Bill Jordan considers begging as a global phenomenon. Drawing on observations from a number of countries, the chapter comments on the significance of global economic conditions and labour markets; the cultural factors which influence just how, where and in what circumstances people may resort to begging; the significance of changes in the nature of welfare states, the distribution of public resources and the growth of 'civil indifference'. The chapter concludes with some speculative hypotheses for future research.

Finally in Part I, contemporary begging – in comparison with begging in the past – is characterised by the relative youth of many who beg, and the next chapter by Bob Coles and Gary Craig focuses on those specific aspects of the social policy context which may help to account for this. It points to those policy changes – in such areas as housing, social security, education, training and employment – that have impacted in recent years upon young people in particular, and it speculates on how these are likely among other things to have exacerbated the number of young people who resort to begging.

Part II begins with a chapter by myself and Margaret Melrose that provides an account of the findings from a small pilot study involving interviews with beggars in London, York and Edinburgh. The study demonstrates something of the diversity and the vulnerability of the people who beg; the complexity of their circumstances and the inadequacies of existing social policy arrangements; and the hazardous and precarious nature of begging as an economic activity. This is followed by a chapter by Julia Wardhaugh and Jane Jones that provides an account of another pilot study, this time involving interviews with beggars, buskers and *Big Issue* sellers in a rural coastal strip of North Wales. The chapter is important, not only because it addresses the phenomenon of street-level economic activity in a rural as opposed to an urban context, but because it considers more generally the time and spatial context in which street-level economic activity occurs. Both the Dean and Melrose and the Wardhaugh and Jones studies are exploratory and primarily qualitative in nature, and they rely on small interview samples. As ever, we must be cautious about generalising from such studies, but the findings presented here provide a valuable basis for reflection and discussion: there is such a dearth of other empirical work on begging upon which to draw and the very purpose of the studies – like that of this book – is to inform the development of further research.

A very different kind of analysis is provided in the chapter by Andrew Travers. The empirical study on which this draws involved ethnographic methods and the development of theoretical frameworks, or 'cartographies', based in symbolic interactionism. The essential argument of the chapter is that the face-to-face interaction between beggar and passer-by exemplifies *in extremis* certain processes by which any one of us may fuel the creation of another's self-identity: it is a highly abstract analysis which, nonetheless, provides insights into what is discomfiting about such interactions. The final chapter in this section is by Margaret Melrose and addresses the practical, methodological and ethical difficulties associated with fieldwork and ethnographic studies of begging and street level-economic activity: in particular, questions of sampling strategy, ethical issues, the very particular personal and emotional hazards involved in such work, and the complex problems associated with gender dynamics and 'placing' in the interview situation.

Part III begins with a chapter by Michael Adler on public attitudes to begging. This presents a wide-ranging discussion of the theoretical issues which the author hopes to address through a forthcoming national study of social attitudes to begging. This is followed by a chapter by Ian McIntosh and Angus Erskine that reports the findings of a local empirical study of public attitudes to begging, based on discursive interviews conducted in Edinburgh. The findings illustrate the ambivalence and moral confusion experienced by passers-by, further illuminating aspects of the discussion in both Chapters Two and Eight.

How then are the sensibilities of public opinion to be addressed? In his chapter, Joe Hermer describes and analyses an innovative scheme in Winchester in which the City Council, high street retailers and the police collaborated to give shoppers the opportunity of making donations to local homeless persons' shelters, while at the same time concerted steps were taken to remove beggars and street-people from the city centre. Finally, Roger Hopkins Burke's chapter provides a discussion of 'zero-tolerance' policing methods and begging and, drawing on a study of begging in Leicester, the author presents his own conclusions about what forms of intervention might be more appropriate.

Notes

[1] The *Big Issue* is a weekly newspaper, first launched in the United Kingdom in 1991, that is distributed for sale by homeless people as an alternative to begging. Vendors are entitled to retain a proportion of their takings and the paper itself champions the cause of homeless people.

[2] I am grateful to Pam Dean and David Berridge respectively for these last two examples.

References

Bauman, Z. (1988) *Freedom*, Buckingham: Open University Press.

Bauman, Z. (1998) *Globalisation*, Cambridge: Polity Press.

Beck, U. (1992) *The risk society: Towards a new modernity*, London: Sage Publications.

Craine, S. (1997) 'The black magic roundabout: Cyclical transitions, social exclusion and alternative careers', in R. MacDonald (ed) *Youth, the 'underclass' and social exclusion*, London: Routledge.

de Schweinitz, K. (1961) *England's road to social security*, Pennsylvania, PA: Perpetua.

Dean, H. (1991) *Social security and social control*, London: Routledge.

Dean, H. with Melrose, M. (1999) *Poverty, riches and social citizenship*, Basingstoke: Macmillan.

DSS (Department of Social Security) (1998) *New ambitions for our country: A new contract for welfare*, Cm 3805, London: The Stationery Office.

European Foundation on Social Quality (1997) *Amsterdam Declaration on the social quality of Europe*, 10 June, Amsterdam.

Fooks, G. and Pantazis, C. (1999) 'Criminalisation of homelessness, begging and street living', in P. Kennett and A. Marsh (eds) *Homelessness: Exploring the new terrain*, Bristol: The Policy Press.

Foucault, M. (1977) *Discipline and punish*, Harmondsworth: Penguin.

Giddens, A. (1990) *The consequences of modernity*, Cambridge: Polity Press.

Hirst, P. and Thompson, G. (1996) *Globalisation in question*, Cambridge: Polity Press.

Hughes, G. and Lewis, G. (eds) *Unsettling welfare: The reconstruction of social policy*, London: Routledge.

Ignatieff, M. (1984) *The needs of strangers*, London: Chatto and Windus.

Kempson, E., Bryson, A. and Rowlingson, K. (1994) *Hard times? How poor families make ends meet*, London: Policy Studies Institute.

Le Grand, J. (1990) 'The state of welfare', in J. Hills (ed) *The state of welfare: The welfare state in Britain since 1974*, Oxford: Clarendon Press.

Levitas, R. (1996) 'The concept of social exclusion and the new Durkheimian hegemony', *Critical Social Policy*, vol 6, no 2, pp 5-20.

Lyotard, J. (1984) *The postmodern condition*, Manchester: Manchester University Press.

Mishra, R. (1984) *The welfare state in crisis*, Hemel Hempstead: Harvester Wheatsheaf.

Orwell, G. (1933) *Down and out in Paris and London*, London: Gollancz.

Powell, M and Hewitt, M. (1998) 'The end of the welfare state?', *Social Policy and Administration*, vol 32, pp 1-13.

Ribton-Turner, C. (1987) *The history of vagrants and vagrancy and beggars and begging*, London: Chapman Hall.

Waldfogel, J. (1997) 'Ending welfare as we know it: the Personal Responsibility and Work Opportunity Act of 1996', *Benefits*, no 20, pp 11-15.

TWO

Begging and the contradictions of citizenship

Hartley Dean and Keir Gale

I am a Victorian value;
Enterprise and poverty.
I'm totally invisible to the state
And a joy to Mrs. T.

And it's a-begging I shall go-o-o,
A-begging I will go. (**Martin Carthy and Dave Swarbrick,**
'The begging song', **from** *Life and limb*, **Topic Records, 1990**)

This adaptation of the traditional English folk song, originally entitled
'The jovial beggar', mischievously conflates the myth that begging is a
time-honoured 'profession' with the reality that the existence of
contemporary begging signals a failure of the welfare state. The beggar
has always been an ambiguous figure (see Chapter Three in this volume):
an ascetic pilgrim or a lawless wanderer; a deserving object of pity or an
undeserving scrounger; a hapless victim of welfare retrenchment or a
venal representative of an emergent modern underclass. In Britain, neo-
liberal economics and welfare retrenchment in the Thatcherite era were
inclined (if they were not contrived) to drive more people into begging,
while the social democratic instincts of old Labour deplored this process
and sympathised with its victims. In the political discourse of the 1990s,
however, a new consensus has been born. The beggar is no longer either
quaint or pitiable, but is universally reviled.

The seeds of this consensus were sown by Margaret Thatcher's successor
as Conservative Prime Minister, John Major. In 1994 Major condemned
begging, describing it as an 'eyesore': "There is no justification for it these
days. It is a very offensive problem to many people" (*The Guardian*, 28
May 1994). The following September, New Labour's Shadow Home
Secretary similarly spoke out, but more specifically against the "winos,
addicts and squeegee merchants ... whose aggressive begging affronts and

sometimes threatens decent compassionate citizens" (*Times*, 6 September 1995). Then, just a few months before his 1997 General Election victory, Labour Leader Tony Blair, in an interview for *The Big Issue* (ironically, a magazine produced for homeless people to sell as an alternative to begging), announced his support for New York style 'zero-tolerance' policing, which would sweep petty offenders, including beggars, from the streets. Referring to the King's Cross area in London, where such an approach had already been tried on an experimental basis (see Fooks and Pantazis, 1999 and Chapter Thirteen in this volume), Blair claimed that he found the area – with its reputation for drug-dealing, prostitution and begging – "actually quite a frightening place. I'm saying we do have to make our streets safe" (*The Big Issue*, 6–12 January 1997).

In his *Big Issue* interview and in an article in its defence in *The Guardian* (8 January 1997), Blair was at pains to emphasise that 'zero-tolerance' should mean tackling the problems of petty crime and homelessness together but, in so doing, he firmly established a chain of association between begging, homelessness and petty crime. Though the tone may have been different, the essence of the new consensus was cemented later the same week by the Home Office Minister, Conservative MP David Maclean, who declared "There are no genuine beggars. Those who are in need have got all the social benefits they require. Every time we go and check, we find they won't go in hostels. Beggars are doing so out of choice because they find it more pleasant" (quoted in *The Guardian*, 11 January 1997).

In England and Wales, begging is still an offence under the 1824 Vagrancy Act. It is important, nonetheless, to distinguish begging – the unlawful solicitation of a voluntary unilateral gift in a public place – both from other forms of informal economic activity (such as busking, pavement art, windscreen cleaning, unlicensed street trading), and from other criminal offences (such as prostitution, drug-dealing, street robbery involving violence or menace). People who beg are likely to be homeless (Murdoch, 1994; Moore et al, 1995), but this is not necessarily the case. There is evidence that young people without automatic social security entitlements and former patients from mental health institutions are among those to be found begging on Britain's streets, but this does not necessarily characterise who begs or what kind of a problem begging is. Begging may intersect with a variety of other phenomena, but as an economic activity and as a means of subsistence, it needs to be addressed and analysed in its own right.

The particular approach that this chapter will adopt is to explore the different ways in which the beggar may be located as a citizen. Is begging to be understood:

- as a failure of integrative citizenship;
- as a phenomenon beyond the pale of citizenship;
- as the subversion of citizenship;
- as the frustration of aspirations to citizenship;
- as a consequence of 'asymmmetries' of citizenship?

The failure of citizenship

The seminal theory of citizenship provided by Marshall (1950, 1981) supposed that citizenship consists of three kinds of rights which are, or ought to be, mutually interdependent. Social integration and cohesion in democratic-welfare-capitalist society rests on the maintenance of political, social and civil rights. People who beg may have their citizenship curtailed in all three dimensions.

At the level of civil rights, though beggars may in theory enjoy rights, for example, to legal redress, their means of subsistence is itself illegal, making it difficult in practice to enforce such rights. Research suggests that people who beg are themselves frequently subjected to verbal abuse and physical violence (Murdoch, 1994; and see Chapters Six and Thirteen in this volume), yet their status as law breakers may inhibit their willingness or ability to resort to law for their own protection. Similarly, people who beg are likely to be disenfranchised from the political rights of citizenship. Not only might they be prevented by their circumstances from registering to vote, but even if they establish the right to vote, their votes are not courted by politicians. Beggars, as we have seen, exist in political rhetoric as a problem to be addressed, rather than as constituents with distinctive needs and interests.

At the level of social rights, there are two considerations. First, begging bypasses the state welfare system and people who beg do not therefore realise their rights or achieve the citizenship status which derives from participation in the welfare state. This is a failure of citizenship in the sense that social policy is not working. Inadequacy of policy or technical faults in the systems of provision for social security, housing or community care mean either that needs are not properly provided for or that provision that is available does not reach those who need it.

The second consideration takes account of the extent to which social citizenship has a disciplinary 'dark side' (Squires, 1990) and, when this fails, the subject ceases to be a citizen and becomes an outlaw. The receipt of welfare benefits has always implied – and, increasingly, explicitly requires – acceptance of reciprocal obligations, for instance, to seek work or to provide care for dependants. People who beg may be sidestepping such obligations, or may appear to be doing so and may, therefore, be subject both to official and popular opprobrium. More particularly, however, it has been argued elsewhere (Dean, 1991, ch 4) that the administration of social rights serves to identify, categorise and 'partition' the poor. Those who exercise certain social rights are constitued as different kinds of citizen to those who do not. Those who qualify for certain kinds of entitlement are constituted differently from those who qualify for others: 'job seekers', lone parents, disabled people, retirement pensioners – all are subject to different and distinctive regimes; to different gradations of status and constraint. Such categories serve to isolate and locate welfare recipients within a wider framework of citizenship. Beggars stand outside that framework. Such rights as they may purport to exercise are not those defined by social legislation, but those which resonate atavistically with the rights of the destitute poor to alms, or with globally conceived notions of natural or fundamental human rights. They escape the control of the democratic-welfare-capitalist state.

In either case, there is a failure of citizenship in the sense that beggars are not effectively integrated.

Exclusion from citizenship

An alternative way to understand begging is not as a failure of inclusion in the Durkheimian sense (see Levitas, 1996), but as the result of an axiomatic exclusion. The nature of the beggar's deprivation is his or her exclusion from the ordinary realm of citizenship (cf Scott, 1994). The beggar lies beyond the pale of citizenship: by their behaviour or their status beggars place themselves, or they are to be placed, on the outside of any society or citizen-community. The contemporary expression of this argument is to be found in the 'underclass' debate.

Notions akin to that of 'underclass' are not new. Since the 19th century, writers as diverse as Malthus, Marx, Mayhew, Booth and Rowntree all sought to define a class of persons beneath the mainstream of social relations (Morris, 1994). Whether explicitly or by implication, beggars have usually been numbered among a tainted and potentially contaminating minority variously descibed as the dangerous classes, the lumpenproletariat, the residuum. Though it was first used by Myrdal (1992), the particular term 'underclass' was popularised in the USA during the 1980s (see Auletta, 1982) and brought to Britain through the writings of the Right-wing political scientist Charles Murray (1990, 1994). Murray's express concern was that there was a mass of people who no longer subscribe to the values of mainstream society, but embrace criminality and/or welfare dependency as a way of life. Such contentions were suspect, first because membership of Murray's 'underclass' was essentially behaviourally determined and could not be objectively defined; second, because there was little evidence that those supposed to belong to this class (such as long-term welfare dependents) do subscribe to a different or distinctive set of values (see Dean and Taylor-Gooby, 1992).

However, Centre-Left commentators like Frank Field (1989) have also advanced a concept of 'underclass', though membership of his 'underclass' was structurally determined, consisting of all those who have been left behind or excluded from mainstream society. It is also difficult systematically to operationalise Field's 'underclass', since it could be held to incorporate almost anybody dependent on social assistance benefits. It would certainly include unemployed people on means-tested benefits, for example, even though such a group can be looked upon as "not so much stable members of an underclass as unstable members of the working class" (Buck, 1991, p 21). 'Underclass' has therefore become a largely rhetorical device (see Mann, 1994), the object or effect of which is the symbolic exclusion of more or less arbitrarily defined social minorities. Beggars are likely to 'belong' to the underclass, not in the sense that they are necessarily locatable in class terms, but in the sense that they are par excellence symbolically excluded.

Whether they be regarded as culpable villains or perishing victims, the members of any 'underclass' are to be regarded as an actual or potential threat to polite society. In some instances the symbolism of their exclusion has spatial connotations in that the 'underclass' may be segregated from the rest of society in 'ghetto' localities or on local authority housing estates. In this respect, beggars are different. Contact with beggars cannot be so easily avoided since they confront polite society in public places. They are a very potent symbol of the enemy in our midst and/or the waif on our doorstep.

The subversion of citizenship

The third way in which one might think about begging is as a form of resistance to or subversion of citizenship. There have always been those who have consciously rejected the norms of citizenship. In medieval times there were those 'lordless men' who chose to live in isolation as hermits, while making occasional forays to beg for alms; and those who claimed to be within but not of a worldly society, in the manner of mendicant friars and pilgrims (Briggs, 1985). However, we would suggest that neither example may be said to be subversive.

In modern times, there have been subversive life-style movements such as the largely middle-class beatnik and hippy counter-culture (Roszak, 1970), the largely working-class punk movement (Hall and Jefferson, 1976) and the new age travellers movement of the 1980s and 1990s (Earle et al, 1994). All have, to varying degrees, sanctioned a rejection of authority and of mainstream citizenship values. However, though numbers of young people in successive generations have purported to 'drop out' and turn their backs on conventional modes of subsistence, they seldom appear to have resorted to begging and certainly have not celebrated begging as an essential element of a subversive life-style.

Bill Jordan, in a discussion of the ways in which poor and subordinate groups may resist their oppression, includes 'organised begging' as a possible strategy. Jordan points to the ways in which the 'hypercasualisation' of labour markets and the retrenchment of welfare provision result in rational survival strategies involving undeclared informal employment and social security benefit fraud. He then suggests that "there is little conceptual distinction between such interactions and other types of predation – organized begging, drug dealing, prostitution, mugging or burglary" (1996, pp 75-6). However, Jordan offers no evidence that organised begging as a conscious strategy of resistance is taking place. Nor does this view take account of evidence that those who do, for example, participate in informal work and benefit fraud tend to subscribe to the values and aspirations of the social mainstream and are engaged, at best, in a very conservative form of resistance (Dean and Melrose, 1997).

The present authors have anecdotal evidence that at least some contemporary beggars may claim positively to enjoy the begging life-style for the freedom it bestows. One man in his late twenties observed begging in London described himself as a traveller, and said he had recently returned from Italy and intended to go there again for the coming summer. Another told us "I know I'm in control – to put food in my mouth, to get myself a few quid, and I'm not hurting nobody". However, such an allusion to freewheeling ideals is not in our experience typical and, taken in context, appeared more as a self-justifying posture than a statement of principle: the same man later said he hated begging and would prefer to work.

There is, nonetheless, a coherent anarchist tradition which, rejecting all authority, would be capable of embracing begging as a strategy of resistance. Arguing that in a post-scarcity society there is no need to compel everybody to work, Peter Marshall has written – "As with the body, so with society: the health of a free community might well be measured by the number of 'parasites' it could support as an organism without going under" (1993, pp 656-7). It is a matter for empirical investigation whether many of those who do beg, in fact, harbour some version of an anarchistic philosophy. The existing evidence, however, suggests it is unlikely.

Aspirations to citizenship

People do not necessarily engage with discourses of citizenship, so much as relate pragmatically to questions which bear upon their own comfort and security. In this context, they generally do value key elements of a collectivised social democratic settlement, while they are at the same time perhaps increasingly predisposed to ideological principles which would underpin a more individualistic notion of citizenship (Dean with Melrose, 1999). There is a considerable body of evidence (for example, McLaughlin et al, 1989; Dean and Taylor-Gooby, 1992; Kempson et al, 1994) that people in poverty – though they may be dependent on state benefits – are no different: they are, in fact, highly motivated to achieve independence through work and they subscribe generally to the same kinds of ambitions and beliefs as the rest of society. There is further evidence which suggests that the same applies at least to some people who beg.

Research carried out on behalf of the homelessness charity, Crisis, involved interviews with 145 people (aged from 16 to over 60) who were or had been involved in begging (Murdoch, 1994). Participants frequently described the difficulties they experienced when they had first started begging, because of the humiliation involved, although many had become inured to this in time. Asked about their hopes or plans for the future, about a third of the respondents said they wanted an improvement in their housing situation and just over a quarter said they wanted work:

these were their highest priorities. By implication, they aspired to the security and the responsibilities of ordinary citizenship. There was, however, a minority within the Crisis sample who cited neither housing nor work as priorities, although the research did not reveal why this was the case.

The present authors also have tenuous anecdotal evidence that some people who beg may be sustaining each other in accordance with citizenship principles within alternative communities. One of the authors was told by a young woman observed begging in the Hungerford Bridge area in London that she and other homeless people operated a rota, begging on behalf of older homeless people unable to beg for themselves. If this were more than an artful myth, it would appear to be a rare instance of the 'organised begging' referred to by Jordan. In the event, subsequent investigation (see Dean and Melrose, Chapter Six in this volume) failed to validate the basis of this woman's account. What is striking about the story, however, is that this collectivised begging was not portrayed as a predatory act of resistance, but a romantically inspired application of common rights and responsibilities within a heterogeneous social group.

Our contention, therefore, is that some beggars, at least, may be regarded, not as non-citizens, but as aspiring citizens. Whatever circumstances may have lead them into this particular mode of subsistence and form of economic activity, they remain essentially a part of the social and cultural mainstream and subject to the same ideological influences.

'Asymmetrical' or contradictory citizenship

Pat Carlen's work on youth homelessness defines what she calls an asymmetry of citizenship, "with young people being punished for not fulfilling their citizenship obligations even though the state fails to fulfil its duties of nurturance and protection towards them" (1996, p 2). Her claim is that a:

> ... significant number of youngsters, having been brought up to expect that citizenship should reside in social rights rather than property rights, resisted punitive attempts to fob them off with meaningless jobs, store them away in state institutions, or force them to live with families wherein they had been sexually or physically abused; or where poverty-induced conflict was making their lives unbearable. (Carlen, 1996, pp 4-5)

If this assertion is sustainable, the concept of 'asymmetrical' citizenship has, potentially, a much wider application than this. Certainly it would apply to those, including young people, who beg – if their experiences at the hands of the welfare state have amounted to persecution, not protection; if their expectations of citizenship have been betrayed. It has been shown that people who resort to social security benefit fraud often have a sense that they have been betrayed by the welfare state; that there is a gap between their legitimate expectations of the welfare state and their actual experiences of it (Dean and Melrose, 1996; Dean, 1998). It may be that those who resort to begging feel similarly. In the face of betrayal, do people who beg regard themselves as defective citizens, as disempowered citizens, or as disillusioned citizens for whom citizenship has been irredeemably devalued? Carlen herself believes, so far as young homeless people are concerned, that to "define them in" to citizenship or society requires more than coercion and more than "offering them stakes in what they have already rejected" (1996, p 5).

Recent research by the authors began to investigate the contemporary nature of begging as an informal economic activity. Over a nine-month period in 1996-97, systematic observation of begging behaviour was undertaken at several sites in central London. Most of those observed begging (as opposed merely to sitting or sleeping in the street) appeared to be young or relatively young men. Though a few begged quite assertively, none were observed to be aggressive and most, paradoxically, behaved in ways calculated to make themselves as unobtrusive as possible. Some begged silently; others, avoiding eye contact, uttered a sometimes barely audible mantra to passers-by – "Can you spare any change please". It is as if they were engaged in a very private performance, albeit in a public place. The interviews reported by Dean and Melrose in Chapter Six have built upon these preliminary observations.

It must, nonetheless, be remembered that the 'style' of begging that is observable in Britain may be fairly distinctive. Anecdotal evidence suggests that begging in other continental European cities, for example, can be more vocal or flamboyant, or else – even when wholly silent or purposefully restrained – it tends to entail more conspicuous and theatrical modes of supplication than those we have observed in London. This reflects different cultures and traditions, no doubt, but also perhaps different expectations and understandings with regard to the basis of social welfare and the rights of citizenship. These are questions we have not even begun to address.

In the meantime, the model provided by Carlen is fairly compelling. The distribution of rights and obligations within contemporary British society is inherently unequal. There is a contradiction between the extent to which social legislation increasingly now enforces social obligations (to seek work, to maintain one's dependants, to be independent) while restricting social rights (to benefits, housing and social care). While our obligations are being collectivised, our rights are being individualised (Fitzpatrick, 1998), as we are compelled to meet more and more of our needs privately. The beggar is almost an emblem of this contradiction.

Fragile citizenship and fearsome strangers

Begging is both a timeless phenomenon and a new moral issue. The purpose of this chapter has been to provide the beginnings of a theoretical framework within which to understand contemporary begging in Western societies. Begging is an informal economic activity which occurs in the context (whether in spite of or because of) the welfare state. Whatever begging may have symbolised in the past, its present significance is inseparable from contemporary issues concerning the scope of citizenship.

We have put forward five ways of addressing this. First, using conventional notions of citizenship we can see the extent to which beggars are deprived of aspects of their civil, political and social citizenship and that the welfare state is failing to integrate them into society. Second, beggars are also symbolically excluded from the citizen-community, and this has lately been given expression in various theories of 'underclass'. Third, it is possible to think of begging as a subversive, anarchistic activity, which undermines citizenship. Fourth, those who beg are not necessarily immune to prevailing ideological values and beliefs and it is important to consider the extent to which they aspire to the norms of citizenship. Fifth, recent changes in the nature of welfare state citizenship have resulted in an asymmetry or imbalance between the obligations which are imposed on the individual and the rights which are supported by the state, changes which may have particular bearing on the reasons why some people beg.

We might speculate about the reasons why politicians of both Britain's major parties should have united against begging. Is it because the beggar's plea is an ironic reproach to the inexorable shift towards what Jessop (1994) has characterised as a Schumpterian workfare state, in which the imperatives of globalised capitalism hollow out the space between the citizen and the state? There is evidence to suggest that popular understandings of citizenship may be becoming, to some extent, disarticulated from the essentially solidaristic values of a social-democratic welfare state and rearticulated with the narrower contractarian values of the emerging neo-liberal workfare state (Dean with Melrose, 1999). However, while the process of economic globalisation is supposed to homogenise life-styles and cultures at the global level, paradoxically it also fragments communities and identities at the local level (see Rustin, 1989; Jordan, 1996 and Chapter Four in this volume). Against this backdrop, the protectionist welfare state of the 'golden' era of welfare (Esping-Andersen, 1996) is being 'downsized' (Davis, 1993) and restricts itself increasingly to the role of fitting the citizen for the labour market. The beggar seeks to manage not only without the labour market, but without the welfare state and, in so doing reminds us that the nature of our own citizenship has been eroded.

As the stranger in our midst, the beggar now perhaps evokes a new fear. In feudal times, the giving of alms to strangers could sanctify the donor and afford some assurance against the risk of hell-fire and damnation (Lis and Soly, 1979). The emergence of capitalism contrived a resurgence of a primaeval fear of strangers until this could be assuaged or at least modified through the development of the welfare state. The modern welfare state served, it has been argued, at one level to suppress begging and the giving of alms (Offe, 1984), but at another to provide a secular apparatus through which to meet our need for sanctification through giving (Titmuss, 1973). According to Giddens, modernity with its infinitely attenuated network of both market and bureaucratic relations, entailed a 'transformation of intimacy' and the transformation of the 'stranger' into just "someone I don't know" (1990, p 119; see also Ignatieff, 1984). It may be that, as the nature of citizenship and of our belonging changes under conditions of late or post-modernity, begging is assuming a new significance; the stranger is once more to be feared.

Note

An earlier version of this chapter was presented as a paper at the annual conference of the Social Policy Association, 'New politics: new welfare?', University of Lincolnshire and Humberside, Lincoln, 15-17 July 1997. The authors are grateful to Margaret Melrose for helpful comments and suggestions.

References

Auletta, K. (1982) *The underclass*, New York, NY: Random House.

Briggs, A. (1985) *A social history of England*, Harmondsworth: Penguin.

Buck, N. (1991) 'Labour market inequality and polarisation: a household perspective on the idea of an underclass', Paper given at a conference, 'The idea of an underclass in Britain', 26 February, London: Policy Studies Institute.

Carlen, P. (1996) *Jigsaw: A political criminology of youth homelessness*, Buckingham: Open University Press.

Davis, M. (1993) 'Who killed LA? A political autopsy', *New Left Review*, no 197, pp 3-28.

Dean, H. (1991) *Social security and social control*, London: Routledge.

Dean, H. (1998) 'Benefit fraud and citizenship', in P. Taylor-Gooby (ed) *Choice and public policy*, Basingstoke: Macmillan.

Dean, H. and Melrose, M. (1996) 'Unravelling citizenship: the significance of social security benefit fraud', *Critical Social Policy*, vol 16, no 3, pp 3-31.

Dean, H. and Melrose, M. (1997) 'Manageable discord: fraud and resistance in the social security system', *Social Policy and Administration*, vol 31, no 2, pp 103-18.

Dean, H. with Melrose, M. (1999) *Poverty, riches and social citizenship*, Basingstoke: Macmillan.

Dean, H. and Taylor-Gooby, P. (1992) *Dependency culture: The explosion of a myth*, Hemel Hempstead: Harvester Wheatsheaf.

Earle, F., Dearling, A., Whittle, H., Glasse, R. and Gubby (1994) *A time to travel: An introduction to Britain's newer travellers*, Lyme Regis: Enabler Press.

Esping-Andersen, A. (1996) (ed) *Welfare states in transition*, London: Sage Publications.

Field, F. (1989) *Losing out: The emergence of Britain's underclass*, Oxford: Blackwell.

Fitzpatrick,T. (1998) 'The rise of market collectivism', in E. Brunsdon, H. Dean and R.Woods (eds) *Social Policy Review 10*, London: Social Policy Association.

Fooks, G. and Pantazis, C. (1999) 'Criminalisation of homelessness, begging and street living', in P. Kennett and A. Marsh (eds) *Homelessness: Exploring the new terrain*, Bristol: The Policy Press.

Giddens, A. (1990) *The consequences of modernity*, Cambridge: Polity Press.

Hall, S. and Jefferson, T. (1976) *Resistance through rituals: Youth sub-cultures in post-war Britain*, London: Hutchinson.

Ignatieff, M. (1984) *The needs of strangers*, London: Chatto & Windus.

Jessop, B. (1994) 'The transition to post-Fordism and the Schumpterian workfare state', in R. Burrows and B. Loader (eds) *Towards a post-Fordist welfare state?*, London: Routledge, pp 13-37.

Jordan, B. (1996) *A theory of poverty and social exclusion*, Cambridge: Polity Press.

Kempson, E., Bryson, A. and Rowlingson, K. (1994) *Hard times: How poor families make ends meet*, London: Policy Studies Institute.

Levitas, R. (1996) 'The concept of social exclusion and the new Durkheimian hegemony', *Critical Social Policy*, vol 16, no 2, pp 5-20.

Lis, C. and Soly, H. (1979) *Poverty and capitalism in pre-industrial Europe*, Brighton: Wheatsheaf.

McLaughlin, E., Millar, J. and Cooke, K. (1989) *Work and welfare benefits*, Aldershot: Avebury.

Mann, K. (1994) 'Watching the defectives: observers of underclass in the USA, Britain and Australia', *Critical Social Policy*, vol 14, no 2, pp 79-99.

Marshall, P. (1993) *Demanding the impossible: A history of anarchism*, London: Fontana.

Marshall, T.H. (1950) 'Citizenship and social class', reprinted in T.H. Marshall and T. Bottomore (1992) *Citizenship and social class*, London: Pluto.

Marshall, T.H. (1981) *The right to welfare and other essays*, London: Heinemann.

Moore, J., Canter, D., Stockley, D. and Drake, M. (1995) *The faces of homelessness in London*, Aldershot: Dartmouth.

Morris, L. (1994) *Dangerous classes*, London: Routledge.

Murdoch, A. (1994) *We are human too: A study of people who beg*, London: Crisis.

Murray, C. (1990) *The emerging British underclass*, London: Institute of Economic Affairs.

Murray, C. (1994) *Underclass: The crisis deepens*, London: Institute of Economic Affairs.

Myrdal, G. (1992) *Challenge to affluence*, New York, NY: Pantheon.

Offe, C. (1984) *Contradictions of the welfare state*, Cambridge, MA: MIT Press.

Roszak, T. (1970) *The making of a counter-culture: Reflections on the technocratic society and its youthful opposition*, London: Faber & Faber.

Rustin, M. (1989) 'The trouble with new times', in S. Hall and M. Jacques (eds) *New times: The changing face of politics in the 1990s*, London: Lawrence & Wishart.

Scott, J. (1994) *Poverty and wealth: Citizenship, deprivation and privilege*, Harlow: Longman.

Squires, P. (1990) *Anti-social policy: Welfare, ideology and the disciplinary state*, Hemel Hempstead: Harvester Wheatsheaf.

Titmuss, R. (1973) *The gift relationship*, Harmondsworth: Penguin.

THREE

Why begging offends: historical perspectives and continuities

Angus Erskine and Ian McIntosh

This chapter draws on both historical accounts and contemporary reports about begging to point to a remarkable continuity in attitudes towards begging. It asks the question – why is it that begging gives offence? Drawing upon an initial analysis of data from a study of attitudes to begging (for more detail, see Chapter Eleven), it concludes by speculating that what we call the 'begging encounter' is problematic for the donor, because it involves making a moral judgement (cf Chapters Eight and Thirteen in this volume). Making such a judgement in a public place and instantaneously is difficult because it involves either the acceptance of the proffered interpretation of the encounter or the construction of an alternative one. Second, it is also problematic for the supplicant because, while at the same time as he or she creates the encounter, it also involves presenting him or herself as helpless and powerless.

We suggest that because poverty is usually understood as being a passive state, the creation of the interaction by the supplicant in a begging encounter raises a question mark over their claim to be poor. People who are poor are caught in a double bind. If a person is 'genuinely' poor they are not expected to be active. Yet, paradoxically, someone who is 'genuinely' poor is expected to do something about it – to be active. This contradiction may account for the consistency of the accounts of begging and attitudes towards it across centuries. This chapter stresses the continuities in accounts of begging in history. Of course, it is the case that at different times begging has been perceived differently, but this chapter concentrates upon the continuities.

The continuity of accounts

When former Prime Minister, Margaret Thatcher, gave the injunction in her 1987 *Women's Own* interview: "It's our duty to look after ourselves and then, also, to look after our neighbour", she was probably unconsciously returning to an old tradition and debate. Rufinus, writing in the 12th century, cited St Ambrose to argue that it was a person's duty "to love first God, then his parents, then his children, then those of his own household and finally strangers" (Tierney, 1958/59). There has consistently been a view about a hierachy of responsibility for those who experience need. The decision as to who is most worthy of help has occupied minds from 12th-century canonists to Victorian philanthropists to contemporary politicians and journalists. History may show that it was only in the early post-Second World War period in Britain that this moral dilemma was briefly removed from individuals. Titmuss' (1970) exposition of the moral, economic and social benefits of an institutionalised gift relationship and Ignatieff's (1990) assertion that the moral relations between strangers have partly been taken over by the welfare state may, in the last decades of the 20th century, be called into question. Ignatieff pointed to how the arteries of the state transferred income between strangers, enforced responsibilities and mediated our relationships. If that is so, then perhaps the presence of people begging in city streets attests to the arteriosclerosis that is afflicting the state today.

Begging has become a focus for politicians' moralising from John Major to Jack Straw and Tony Blair (see Chapter Two). Reports in newspapers, at regular intervals, reflect a negative perception of begging (see below). Rather than explaining the possible causes of increasing begging, reports consistently portray people who beg as dishonest and undeserving of the sympathy or generosity of the passer-by. These accounts appear to hold some influence in the construction of public attitudes towards begging. A typical example of this is a *Sunday Times* story which set out to expose a fraudulent beggar, who drove a new car to his begging stance, changed into old clothes and then, faking a disability, begged for the day. The *Sunday Times* suggested that such frauds were costing the taxpayer "billions of pounds a year". The story concluded that:

> ... [this] illustrates the cynicism of many of his [the supplicant's] generation who, for whatever reason, are without education or obvious prospects. They are brought up believing that to help oneself, even to other people's money, is acceptable. (*Sunday Times*, 20 February 1994)

In 1993, *The Guardian* carried an article about an English vicar who claimed that beggars "earn £50,000 a year". He is reported as saying:

28

> I've heard of beggars who collect £100 in a few hours ... I once
> refused to give money to someone who claimed that they were
> homeless, but directed them instead to the nearest shelter building.
> They just wandered off in the opposite direction. (*The Guardian,*
> 17 July 1993)

There are two particular features of these sorts of stories which are
interesting: that those who beg may not be what they seem, and questions
about the amount of money that they make.

Fraud and riches

These attitudes have a long pedigree. Just as the *Sunday Times* reported a
beggar faking disability, so does Harman, who, living in Elizabethan
England, classified and studied beggars and vagrants. Harman recounts
the story of one Nicholas Jennings as an example of the wiles of people
begging who appear to be disabled. Jennings claimed to Harman to be
epileptic.

> "A good maister", quoth he, "I have the grevous and paynefull
> dysease called the falynge syckenes". (Viles and Furnivall, 1869,
> p 52)

Harman had his servants follow Jennings and discovered that he was a
fraud. The story of Nicholas Jennings is one that is retold by, among
others, Salgado (1977), Aydelotte (1913) and Pound (1986). From this,
faking epilepsy is portrayed as a popular tactic. Harman claims:

> ... they ... never go without a péece of whyte sope about them,
> which, if they sée cause or present gaine, they wyll prively convey
> the same into their mouth, and so worke the same there, that
> they wyll fome as it were a Boore, and marvelously for a tyme
> torment them selves; and thus deceive they the common people,
> and gayne much. (Viles and Furnivall, 1869, p 51)

Hotten, writing in the 19th century, reports:

> The trick of placing soap in the mouth to produce froth and
> falling down before passers by as though in a fit, common enough

> in London streets a few years ago, is also described [by Martin
> Luther] as one of the old manoeuvres of beggars. (Hotten, 1860,
> p 52)

Garraty, in 1978, commenting on 16th-century beggars, also writes:

> **Beggars often feigned illnesses, for example, by eating some soap
> and then throwing themselves on the ground in convulsions, as
> though epileptic. (Garraty, 1978, p 28)**

It may be that these tales of epilepsy all have their common roots in one
source but their credibility rests upon the willingness of the reader or
listener both to believe the account and to find it shocking. Reading
these accounts from the perspective of the late 20th century, there seems
something wrong with the tale of epilepsy in that the first reaction of
most people to epilepsy is not to give money to the person experiencing
the fit. What it might reveal is Hotten's gullibility. Evidently there was a
potential benefit in faking a fit in medieval times (Temkin, 1971, p 114),
but not in the 19th century. Aydelotte (1913, pp 34-5) reports the case of
Miles Rose, who in 1517/18 confessed to faking epileptic fits because
the sufferer might have a silver cramp ring placed in their hand to relieve
the fit, and they could subsequently make off with the ring. However, it
is both the durability of the tale of the epileptic and the claimed connection
between a faked disability and begging which are interesting: the same
connection as is recounted in the above-mentioned *Sunday Times* story.

The second feature which appears in both the *Sunday Times* and *The
Guardian's* accounts is the amount of money being made by people who
beg. This, too, has a long history. Pound (1986, p 31) suggests that in
Tudor England "some of the vagrants were able to prosper exceedingly".
He provides evidence from two examples. The first, a beggar referred to
by Aydelotte (1913), allegedly made 14/- a day from begging. And who
made 14/- a day? – the same Nicholas Jennings upon whom Harman
reports. It was after Harman had the local constable take Jennings into
custody that they found that he had 14/- on him (Viles and Furnivall,
1869, p 55, and also reported by Salgado [1977] and Aydelotte [1913]).
Harman assumes it was all made in the one day. The second, a woman
who, according to contemporary records in Norwich in 1562, had £44
when brought before the courts for begging. Pound (1986, p 31) uses
these two examples to claim: "many men and women found life on the
road congenial". These judgements are based upon very limited material

and yet are blown up to be representative. We found this among the respondents in our own present day study as well:

> "... there's things in the paper that you read about, things in the paper every night.... I was sort of swayed by the *Evening News* without really sort of going into it for myself."

> "... 'cos the *Evening News* did a thing a while ago and they took photographs of them and they followed them home and they all lived in houses. Nobody knows who is a true beggar."

Moral suspicion and classification

Contemporary and historical accounts convey an enduring antipathy towards begging. In 1528, Martin Luther wrote in his Preface to *The book of beggars* (a work which first appeared around 1509):

> ... princes, lords, counsellors of state, and everybody should be prudent, and cautious in dealing with beggars, and learn that, whereas people will not give and help honest paupers and needy neighbours, as ordained by God, they give, by the persuasion of the devil, and contrary to God's judgement, ten times as much to vagabonds and desperate rogues. (Hotten, 1860, pp 63-5)

Four hundred years later, in the United States, the Wenschler Children IQ Test in 1949, asked examinees:

> Why is it generally better to give money to an organised charity than to a street beggar. (Blau, 1992, p 5)

The three possible correct answers, which were assumed to be indicators of innate intelligence, were: that it assures that money goes to really needy people; or that public charities are in a better position to investigate the merits of the case; or that it was a more orderly way for the donor to contribute.

Why are these moral attitudes towards begging so long-standing and durable? In almost all major religious traditions (Christianity, Islam, Judaism and Buddhism), the giving of alms to strangers is an indication of goodness on the part of the donor. However, in Europe, particularly in the Protestant tradition, the seeking of alms was a sign of weakness. So while to give was good, to receive was a moral failing.

To help avoid the difficulty for passers-by of making decisions on a case-by-case basis, there is a long tradition of classifying beggars by different types. In 1627, an Italian monk published a description of 33 types of false beggars (*Allacrimati* – who burst into tears; *Attarantati* – who pretend to be mad, etc) (Garraty, 1978, p 28). Harman published his 'Caveat or Warening for common cusetors' which classified beggars in the late 16th century (Viles and Furnivall, 1869). Frequently referred to is Luther's *Book of beggars* (Hotten, 1860), which classifies beggars and articulates a commonly held ambivalent attitude towards begging. The book describes 28 different types of beggars. Of these, people are advised to give to a group called 'bregers':

> ... they come plainly and simply to people and ask an alms for God's, or the Holy Virgin's sake: perchance honest paupers with young children, who are known in the town or village wherein they beg, and who would, I doubt not, leave off begging if they could only thrive by their handicraft or other honest means....
> (Hotten, 1860, 69)

There are features to note in this description of honest beggars. Firstly, they come plainly and simply to people; in other words, they are not suspected of using any guile or trick. Secondly, they are known to the donor, which presumably acts as a way of checking whether they are, or are not, 'coming plainly or simply'. Thirdly, they would work if they could. On first sight it may seem that this is the traditional view of the 'deserving poor', but it is interesting to explore further the characteristics of who is undeserving before concluding that being known to the donor or willingness to work are the key aspects of being deserving.

There are five types of beggars which the book recommends the donor may give to after exercising discretion: some vagrants who won't work; poor clergy from nearby churches; those suffering from a curse and having to present gifts to the Saints for a cure; blind beggars; and ex-hangmen. There are two common characteristics of those who can be given to – they are known to the donor and they don't have elaborate stories. In these cases it is not that they would work if they could, because some won't, but it is that they are known and their stories are not complex.

There are eight types of beggar to whom it is recommended that the reader should refuse to give under any circumstances – sometimes with a strong rebuff. The recommendation for 'Klenckners' who sit at church doors with broken legs or missing limbs, claiming to have been imprisoned by heathens or to have had their limbs chopped off in battle, is 'to give them a kick in their hind parts'. Sexual behaviour is also a matter for the donor's consideration, since Klenckners, Luther claims, have the best looking women. Or there are 'Kammesierers' who are young students who gamble and drink – not giving to them is in their own interest.

The descriptions of the remaining types are not accompanied by a recommendation about giving, but the implication is that one should not give to them. Among them are women who appear pregnant; people who seem to be lepers; women who say they have been converted from Judaism to Christianity; people who appear to be pilgrims; and, people with diseases. It is not clear from the *Book of beggars* how the potential donor can distinguish between what the supplicant seems to be (pregnant, diseased, converts etc) and what they are. Therefore, presumably, the decision to give or not to give can be made either on the basis of indiscriminate non-giving by the donor, or by only giving to those who are known to the donor and whose stories therefore can be verified by the donor themselves.

The *Book of beggars* exhibits many of the enduring characteristics of attitudes towards begging and beggars. De Swaan (1988) suggests that there are three dimensions of poverty among the poor in early modern Europe – proximity, disability and docility. These are reflected in Luther's categorisation and that referred to above – the most deserving are those who are near, incapable of work and docile (see Chapter One for discussion of the role of classification in the regulation of the poor). Those who are least deserving are those who are vagrants from elsewhere, capable of working and least law abiding. The characteristic of the deserving is that their lives are transparent and open to inspection. In part this is because the deserving are known to the donor. But also because their rationale for begging is not complicated by a detailed tale of woe. It is this passivity or docility which is central to understanding the distinction between the deserving and the undeserving poor. Where the supplicant is perceived to not be a passive victim, then there is an additional characteristic added to that of workshy in describing them. They may be dangerous. Another way of understanding this focus on deceit is that if the supplicant is unknown to the donor, then they must have moved. In moving they become active and therefore less worthy of alms.

In medieval Europe many of the landless able-bodied poor and ex-servicemen travelled across the country seeking work or returned home and begged. Passports were issued to such vagrants to travel and to seek alms during their travel. These passports provided evidence that they were who they claimed to be. But there is evidence that even the possession of a passport itself, rather than becoming a means of ensuring that only the known begged, resulted in the possessor of the passport becoming suspected of having obtained it fraudulently (Hufton, 1974, p 229).

Moral ambivalence and the beggars' double bind

The double bind within which people who beg were trapped represents a durable ambivalence towards those who are seen as being outside the confines of settled organised societies and social relationships. A feature of many accounts of begging which displays such an ambivalence is that those who beg are imagined as asocial and amoral and, at the same time, being part of an alternative tight knit community with its own social codes and secret language. This moral ambivalence towards beggars is a feature of literature on begging across countries and across centuries (see Chapter Eleven for examples of this ambivalence today).

What is of interest is that, that which gave offence to Harman in the 1600s clearly gives offence to Pound in the 1900s. What offended Luther in the 1500s, offends Hotten in the 1800s, and the *Sunday Times* in the late 1900s. What is the offence and what can old and new tales of beggars tell us of this matter? There may be a truth in these accounts of begging. But, an agnostic analysis needs to reconcile scepticism with these interpretations of begging with the endurance of the accounts and explore the nature of the objections to begging being put forward.

Hotten returns time, and again, to the parallels between Victorian Britain and 16th-century Germany:

> ... they [the tricks] should still be found amongst the arts to deceive thoughtless persons adopted by rogues and tramps at the present day. (Hotten, 1860, p 50)

> ... it is remarkable that many of the tricks and manoeuvres to obtain money from the unthinking but benevolent people of Luther's time should have been practised in this country at an early date. (Hotten, 1860, p 51)

> ... these half-famished looking impostors, with clean aprons, or

**carefully brushed threadbare coats, who stood on the curbs of
the public thoroughfares begging ... were known in Luther's time.
(Hotten, 1860, p 51)**

The central interesting element of Hotten's hostility is based on his
assumption that what people say is untrue, that it is a trick or a strategy
to get the sympathy of the donor – that they are not 'genuine' (cf Chapter
Eleven). The example of the coats or aprons is perhaps the most revealing.
Because their coats have been brushed, because their aprons are clean,
then they must be impostors. What could be interpreted as a sign of
virtue is in fact a proof of vice. This double bind is also found in Harman
writing of 'the Ruffler'. He suggests that while such men claim to be
maimed, discharged soldiers, they are in fact impostors:

**... some wyll shew you some outward wounde, whiche he gotte
at some dronken fraye, eyther haltinge of some preuye wounde
festred with a fylthy firy flankard. For be well assured that the
hardist souldiers be eyther slayne or maymed, eyther and they
escape all hassardes, and retourne home agayne ... [they] disdayne
to beg or aske charity. (Viles and Furnivall, 1869, p 29)**

So far this chapter has argued that there are enduring features of the
attitudes towards and portrayal of people who beg which are based, as de
Swaan pointed out about early modern beggars, upon their docility, their
proximity and their disability. The categorisation of people who beg as
'genuine' or not was something which respondents in our own present-
day study (see Chapter Eleven) returned to time and time again. For
example:

**"Two reasons [why people beg]: one well they've just no got the
money and they can't get a job and then the other reason as I
said to you that they are just at it, you know they are no really
needing to beg but they have got it down to a fine art."**

A secret society

Many historians' accounts of begging (for example, Pound, 1986) are
remarkable in that they lack any attempt to connect the historical evidence
with the biography and lived experience of those about whom they

write. They take the extant contemporary accounts written by the powerful and use them to relate to us the way of life of the vagrant and beggar. Pound goes as far as insisting that Harman is believable, because:

> **There seems no good reason for a person of his social standing to have deliberately invented the types of vagrant he describes so graphically. (Pound, 1986, p vii)**

Others, such as Beier (1974, 1983, 1985) and Slack (1974, 1988), suggest that Harman's picture of bands of vagrants wandering the Tudor countryside and living an alternative life-style is not accurate. Instead they suggest that most vagrants were young, travelling alone and looking for a job rather than being engaged in criminal activity.

Many historical and contemporary accounts of begging focus upon the ways in which people who beg are part of an organised social group who share in common customs and in some cases a secret language. That people who beg are well organised seems to be another understanding of the fact that they are living on the margins of, or outside, normal society. As outcasts, they are understood to be part of an alternative and competing social order. Salgado writes:

> **... in response to the dire social conditions ... [beggars] developed their own society and hierarchy, their own intricate and elaborate strategies which enabled them to take advantage at every turn of the society from which they had been excluded. (Salgado, 1977, p 12)**

On the other hand, Slack (1974, p 360) suggests that we should resist the temptation to see vagrants as a sub- or counter-culture, arguing that "vagabonds become the scapegoats of all social problems". He bases this upon an analysis of historical records and concludes that:

> **... vagrant bands of beggars and gypsies, with a canting language and a structured hierarchy, may sometimes have existed behind our evidence of individual vagabonds. But they were by no means as common as Harman and particularly his later plagiarists suggested. (Slack, 1974, p 377)**

He suggests that they romanticised the vagrant phenomenon, to make the reality more explicable. Beier's interpretation of the evidence is similar to Slack's and suggests that "there is no evidence that they operated in a gang" (Beier, 1974, p 9). Slack and Beier contest this point with Pound (Pound, 1976), who brings with him a modern morality to interpret an Elizabethan world. Relying upon Harman, he argues that:

> ... the bands were led by the so-called upright man, a beggar stronger and imbued with a greater sense of leadership than his fellows. It was he who ... had the lion's share of the loot and had the pick of the doxies or bawdy baskets as the women members of the band were known.... Some, ostensibly tinkers or pedlars ... [were] ... the products of illicit unions between men and women of the same breed.... Men such as this seldom starved. (Pound, 1986, p 29)

The point here is not the accuracy of the portrayal by Pound but that by echoing Harman, he focuses upon their social organisation as involving an alternative social order. The enduring images of beggars and vagrants present them as both an organised tight knit society and an asocial rabble.

Begging and social control

Beier (1974, pp 26-7) argues that in Tudor England there were reasons of state for repressing vagrants. State officials were frightened of plots and rebellions. Society was ordered in hierarchies that were unified by paternalism. 'Masterless men' had broken away from this established order.

While people who begged, and people who wandered, may have had the potential to pose an immediate threat to the state in Tudor and Stuart England, that is clearly not the case in the 19th and 20th centuries. People begging do, however, represent at least a breakdown in social order and at worst, in the images of an alternative social organisation, a different set of norms and a different way of life from those which are dominant. As some of our present-day respondents described it to us, it was seen as a life-style choice. For example:

> "I mean at the end of the day do some of them really want to go out to work and earn a living? You know some of them are maybe quite happy on the streets begging...."

Contemporary and historical accounts of begging reflect a concern with social order. For example Aydelotte refers to:

> ... **the vagrants and masterless men who roamed from place to**
> **place like modern tramps and gipsies, begging and stealing by**
> **turns, and,** *in the absence of regulation, living a merry life.* **(Aydelotte,**
> **1913, pp 1-2; our emphasis)**

A contemporary version of this is to be found in a front page article in the *Glasgow Evening Times* of January 1992. This tells the story of three people who were begging in the centre of the city and claims these were 'professional' beggars.

It is worth pausing to consider this contradictory notion of the 'professional' beggar. It would imply that someone makes their income by begging, yet it also implies a deceit beyond that of an 'ordinary' beggar. Yet if someone is to beg, while already receiving their income from elsewhere, they might be considered less deserving than the person resorting to begging to gain their income. This is another example of the double bind within which people who beg are trapped. If you make a living begging, you may be condemned as a professional. If you beg to supplement your income you are not really in need. The story headline in the *Evening Times* claimed that beggars could make £350 a week begging. Yet, within a paragraph of claiming that the operation can "net over £700 a week", it quoted one of the beggars as saying "I work only half an hour to get some money". So while extrapolating their short-term takings to a full working week would result in a large sum of money, that is not what is being practiced. The article acknowledges this by observing that the beggars live under a motorway bridge.

As one of our respondents expressed it to us:

> **"... like they've got good gear on and you think, you know there**
> **are things in the papers there are always wee stories about, this**
> **guy makes £2,000 a week begging, and you think well, I mean,**
> **I never believe those stories but I suppose some of them must be**
> **true. But if somebody came up to me wearing like an Adidas**
> **track suit and trainers on I'd think well wait a minute he doesn't**
> **look short of a bob or two."**

But it is the image of the 'merry life' which we suggest is one of the reasons that begging offends. We return time and again to this portrayal of beggars as, at best wealthy cheats, and at least free from the constraints of society (Pound, 1986; Aydelotte, 1913). There is almost an element of jealousy here. They are part of an alternative tight knit group who speak a secret language. They are alcoholics, or today – drug addicts – and they are sexually immoral. Above all they may be dangerous – the aggressive beggar of contemporary tabloids.

Yet these views are counter-intuitive. The *Evening Times* reports that the £700 a week beggars had egg and chips for breakfast (perhaps they invest the remainder of their gains in stocks and shares!). If vagrancy was such a good life, why don't we all do it? At a time of economic prosperity, we could expect a growth in people begging; siphoning off the excess income of the prosperous. But begging grows at times of social and economic crisis.

Passivity

Dyer observes (1989, p 235) that in medieval England, the poor were not defined in economic terms, but politically and legally: they lacked power. Poverty was the lot of the majority of the population and the poor, by providing a locus for the giving of alms, were integrated into the social order. In contrast, in the post-reformation Christian tradition, poverty is deserving of good from those who are not poor, while it is a sign of weakness on the part of those who are poor. As Woolf (1986, p 28) points out, both Protestant and Catholic cities and states treated beggars harshly. Poverty was also conceived of as a passive state. Financial poverty becomes associated with personal inadequacy and a lack of ability. The poor are acted upon as passive victims.

Begging does take its passive forms. The person with the 'hungry and homeless' sign is symbolically proclaiming their loss of voice. Contrast this with a stranger walking up to another person in the street and asking for money, which is likely to be experienced as an aggressive or threatening act and at least always an uncomfortable one. The supplicant initiates the interaction with the donor and thus creates an encounter. This is at the heart of the ambiguity of begging encounters. The deserving poor are conceived of as passive victims. Yet, no one, no matter how poor, is a passive victim, unable to create social interactions. And begging is a deliberate action, which involves a conscious choice by the person seeking alms. Begging strategies are dismissed as involving guile because they involve an interaction generated by the supplicant.

From the perspective of the supplicant, the encounter is problematic.

A study of begging in London (Murdoch, 1994) reported that 76% of those questioned had initially found it extremely difficult to beg. The consistent element of accounts of fraudulent begging is that there is a consciousness in the presentation of the beggar. Yet a begging encounter must involve a deliberate strategy by the supplicant. These strategies are variable but they contain enduring characteristics. Hotten, in drawing parallels between Luther's accounts and his own experience in Victorian England, provides the examples of the selling of counterfeit goods, card sharps, and pretend distressed gentry writing begging letters (1860, pp 50-1). Hotten widens the definition of begging to involve all strategies which seek a gift from a stranger, whether or not the donor is aware that the transaction has no intrinsic value.

At its extreme, it would include all con tricks and the sale of worthless goods under a definition of begging. This would lead us into an investigation of many commercial transactions today! Begging strategies do contain within them an alternative understanding of the encounter. Whatever the intentions of the supplicant, or interpretations of the donor, a request for a gift from a stranger is fraught with ambiguity. These ambiguities invade the understandings both of the supplicant and the donor. For the supplicant, in many cases, they do not wish to see themselves as begging, and therefore present their behaviour in such a way which gives both themselves and the potential donor an alternative understanding of the interaction. The understanding of the interaction has to draw parallels with other interactions to make sense of it. For example, a long-standing and common one is that of asking for loose change for the telephone, train or bus. Many of us will have experienced this, both asking and being asked. The donor makes a judgement about the request based both on the request and the supplicant. Another begging strategy is the sale of a flower or piece of heather. Again a common sense interpretation is made by the donor about the interaction. Busking and street entertainment, flag days and collection cans, *The Big Issue* and doorstep selling for charity are seen as begging depending upon the interpretation given to the interaction by the donor (see Chapter Eleven). One interpretation is that a supplicant is seeking a gift from a stranger, another that goods or services are being provided. De Swaan argues (1988, p 16) that there is a "human tendency to construct interpretations that compensate for relational asymmetry".

These ambiguities help us to understand the hostility towards begging and in particular to the most straightforward request for a gift. In a society based upon reciprocal exchange, unsolicited, unilateral transfers are unusual and difficult to understand on an everyday level (for example, unreciprocated gifts, leaflets in the street). But begging encounters are more than unusual, they threaten the core assumptions of market economies and societies. Furthermore, because the encounter is initiated by the supplicant, the supplicant chooses how to create the encounter and provides the understandings which can be drawn upon to make sense of it. Because of this, all begging encounters can be seen as involving an element of an act, because they are staged by the supplicant and could not be otherwise. This explains why they are so frequently suspected of being fraudulent.

The encounter is problematic both for the supplicant and the potential donor. The donor is faced with making a judgement. Unless we decide before an encounter that all requests for gifts are met with the same response, then a judgement has to be made. While some people are more prone to give than others, few people either consistently give or consistently don't give when asked for a gift from a stranger, or are asked to enter into a quasi-commercial transaction for a product which they had not been seeking. The judgement involves a discretion about a value which is neither aesthetic, nor useful, nor commercial, but moral. The value is not derived from the transaction but lies either in the transaction itself (the act of giving) or in the individual to whom the money is given.

This chapter has focused upon the continuities in attitudes towards people who beg. These attitudes seem to be ambivalent and at times contradictory, but an analysis of them does demonstrate that the begging encounter is never unproblematic. This chapter has illustrated the remarkable continuities in attitudes and reactions towards begging. Contemporary attitudes towards begging is a theme that we pick up upon in Chapter Eleven, where we explore people's understandings, today, of the nature of the begging encounter.

References

Aydelotte, F. (1913) *Elizabethan rogues and vagabonds*, Oxford: Clarendon Press.

Beier, A.L. (1974) 'Vagrants and the social order in Elizabethan England', *Past and Present*, no 64, pp 3-29.

Beier, A.L. (1983) *The problem of the poor in Tudor and early Stuart England*, London: Methuen.

Beier, A.L. (1985) *Masterless men. The vagrancy problem in England 1560-1640*, London: Methuen.

Blau, J. (1992) *The visible poor: Homelessness in the US*, Oxford: Oxford University Press.

de Swaan, A. (1988) *In care of the state*, Cambridge: Polity Press.

Dyer, C. (1989) *Standards of living in the later Middle Ages*, Cambridge: Cambridge University Press.

Garraty, J. (1978) *Unemployment in history: Economic thought and public policy*, New York, NY: Harper Row.

Hotten, J.C. (1860) *The book of vagabonds and beggars; with a vocabulary of their language; edited by Martin Luther in the year 1528*, London.

Hufton, O. (1974) *The poor of eighteenth century France 1750-1789*, Oxford: Clarendon Press.

Ignatieff, M. (1990) *The needs of strangers*, London: The Hogarth Press.

Murdoch, A. (1994) *We are human too*, London: Crisis.

Pound, J. (1976) 'Debate: vagrants and the social order in Elizabethan England', *Past and Present*, no 71, pp 126-9.

Pound, J. (1986) *Poverty and vagrancy in Tudor England*, Harlow: Longman.

Salgado, G. (1977) *The Elizabethan underworld*, London: JM Dent & Sons Ltd.

Slack, P. (1974) 'Vagrants and vagrancy in England, 1598-1664', *Economic History Review*, 2nd Series, vol xxvii, no 3, pp 360-79.

Slack, P. (1988) *Poverty and policy in Tudor and Stuart England*, Harlow: Longman.

Temkin, O. (1971) *The falling sickness*, London: The Johns Hopkins Press.

Tierney, B. (1958/59) 'The decretists and the deserving poor', *Comparative Studies in Society and History*, no 1, pp 360-73.

Titmuss, R. (1970) *The gift relationship*, London: George Allen & Unwin.

Viles, E. and Furnivall, F. (eds) (1869) *Awdeley's fraternity of vacabondes, Harman's caveat, Haben's sermon &c*, Oxford: Early English Text Society/Oxford University Press.

Woolf, S. (1986) *The poor in Western Europe in the eighteenth and nineteenth centuries*, London: Methuen.

FOUR

Begging: the global context and international comparisons

Bill Jordan

This chapter tries to put the phenomena analysed in other chapters – varieties of British begging – into an international context. It would be absurd to attempt a classification of national begging cultures, or even a categorisation of global begging practices, and I have neither the knowledge nor the desire to embark on such a task. What is feasible and useful is a comment on those factors in the global economy that contribute to the re-emergence of begging as a widespread social phenomenon in Britain and the USA in the 1980s, when it had largely disappeared during the 'golden age' of welfare states (Esping-Andersen, 1996). And it also seems relevant to comment on the specific features of this phenomenon, both in an historical and geographical comparative perspective.

Begging as a street-level economic activity represents a return to practices that were common in previous centuries in all the developed economies, and which both welfare states and state socialist systems sought to eliminate. The cultural context of begging was one of alms-giving as the predominant form of poor relief, and one which was embedded in systems of religious belief and duty, and in interactions between fellow members of the great religious faiths. In so far as begging is still a highly visible feature of social life in some developing countries, it retains many of these connotations, and hence lacks the stigma attached to it in developed ones.

In this chapter I shall argue that new global economic conditions, because they fundamentally change the bargaining position of unskilled workers throughout the developed (and much of the developing) worlds, are now contributing to a reappearance of many forms of street-level economic activity. The prevalence and forms of begging in any city or rural area are explicable in terms of the informal alternatives available, and the cultural resources of the economic actors. At the end of the chapter, I shall go on to look at interactions between beggars and their fellow citizens – and the moral dilemmas that are posed by and reflected through them – in the context of policy regimes once designed to relieve poverty through collective welfare systems, but which increasingly seek to promote welfare through paid work.

During my adult life, these dilemmas have become more pressing aspects of social policy. In my early experiences as a social worker in the 1960s, demands for money were uncomfortable reminders of the persistence of homelessness and poverty, mainly among middle-aged single men. My first book contained a detailed account of such a transaction (Jordan 1970) leading to a very educational 10-year relationship, punctuated by mishap and mayhem (Jordan, 1979). In that era the problems that led to such exchanges were still seen as issues to be tackled through personal relationships with professionals in public services – as individual problems, rather than manifestations of wider economic and social phenomena. Thirty years later, begging has become so widespread and so visible that it requires a different analysis. It also has a different kind of personal significance. When a beggar was murdered (allegedly by a 'beggars' mafia') almost outside my flat in Budapest, I was uncomfortably reminded of the anonymity of extreme distress, and the social distance that has developed between the mainstream and those who live on the streets. The global economic forces that washed *me* up as a teacher of social work in the Hungarian capital had exposed *the beggar* to risks that would have been unimaginable during the socialist era.

The origins of begging and its regulation

In medieval Europe, as in the Orient and the Middle East, the faithful were exhorted to give alms not merely to relieve the poor, but also to support travellers and (above all) pilgrims to religious sites and shrines – as Muslims did to pilgrims to Mecca. Furthermore, Christian monastic orders included mendicant friars, who travelled the roads in the pursuit of their missions of education or healing, and survived by begging. As in the Buddhist tradition, therefore, begging was in a religious context and (when practised by appropriately licensed groups) the reverse of a shameful activity; it denoted a spiritual calling or an evangelistic task.

As has been touched upon in Chapters One and Three, the break-up of the feudal system and the Protestant reformation gave rise to concerns about 'organised begging' as an informal (or criminal) alternative to peasant self-sufficiency or waged labour. But it would be a mistake to suppose that this implied disapproval of all forms of begging in the Protestant countries of northern Europe. Even writers of a strongly liberal, progressive and commercial turn of mind, such as John Locke, recognised that begging might still be located in a context of moral obligation on the alms-giver, and moral right for the beggar: "*Charity* gives every Man a Title to so much of another's Plenty, as will keep him from extreme want, where there is no means to subsist otherwise" – God had given the needy the right to a share of the surplus from capitalist production, "so that it cannot be justly denied him, when his pressing wants call for it" (Locke, 1698, section 42).

Although Locke (and his successors in this intellectual tradition, such as Daniel Defoe) were strong in their condemnation of idleness and fraud, and prescribed harsh penalties for those beggars guilty of such practices, the moralists and theologians of the 18th century remained ambivalent and ambiguous about begging, its origins and consequences. Adam Smith's famous aphorism about the 'invisible hand' that moved the rich to "make nearly the same distribution of the necessaries of life, which would have been made, had the earth been divided into equal portions, among all its inhabitants" (Smith, 1759, part IV, ch i) was immediately followed by a comment that, in the commercial societies of his era (notably England and Holland, more than his native Scotland) "the beggar, who suns himself by the side of the highway, possesses that security which kings are fighting for" (Smith, 1759, part IV, ch i). Here Smith contrasts the 'selfishness and rapacity' of the rich with the simplicity of the poor. It has been suggested that the last sentence is purely intended to convey Smith's stoic contempt for materialism and luxury, but the context reveals that it was (like Locke's productivity principle, by which he justified wealth in private property) also an early example of the claim of a 'trickle down effect' from the gains of the rich to the incomes of the poor – even of the least industrious of the lower orders.

Of course, what this implied was that certain forms of begging were morally justified or morally neutral, while others were vicious and corrupting of good character. As an alternative to real starvation, or as an expression of simple tastes and easy contentment, begging need not offend bourgeois sensibilities, or contravene the Protestant work ethic. But this was contrasted with the violence and fraud practised on a large scale in cities, which were to be eradicated. Nineteenth-century philanthropists made it their main business to distinguish between deserving and undeserving alms-seekers. The whole profession of social work – as the investigative arm of charitable giving – was grounded in this distinction, and the skills of distinguishing between these two groups.

Early social work therefore sought to transform begging from a street-level encounter between citizens to a formal application to a professional, skilled in assessing need. Social theorists of the day argued that the 'maudlin philanthropy' of the thousands of charities that had grown up to relieve distress bred "an increasing population of imbeciles, idlers and criminals" (Spencer, 1869, p 340). The Charity Organisation Society's (COS) aims included "the repression of mendicity and imposture, and the correction of the maladministration of charity" (COS, 1875, pp 5-6). But the organised charity that imposed this new system dealt selectively with those who applied to it, leaving the 'unhelpable' majority to the Poor Law authorities.

The 20th-century history of social policy has been of the expansion of professional services to take such problems off the streets and out of the workhouse (see Chapter One in this volume). In Britain these services were provided by local authorities; in most other countries they were funded by the state, but provided by voluntary organisations (Jordan, 1997). Under such regimes, begging, homelessness and other street-level phenomena were seen as evidence that "any sound system of comprehensive general social service will need to be supplemented by a more intensive, selective case-work provision" (Cormack and MacDougall, 1950, p 34). Yet – despite the enormous expansion of such services – begging and these other activities have re-emerged as strong features of first-world societies at the end of the century of welfare provision. The explanation for this will be sought in the next section.

Global forces and street-level activity

The re-emergence of begging in first world and second (post-Communist) world countries is clearly related to the surplus of unskilled labour in all these economies, the reappearances of mass unemployment, and the erosion of welfare entitlements. The rise in begging correlates with increases in homelessness, in poverty and income insecurity, and in a whole range of survival activities taking place outside the formal labour market. This change has been most dramatic in the former Soviet Union and its satellites in Central and Eastern Europe, where economies with very high levels of employment suddenly found themselves with massive labour surpluses, especially among those unskilled groups of workers whom their regimes most favoured and protected. In countries such as Russia and the Ukraine, the result has been a return to subsistence production of fruit and vegetables as the main economic activity and output, even in large cities (Revenko,

1997). Begging should be analysed in this context; its prevalence can be understood in terms of the extent of informal activity, and the opportunities for alternative survival strategies.

Both welfare states and state socialist regimes aimed to minimise informal street activity, and to eliminate begging by regulating the volume and conditions of employment (including wages), and by providing benefits and services to their populations. Policies for welfare (including social housing) provision were complemented by measures to control trading, performing and soliciting in public spaces, and to police those who hung around on the streets. In first world countries, there was much evidence that these policies were differentially implemented (Hall et al, 1978); policing focused on young black and other ethnic minority groups, and on certain districts and activities (such as prostitution), while turning a blind eye to the growth of other activities (such as busking and rough sleeping in London, for example).

Standards of public order and restrictions on street-level activity varied greatly between countries, and between cities within countries. In general, the state socialist regimes maintained very strict standards of public behaviour, which were reinforced by citizens' cultures of civic conduct (allowances being made for those suffering from alcoholic excesses). As someone who has lived for extensive periods and travelled widely in Central Europe, I can testify to the remarkable survival of these cultures in most regions. Even though enforcement by officials is now discreet or absent, the tower blocks that characterised accommodation in towns and cities are still orderly, clean and relatively safe places to live (with the exceptions of those unsalubrious ghetto quarters to which Roma gypsy families have been consigned). Standards of politeness on public transport are high, and there is a noticeable absence of litter and graffiti in most city environments.

During the 'golden age' of welfare states, variations in the visibility of social problems, and enforcement of controls on street-level activity, were similarly explicable in terms of policing, regulation and civic culture. Very high standards of cleanliness and orderliness in the city centres in Austria, Switzerland and New Zealand, for example, and more relaxed ones in Britain, Ireland and France, reflected cultural differences more than economic factors.

An interesting example of a steady rise in street-level activity is provided by South Africa. The paraphernalia of 'petty *apartheid*' consisted in the strict enforcement of rules excluding black people from most facilities and amenities, and segregating them in the use of services. This was at its height in the late 1950s and early 1960s. However, it was gradually worn down by economic forces, as informal suppliers of transport ('African taxis') and various goods and services (street traders) were gradually drawn into a flourishing informal economy in the towns and cities. The formal economy came to rely on these activities, and eventually commercial forces (which were blocked by *apartheid's* restrictions on profitable exchanges) burst through these fetters, overwhelming even the fundamental codes of the *apartheid* regime, the pass laws and Group Areas Act (Kane-Berman 1991). In this case, it was the rise of black entrepreneurialism and the growth of the black consumer market, not an increase in poverty, that led to increased street-level activity. Black incomes were rising and white incomes falling during the 1980s, when this process was at its height.

However, in general terms, the rise in street-level informal activity can be understood in terms of the declining share of national income going to labour, and the rising share to capital, as a result of global economic changes in the 1970s and beyond (Dore, 1998). Between the end of the Second World War and that time, post-war settlements had given organised labour a platform from which to exert economic power, and increase its share of national product, throughout that period – a tendency that continued for the longest in countries like Sweden and Austria, where corporatist institutions survived until the 1990s (Mishra, 1984; Esping-Andersen, 1990).

Meanwhile, first in the UK and USA under Thatcher and Reagan, then in New Zealand, and eventually in Western Europe and Australia, trade unions' power was broken, and national governments abandoned systems for protecting the employment levels and incomes of their whole populations. Systems under which high levels of overall (male) employment, secure and growing public-sector jobs, and adequate minimum wages had been sustained were destroyed through capital's increased mobility, the expansion of industrial production in the newly developing countries, and the impact of technological change (Jordan, 1996). Under competitive pressure, from the rising South-East Asian economies in particular, welfare states sought to contain social provision and to make labour markets more 'flexible' (Held and McGrew, 1994; Esping-Andersen, 1996).

Responses to global pressures

With hindsight, it is easy to recognise two distinct strategies (each with its own variations) pursued by national governments in the face of these pressures. In the US and UK, New Zealand and (to a lesser extent) Australia, neo-liberal regimes sought to deregulate the labour market, and drive down wages and other forms of job protection, especially for unskilled workers. The result has been the now-familiar syndrome of 'flexible insecurity', poverty and exclusion. The service sector has expanded, through the increase in part-time, short-term and sub-contracted work, and self-employment. This work has mostly been taken by married women (to make up mainstream household incomes) and younger people. In a large number of households – one in five in the UK (DSS, 1998) – no adult of working age has formal employment. These get by on means-tested benefits, but evidence from qualitative research suggests that a high proportion of them do occasional work for cash in the informal economy (Evason and Woods, 1995; Rowlingson et al, 1997). They justify this as the only way to sustain family incomes, and to meet occasional unpredictable costs, in the face of inadequate and unreliable benefits provision (Jordan et al, 1992; Dean and Melrose, 1997).

Studies in the USA draw attention to the links between insecurity of employment, low wages, inadequate means-tested benefits, and the phenomena of social exclusion. William Julius Wilson (1989, 1996) has used the example of the black ghetto in Chicago to study how changes in the labour market and in social insurance cover have made black men less able to earn a 'family wage', and hence to support a partner and children. He links this with the rise in both the prison population (over 1.5 million, disproportionately black, now in the USA), and the increase in one-parent female-headed households. Homelessness, begging and street-level activity involving drugs all relate to these structural changes that deteriorate the earning potential of younger (and especially black) men. The streets of Washington, for example, have borne witness to the impact of these forces since the early 1980s; in many districts, they have continually been lined with black men politely asking passers-by for spare change.

On the other hand, the continental European countries, which had predominantly Christian Democratic regimes during this period, have adopted a different strategy, based on maintaining social solidarity through post-war benefits structures. Industrial employment has contracted, as firms have shed older and less skilled workers through various state schemes for early retirement and disability pensions (Esping-Andersen, 1996). Both total expenditure on benefits and the social contributions required from a smaller number of workers have grown rapidly. In face of these rising social costs, employers have not created new jobs, and in particular the service sector has not expanded as rapidly as in the US and UK. Married women still participate less in formal employment than in those countries, and there are lower proportions of lone-parent households. Even so, social exclusion has become a recognisable phenomenon (Pangum, 1998), and – in the 1990s – poverty is becoming a concern for researchers and governments (Leibfried and Leisering, 1998). Because there is a new generation who have never been absorbed into the labour market, and many districts with high levels of unemployment, new adaptations to these exclusions occur, with informal economic activity (especially among recent immigrants from Central and Eastern Europe, and from North Africa) prominent among these.

In these countries, begging by citizens (as opposed to denizens or aliens who lack full citizenship rights) is a much less visible phenomenon in most cities, and mainly confined to long-term homeless people and people with drug and alcohol problems. Some reasons for this will be explored in the next section.

Finally, the special case of the post-Communist 'transformation' countries has already been mentioned. The extremes of impoverishment these have suffered are best illustrated by reference to the Ukraine, previously both the 'bread basket' of the Soviet bloc, and a region of industrial production. The present level of national income per head of population has fallen to below that of countries such as Sri Lanka and India, and on a par with Papua New Guinea. The incomes of 90% of the population are now equivalent to those of the poorest 10% at the end of the Communist period. Such has been the collapse of manufacturing industry and public-service employment that the largest category in the outputs of Kiev and other cities is fruit and vegetables (Revenko, 1997).

However, because both industrialisation and urbanisation were comparatively recent (and forced) processes in countries like Romania, Bulgaria, Slovakia and parts of the former Soviet Union, almost all inhabitants of towns and cities have close relatives in the countryside, and skills of subsistence horticulture and animal husbandry have not been lost. Hence urban households are able to rely on food (and sometimes even fuel) from the rural areas, where they return intermittently for visits; and they can deploy these skills in urban settings. Even in the more prosperous and economically advanced countries of Central Europe, such as Slovakia in particular, subsistence production is a well-recognised aspect of survival strategies, with descendants of peasants reverting to the extended family reciprocities and cultural patterns of the pre-war generation (Kusá, 1997).

In most Central European towns and cities, begging is uncommon, except by a few Roma people (mainly women and children) whose plight has deteriorated far more dramatically than the rest of the population since the end of Communism. However, begging by old people, people with disabilities and by working-age men is a very extensive and striking feature of street life in Budapest, the Hungarian capital. This appears to be related to two factors. Budapest was a huge and sophisticated bourgeois city before Communism, and since 1989, has experienced social and residential polarisation closer to those of London or Frankfurt than to nearby cities, such as Bratislava (or even the Hungarian provincial cities). Second, Budapest attracts a high volume of migration from rural Hungary, and has experienced a rapid growth in homelessness since the end of Communism. Whereas rural skills are at a premium in Lvov or Kiev (pauperised former industrial centres), they are of little use in Budapest, a thriving commercial and tourist centre. This illustrates the fact that begging becomes prevalent when there is a large volume of impoverished and socially excluded population, but other possibilities of informal economic activity are blocked.

Alternative street-level activities

In the introductory section of this chapter, I pointed out that begging practices were a cultural resource by which poor and powerless people survived in societies with radical inequalities of wealth and power. Whereas in simple (for example, hunter-gatherer) communities, redistribution was built into the roles and norms through which cooperation among members took place (Sahlins, 1974), in peasant economies with military-theocratic or feudal socio-political structures, redistribution became a religious duty of the rich and powerful. Begging was one way to remind them of their obligations, when other strategies provided insufficient resources for subsistence.

Classically, begging is one of the "weapons of the weak" (Scott, 1985, 1990; Jordan, 1993); whereby the very disadvantaged and subordinate take action in pursuit of their interests which involves the minimum energy, risk and organisational skill. Whereas skilled workers in urban, commercial societies quickly organised themselves into guilds, creating bonds of solidarity through loyalty and restrained competition, unskilled rural labourers and those who migrated between towns lacked the bargaining power or the organisational resources to do so. Begging allowed them to make claims on their 'betters' in terms of the conservative religious ideologies of the countryside, or the emerging power hierarchies of the towns. While seeming to express nothing but humility and compliance, and whispering only the homilies of religious orthodoxy, it subverted the traditional order in covert, underground ways. Pretending only destitution, sickness or disability of the most miserably isolated kind, beggars could secretly coordinate their activities, so as to exercise maximum leverage on the rich with least risk of punishment.

Scott's study of poor people's strategic resistance to the progress of agricultural capitalism in rural Malaysia locates begging in a whole range of practices that include petty theft, malingering, sabotage and slander (Scott, 1985). His historical review of resistance practices shows how subordinates used the rhetoric of the rich and powerful (ideas of duty, desert or charity, through which they justified their wealth and power) to extract payments from them, when they could not gain advantage or resources in other ways (Scott, 1990). Notions of a moral right to alms were mobilised when, for example, attempts to steal a landowner's surplus stores were unsuccessful. Conversely, poor people used force or threats of force (riot, arson) when this proved more advantageous than begging, as for instance during the 'Swing' unrest in England in the early 1830s (Wakefield, 1832), when hayricks were systematically burned if farmers refused aid; or in the urban riots in the USA during the Depression (Piven and Cloward, 1977).

These connections between economic dislocation and disorder were not lost upon the authorities in late-medieval European society, or (no doubt) in the present-day developing world. The preambles of all the early Poor Law legislation start with sentences such as one which introduced the Act of 1597:

> ... whereas a good part of the strength of this realm consisteth in the number of good and able subjects ... and of late years more than in times past, there have been sundry towns, parishes and houses of husbandry destroyed and become desolate, whereof a great number of poor people are become wanderers, idle and loose, which is a source of infinite inconvenience. (39 Elizabeth c4, 1597, preamble)

Such Acts went on to list various categories of 'sturdy beggars and vagabonds' to be whipped or incarcerated in Houses of Correction, the forerunners of those 'small minorities' of claimants who discredit any system of poor relief by abusing it and making public mischief. These categories listed street-level activists such as musicians, minstrels, entertainers, prostitutes, fortune-tellers and owners of various wild animals such as bears and monkeys. (It is interesting that a present-day list in Bulgaria or Romania would contain all these activities.) Furthermore, these Acts referred to 'bands of beggars' who threatened residents, anticipating present-day concerns with organised begging.

In Catholic countries, begging practices still evoke religious tradition in their posture (often kneeling, with head bowed) and their location (sometimes in church doorways). In Catholic cultures, women and children are as likely to be beggars as men with disabilities or impairments; in Britain, for instance, women beggars with children are often Romany or Irish by origin. Women accompanied by children are the begging members of destitute Roma gypsy families in Central Europe. But these practices are closely related to other street activities, such as pavement sales of fruit, vegetables or clothes, or door-to-door sales of lucky charms (or trivial services, such as tool-sharpening by men). In other words, begging is a practice that takes its place at the bottom of a hierarchy of survival strategies that include the offer of services to passers-by, or by itinerants to householders, and often practised by women. In South Africa, destitute black women with children walk miles in white residential districts, offering to do washing or other household chores, but asking for money if no chores were available.

In Northern Europe and the more developed post-Communist countries, prostitution may be a more culturally acceptable form of street-level economic activity than begging for most young women (Melrose et al, 1999). By contrast, young men appear to find begging less degrading than 'renting', while those who do engage in male prostitution are more likely to disguise it behind the public façade of begging activity (Hendry, 1998).

These themes and observations will be drawn together in the conclusions to this chapter, in which a series of hypotheses about the role of begging in informal economic activity will be advanced. But first, it is appropriate to address the interactions between beggars and those they ask for alms, to understand how these contribute to new politics of welfare and social control.

Civic indifference and begging practices

It appears that poor people with personal and social resources for other street-level activities choose these in preference to begging, and that begging draws down particularly strong moral responses from mainstream citizens and from civic authorities. Why is begging so low in the hierarchy of street-level economic activities, given that it is both less energetic and more direct than busking or other forms of street entertainment, and less risky than drug-dealing or picking pockets? And why has begging provoked strong political reactions (see Chapter Two in this volume), and does it provoke such strong emotional response (both against beggars and against the social system that produces them) among the public (see Chapters Ten and Eleven)?

Other chapters in this book deal more substantively with the stigma of begging in a contemporary economy (especially in a liberal polity whose political culture emphasises self-responsibility and moral autonomy), and with the roots of cultural antagonism to begging. This section will focus on those aspects of the interactions between beggars and passers-by which evoke ideas and feelings over citizenship, mutuality and social solidarity. As in all interactions – even brief and casual encounters between strangers in the street – the 'exchange' between a beggar and a pedestrian involves 'face work' (Goffman, 1969; and see Chapter Eight in this volume). However apparently one-sided a murmured request for spare change, ignored by the passer-by, may seem, the question itself involves an involuntary transaction, in which social value (positive or negative) is transferred. The averted gaze and hastened step conveys as much to the fellow citizen on the pavement as the smile, the greeting and the willing donation. Begging challenges the pedestrian to face up to destitution (pretended or real), and to communicate something about the value of a human being expressing distress and need, albeit in the most self-demeaning way.

It seems to me that it is precisely because of this challenge that begging occupies its particular niche in street-level activity. To beg is to conduct a series of encounters in which the basic value of one's life as a human being, and as a fellow citizen, is on the line over and over again. It is to court rejection of the most humiliating kind, because it is rejection of the person, rather than of a performance (as in busking or pavement art) or a of product (as in street trading). Although the rituals of begging partially soften and nuance this element in the transaction – for instance, by the repetitiveness of the incantation about small change – the effectiveness of the plea rests on its communication as a message from a person about that person, and its demand for a face-to-face response. (One has only to imagine how differently one might feel about a tape recording of the beggar's voice repeating the same message, or a video of a beggar projected onto a wall at pavement level, to appreciate this point.)

From the standpoint of the passer-by, the impact of begging – as an assault on their expectation of peaceful and uninterrupted progress towards a shop, an office, a parked car or a lunch appointment – is a violation of what might be called a negative right of citizenship (see Chapter Thirteen in this volume). In a first world country, and especially in a welfare state, relatively high taxes and social insurance contributions are the price paid by mainstream citizens for the right to treat their fellow citizens with civic indifference. In other words, they are regarded as a cost of living in a complex and unequal society, but one which buys them peaceful enjoyment of its amenities, without such interruptions, and without unchosen reminders of the problems endured by others.

This can be seen as particularly relevant in a society such as Britain where, during the Thatcher years in particular, social polarisation and the widening gap in incomes between mainstream citizens and the poor led to severe tensions between the former's political beliefs and their everyday decisions. Research has shown that many comfortably-off people were aware of a growing split between the aspirations towards solidarity, equality and social justice that they espoused, and the consequences of their choices – for example, to live in exclusively middle-class districts, to take out private health insurances and private pensions, to send their children to selective or fee-paying schools, and so on (Jordan et al, 1994). The same tendency would be seen in the British Social Attitudes Survey findings in the late 1980s and early 1990s that most people claimed to want to see improved benefits and services, and to be willing to pay more taxes, but the Conservatives still won the elections of 1987 and 1992 (Lipsey, 1994; see also Taylor-Gooby, 1995). This dissonance between 'values' and preferences is uncomfortable, and begging can be a reminder of it.

To encounter a beggar is to be asked to make a judgement about a fellow citizen's plight. Are they a 'genuinely' destitute, homeless and freezing (in which case, how can one withhold a small payment)? Or is there a 'hidden reason' (such as alcoholism, drug-use, gambling, criminality or idleness) that explains their situation? Welfare states collect taxes and contributions from citizens to employ officials – bureaucrats and professionals – to make such judgements, in the distribution of benefits, services, treatment, training and punishment. Citizens pay good money *not* to make such judgements, and to experience the moral perplexities and pains of framing and communicating them. Hence they resent the serial experience of being asked to decide whether to give. It is like having paid once as a taxpayer, and then being asked to pay again and again (see Chapter Eleven in this volume).

Conclusions

The general hypotheses of this chapter (and this book) require further refinement and testing through research. Provisionally, we might assert that there are already some indications:

- that begging activity in Britain and North-West Europe is engaged in mainly by those with the least personal and cultural resources for survival practices, such as young people who have been recently in care or in mental hospitals, homeless single people, and people with serious mental health, alcohol or drug problems;
- that older or more resourceful and better-connected people engage in activities such as busking, street trading, drug-dealing, petty crime, working-while-claiming or prostitution in preference to begging, though these activities are not necessarily mutually exclusive, and individuals may graduate (or sink) from one to the other;
- that cities in which there are established, stable networks and communities in which other informal economic activities of many kinds have been rather successfully practiced (for instance, because of long-term industrial decline, as in Glasgow or Newcastle), manifest relatively little begging activity;
- that cities with wide disparities of income between rich and poor, and with large number of tourist visitors, manifest relatively high levels of begging activity (for example, Bath). Some such cities have large numbers of young and vulnerable beggars near their centres *and* established networks of other informal activities (drug-dealing, crime and working-while-claiming) by settled residents around their outer perimeters (for example, Edinburgh);
- cities (and societies) with strong traditions of collective solidarity, little residential polarisation and relatively equal incomes (except for a small elite), such as are found in most of the post-Communist countries, are less likely to have high levels of begging than those with great

inequalities of income, residential polarisation and low solidarity (such as most cities in the USA, and Budapest).

All these hypotheses must, of course, contain provisos about policing practices and public toleration. Variations in policing between cities can (at least temporarily) explain some of the variations in begging activity. Some rich, polarised cities with many tourists are prepared to spend money on policies for diverting or concealing begging, in order to present a more acceptable public face (see Chapter Twelve in this volume).

As a form of street-level economic activity, the return of begging to the cities of first world countries can be understood as part of the erosion of Keynesian, productivist economic management and welfare states. The figure of the beggar symbolises the failures of social policies of that era in many ways – someone who is rootless, homeless, destitute, without a work role, who may remind the passer-by of news stories about the problems of community care for mentally ill people, of prison aftercare, of drug addiction or alcoholism, of children leaving care, or of minority groups and asylum seekers. The figure of the beggar is an unsettling and reproachful reminder, both of the mainstream citizen's comfort and contentment, and of the welfare system's capacities and coverage (see Chapter Two in this volume).

But begging is symbolic in other ways too. As Bauman (1998) points out, welfare states incorporated the mainstream working class and its marginal outreaches as *workers*, and they then made their claims on society (especially during infancy and old age) on the basis of their work contributions. Since the onset of the welfare state's decline in the 1970s, poor people have been reconstructed as failed *consumers* as much as discarded workers. In an age when unskilled workers are worth less than the costs of their subsistence, and require heavy subsidisation to be worth employing, claiming from the need to consume (and hence claiming needs-based, means-tested benefits) is their only option. Beggars turn their identities as failed consumers and needy citizens into income-generating assets; in this sense, begging is ironically an economic activity that is well suited to an age of consumerism, especially when the beggar can confront the consumer at the paradigm moment of their public identity – as a shopper.

In Britain, the New Labour government has based its welfare reforms on a return to the productivist ethos of the post-war period (Jordan, 1998). Policies for social justice through social inclusion will be pursued almost entirely through increased labour market participation, because "paid work is the surest route out of poverty" (DSS, 1998, p 3). The various New Deals through which this will be accomplished are aimed at making claimants more employable, and providing them with stronger reasons for taking formal employment, mainly by threats of losing benefits. Tighter conditions around claims will be reinforced by an approach based on 'tough love' in the education, criminal justice and personal social services systems; the benefits system itself will be staffed by this new breed of 'tough luvvies' who will offer "individuals, flexible advice" and "tailor-made packages of help" (DSS, 1998, p 3). Under the Rough Sleepers Initiative officials will have the power to compel claimants to enter hostel accommodation. 'Zero-tolerance' in policing will apply especially to the kinds of visible manifestations that citizens confront in the streets (see Chapter Thirteen in this volume).

I have argued elsewhere (Jordan, 1998, chs 2 and 3) that these reforms have dubious foundations, in terms of ethics and efficiency. In an age of *global* labour surplus, the beggar's claim against a fellow citizen, like the social assistance claimant's against a taxpayer, is from their citizenship, consumption needs and humanity, not as a worker or potential worker. As a consumer, the passer-by prefers British companies to relocate to China as their production bases, in order to supply cheaper goods in the shops. As a saver and investor, mainstream citizens prefer capital to be sufficiently mobile to earn a better return in foreign markets. Ethically, this implies compensation for those less skilled and mobile workers on whom the costs associated with these improvements in the welfare of mainstream citizens fall. Since it is Chinese (or Indian or Brazilian) workers whose welfare is increased by mobility of productive capital, and their labour which contributes to growth in *global* income, it cannot be from work efforts that British (or German or French) claimants make their claim. It must stem from membership of a common-interest system of mutual protection of human values and needs, not common contributions to a national system of productive cooperation.

Furthermore, the reforms under which claimants will be persuaded or coerced back to work cannot provide incentives for voluntary, as opposed to forced, labour. Heavy subsidies paid to employers and workers/trainees betray that the market value of the work performed is insufficient to give rise to a mutually-advantageous contract. The Conservative opposition has already pointed out that the first 30,000 jobs created under the New Deal for Young People have cost £11,000 each (BBC Radio 4, 26 November 1998). This is unlikely to have taken account of all the enforcement costs, such as the increase in crime among those disqualified for benefits (the prison population now stands 66,000 at the time of writing, compared with around 40,000 when the present wave of 'tough love' began). In terms of efficiency, therefore, New Labour's programme (like that of the workfare regimes in the USA) is likely to be more expensive than conventional social assistance.

Begging will be one of the main targets of New Labour's policies, and a test of its performance. I would argue that begging is a challenge to any attempt at welfare reform, because it parades the paradoxes of work and well-being. It is only when people have their basic needs satisfied that they can be in any sense responsible contributors to systems of cooperation. An income sufficient for survival is therefore a necessary condition for work, not the other way round, in today's global economy. And a system that gives income security is a necessary condition for any viable attempt to re-include citizens in mainstream society.

References

Bauman, Z. (1998) *Work, consumerism and the new poor*, Buckingham: Open University Press.

COS (Charity Organisation Society) (1875) *Fifth Annual Report*, London: COS.

Cormack, U. and MacDougall, K. (1950) 'Case-work in social service', in C. Morris (ed) *Social casework in Great Britain*, London: Faber & Faber.

Dean, H. and Melrose, M. (1997) 'Manageable discord: fraud and resistance in the social security system', *Social Policy and Administration*, vol 31, no 2, pp 103-18.

Dore, K. (1998) 'Labour markets, employment relations and pension prospects: must the capital share grow and grow?', Paper given at seminar, 'Capital, labour and citizenship', Citizen's Income Trust, London School of Economics, 9 July.

DSS (Department of Social Security) (1998) *New ambitions for our country: A new contract for welfare*, Cm 3805, London: The Stationery Office.

Esping-Andersen, G. (1990) *The three worlds of welfare capitalism*, Cambridge: Polity Press.

Esping-Andersen, G. (1996) 'After the golden age: welfare state dilemmas in a global economy', in G. Esping-Andersen (ed) *Welfare states in transition: National adaptations in global economies*, London: Sage Publications.

Evason, E. and Woods, R. (1995) 'Poverty, deregulation of labour markets and benefit fraud', *Social Policy and Administration*, vol 29, no 1, pp 40-54.

Goffman, E. (1969) *Interaction ritual*, New York, NY: Doubleday Anchor.

Hall, S., Critcher, C., Jefferson, T., Clarke J. and Roberts, B. (1978) *Policing the crisis*, London: Macmillan.

Held, D. and McGrew, A. (1994) 'Globalisation and the liberal democratic state', *Government and Opposition*, vol 28, no 2, pp 261-85.

Hendry, T. (1998) An intervention during discussion at a Social Policy Association sponsored day-workshop, 'Begging and street-level economic activity', University of Luton, 24 September.

Jordan, B. (1970) *Client-worker transactions*, London: Routledge and Kegan Paul.

Jordan, B. (1979) *Helping in social work*, London: Routledge and Kegan Paul.

Jordan, B. (1993) 'Framing claims and the "weapons of the weak"', in G. Drover and P. Kerans (eds) *New approaches to welfare theory*, Aldershot: Edward Elgar.

Jordan, B. (1996) *A theory of poverty and social exclusion*, Cambridge: Polity Press.

Jordan, B. (1997) 'Social work and society', in M. Davies (ed) *The Blackwell companion to social work*, Oxford: Blackwell.

Jordan, B. (1998) *The new politics of welfare: Social justice in a global context*, London: Sage Publications.

Jordan, B., James, S., Kay, H. and Redley, M. (1992) *Trapped in poverty? Labour-market decisions in low-income households*, London: Routledge.

Jordan, B., Redley, M. and James, S. (1994) *Putting the family first: Identities, decisions, citizenship*, London: UCL Press.

Kane-Berman, J. (1991) *South Africa's silent revolution*, Johannesburg: Southern Book Publishers.

Kusá, Z. (1997) *History of family poverty in Slovakia*, Bratislava: Slovak Academy of Sciences.

Leibfried, S. and Leisering, L. (1998) *Time and poverty*, Cambridge: Cambridge University Press.

Lipsey, D. (1994) 'Do we really want more public spending?', in R. Jowell, J. Curtice, L. Brook and D. Ahrendt (eds) *British public attitudes: The 11th report*, Aldershot: Dartmouth.

Locke, J. (1698) *Second treatise of government* (edited by P. Laslett, 1957), Cambridge: Cambridge University Press.

Melrose, M., Barrett, D. and Brodie, I. (1999) *One way street: Retrospectives on childhood prostitution*, London: The Children's Society.

Mishra, R. (1984) *The welfare state in crisis: Social thought and social change*, Brighton: Wheatsheaf.

Pangum, S. (1998) 'Poverty and social exclusion: a sociological view', in M. Rhodes and Y. Meny (eds) *The future of European welfare: A new social contract?*, Basingstoke: Macmillan.

Piven, F. and Cloward, R. (1977) *Poor people's movements: How they succeed and why they fail*, New York, NY: Vintage.

Revenko, A. (1997) 'Poor strata of population in ukraine', Paper given at Third International Conference on Social Problems, 'Social history of poverty in Central Europe', Lodz, Poland, 3-6 December.

Rowlingson, K., Wiley, C. and Newbrom, T. (1997) *Social security fraud*, London: Policy Studies Institute.

Sahlins, M. (1974) *Stone age economics*, London: Tavistock.

Scott, J.C. (1985) *Weapons of the weak: Everyday forms of peasant resistance*, New Haven, CT: Yale University Press.

Scott, J.C. (1990) *Domination and the acts of resistance: Hidden transcripts*, New Haven, CT: Yale University Press.

Smith, A. (1759) 'The theory of moral sentiments', in H.W. Scheider (ed) *Adam Smith's moral and political philosophy*, New York, NY: Harper.

Spencer, H. (1869) *The study of sociology* (edited by S. Andreski, 1969), London: Macmillan.

Taylor-Gooby, P. (1995) 'Comfortable, marginal and excluded: Who should pay for a better welfare state?', in R. Jowell, J. Curtice, L. Brook and D. Ahrendt (eds) *British social attitudes: The 12th report*, Aldershot: Dartmouth.

Wakefield, E.G. (1832) *Swing unmasked*, London: E. Wilson.

Wilson, W.J. (1989) *The truly disadvantaged: The underclass, the ghetto and public policy*, Chicago, IL: Chicago University Press.

Wilson, W.J. (1996) *When work disappears: The world of the new urban poor*, London: Vintage.

FIVE

Excluded youth and the growth of begging

Bob Coles and Gary Craig

This chapter explores the social policy context in which a growing number of young people have become so excluded from mainstream forms of economic and social support, that they have had to turn to alternative – and inherently risky – sources of income. Two important contextual issues need to be recognised. First, the main focus here is upon *young people* who may resort to begging, rather than begging by other age groups. The intention of this chapter is not, however, to provide a detailed review of young beggars themselves, but of the social policy context that has produced forms and patterns of social exclusion among the young in which begging can and does occur. Second, begging is only one of a range of different activities to which young people in poverty turn. Indeed, as Carlen (1997) has documented, many young people in the most extreme circumstances of unemployment and homelessness regard begging as an activity they would never contemplate. The main aim of the chapter is therefore to set begging in two main contexts: first, to see it as part (albeit an extreme part) of a range of different behaviours by those who are socially excluded and in poverty; second, to see this wider syndrome as the result of social and economic policies and processes that have led to their poverty and social exclusion. The chapter does, however, also identify those groups of young people most at risk of having to resort to begging, and social policy areas which need to be addressed to reverse poverty and social exclusion. It suggests ways of creating a social and economic environment in which begging may cease to be accepted as a necessary option by some young people.

The social and economic context of social exclusion

Other chapters in this volume testify that begging has a long history. Yet it has increased substantially in both extent and visibility in Britain in the last 20 years; and among those who beg are an increasing number and proportion of young people. The characteristics of those who beg also reveal an association between begging and a lack of involvement in the formal labour market, homelessness in its various guises, detachment from families, having been in the formal childcare ('children looked-after') system, and periodic involvement in crime and the criminal justice system, including imprisonment. Although those who beg include many who are middle-aged or in later stages of the life-course, many of the processes which have driven these groups to the margins of society are set in train (and increasingly so) during their 'youth'. In examining the social and economic contexts of begging, therefore, it is important to begin with a description of the processes of 'youth', and the ways in which difficulties in managing the transitions of youth have been exacerbated in the past two decades.

Youth is often defined as a series of transitions from childhood dependency to adult citizenship. In this sense, 'youth' covers a series of social processes, and 'young people' are those undergoing them. As late as the mid-1970s, transitions were typically 'traditional', involving leaving full-time education (in the 1970s, two thirds left at minimum school-leaving age), finding work, forming relationships, getting married and, upon marriage, moving away from the parental home to form an independent household. Within traditional youth transitions, two main strands were regarded as of fundamental importance: leaving education to enter the labour market, and leaving the 'family of origin' (that is, no longer living with parents) to start 'families of destination' (Wallace, 1987). 'Extended' transitions – now much more the norm – refer to the ways in which young people enter the labour market and/or leave home at a much later age than in previous decades. Yet much of the evidence on the growth of extended transitions is based on an examination of educational and labour market experience alone, with little attempt to examine the consequences for families of longer periods of family dependency (Roberts, 1995; Furlong and Cartmel, 1997; Seavers and Coles, 1998). This relegates the importance of the other two transition strands concerning housing and family relationships even though both underwent profound change during the last quarter of the 20th century.

Youth research in the 1980s and 1990s has helped to document the growth of both 'extended' and 'fractured' transitions (Jones and Wallace, 1992; Coles, 1995; Morrow and Richards, 1996; Furlong and Cartmel, 1997). Research on fractured transitions encompasses the study of youth unemployment and youth homelessness and recognised that many young people may leave full-time education and training without obtaining employment, and/or leave the parental home without securing alternative accommodation, becoming isolated from familial or surrogate family and welfare state support. Routes into youth unemployment are well known to be associated with social class, gender, ethnicity and region. Class background is important, mediated often through poor or no qualifications attained at the age of 16; for example, young people from working-class backgrounds are more than twice as likely to experience 'failure' on the school-to-work transition (and unemployment) at some stage (Banks et al, 1992; Furlong, 1992; Roberts, 1993). Minority ethnic, particularly African-Caribbean, young men are also known to be over-represented among the young unemployed. In Liverpool, for instance, Connolly et al (1991) found that while 20% of white youth were unemployed by the age of 18-19 and 50% were in employment, these figures were almost exactly reversed for the city's black youth. Nor could this be accounted for in terms of educational attainment or their residential concentrations adjacent to collapsed labour markets. Other evidence bears testimony to the over-representation of certain minority ethnic groups among the long-term unemployed (Modood et al, 1998; Craig, 1999).

There is also evidence of the ways in which training schemes and vocational education have served merely to reflect and reproduce both a gender-stratified labour market and differential access to secure work and rewarding pay levels. Thus, it is claimed that girls are socialised into 'caring jobs' or secretarial, catering, selling and personal services, and boys into a wide range of jobs in industry or trades (Griffin, 1985; Ashton et al, 1990; Bates and Riseborough, 1993; Coles, 1995; Skeggs, 1990, 1997). This locking of male and female into distinct gendered youth labour markets left young men especially vulnerable to unemployment as unskilled jobs in manufacturing industry disappeared in the 1980s. Regional differences in unemployment were also very marked, especially at the height of the mid-1980s recession. Ashton et al (1988) found that the chances of unemployment among young men in Sunderland were one in three compared to one in 33 in St Albans, differences of magnitude far outweighing class differences.

Within these broad patterns of inequality associated with class, ethnicity, gender and region, some groups were much more likely to experience 'fractured' transitions than others. Care leavers, for instance, were almost invariably required to live independently at the age of 16 or 17 (Biehal et al, 1995). This meant that their paramount concern was trying to secure accommodation rather than the search for jobs, although they have nevertheless been found to be vastly over-represented among the homeless (Baldwin et al, 1997; Pleace and Quilgars, 1999). Furthermore, research shows that three quarters of this group gain no qualifications by the age of 16, a factor further decreasing their chances of finding employment (Garnett, 1992; Biehal et al, 1995; Broad, 1998). Stein and Carey (1986) found that within one year of leaving care, half of this group had become unemployed and four out of five were without a job by the end of the second year. Young women leaving care are also much more likely than other groups to become prematurely or inadvertently pregnant. A third of the sample and nearly half of the female sample studied by Biehal et al had become parents within two years of leaving care. In these circumstances, attempting to secure accommodation and stabilise domestic circumstances left them unemployed and in considerable poverty (Baldwin, 1998).

In the late 1980s and 1990s there has been a growing concern about a much wider group of 'status zero' 16- and 17-year-olds (Pierce and Hillman, 1998; Select Committee on Education and Employment, 1998), a term coined to identify young people who are not in any form of education, work or training and have no known independent form of income (Williamson, 1997). Estimates of the size of this group vary. Early studies of the phenomenon in South Wales suggested that it may cover as many as 23% of the 16- to 17-year-old age group. Analysis of the Survey of English Housing suggests a concentration of status zero young people in social housing, with 23% in council houses and 29% in housing association properties. The Unemployment Unit estimates that 170,000 16- and 17-year-olds are not in any form of education, training or employment, yet only 12% of this number are in receipt of any welfare benefit (Chatrik and Convery, 1998).

The Department for Education and Employment now accepts that over 100,000 of the age group are not in education, training or work and have announced an initiative to entice them back into education (*The Guardian*, 1 October 1998). Yet many of this group are disaffected from school well before this age, and the degree to which the new initiative will be successful in enticing them back for more after minimum school-leaving age remains to be seen. The complexity of their circumstances remains under-researched and the government's Social Exclusion Unit (SEU) is now addressing the issue. The SEU estimate is 160,000, one in 11 of the age group (SEU, 1999). Many of this group also experience homelessness and detachment from families (Hall, 1996). The dynamics of how this occurs remains unclear, although one study indicates that it is a result of numerous small and often unplanned, chaotic events in young people's lives, some of which are more related to their family circumstances than part of a deliberate attempt to shun employment, training or education (Williamson, 1997). All this suggests that social research needs to be careful and more vigilant about the interaction of family and housing factors with education and labour market experiences (Catan, 1998).

Socioeconomic and policy trends and youth transitions

Three sets of factors have been important in shaping the changing pattern of youth transitions: labour markets, changes in family structure and welfare reforms. The first relate to the growth of extended transitions in which young people find themselves dependent upon families for longer periods of time. Extended transitions are largely the result of changes in the youth labour market, the housing market and systems of education and training. Much of the relevant research has focused on ways in which these have been caused by changes in the youth labour market, in youth training and post-compulsory education. As Roberts has noted (1984, 1995), whereas in 1974, nearly two thirds of 16-year-olds were in employment, by 1984 the proportion in work had reduced to less than one in five, and 10 years later reduced to one in 10. The collapse of the youth labour market in the 1970s resulted initially in a very rapid expansion of youth training in which more than a quarter of 16- and 17-year-olds participated in the mid-1980s.

The impact of youth training has been far reaching, especially in substantially reducing the income available to young people and increasing their risk of poverty. The 'training allowance' paid to 17-year-olds remained fixed at the same level of £35 and for 16-year-olds at £29.50 from 1986-89, when it was finally increased – by £0.50. Convery has recently estimated that, had these weekly allowances been upgraded in line with the average earnings of their age group, 16- and 17-year-olds would now be receiving £81 and £108 respectively. Furthermore, in circumstances where young people *are* entitled to benefit, these rates have deliberately been set below 'training allowances' in order to retain 'incentives' to be in training. Even when first introduced, training schemes were regarded by young people as 'slave labour' (Coles, 1988). The failure to upgrade allowance rates goes some way to explaining why, when a choice is realistic, young people have turned to post-16 education and part-time employment, rather than youth training, that now caters for less than one in 10 of the age group.

The recent rapid expansion of post-16 education led to nearly four in five 16- to 18-year-olds being in full-time education in most parts of the country in the late 1990s and a third of young people over the age of 18 being in higher education (CSO, 1997). The number of over-16 year-olds who are financially dependent upon their parents for substantially longer periods has, therefore, more than doubled in less than a decade.

Changes in the labour market have also been matched by changes in the housing market. There has been a reduction in the types of property young people were able to access in previous decades, and their ability to afford the rents charged in the private rented sector. Most young people are not a priority group in housing allocations in social housing, and stocks of suitable housing which they may be able to afford have been reduced. Clearly, extended transitions into the labour market serve to limit young people's access to an income through which to purchase independent housing until their early twenties. Even when in employment, the income levels of young men are less than the average for all men in manual groups and those of young women considerably less again (Seavers and Coles, 1998). Unless other family members are able to subsidise a young person's attempt to live independently, it is highly unlikely that they will be able to afford to do so until they have both obtained secure and well-paid employment, and saved sufficiently to afford the start-up costs of an independent home. In all housing sectors, therefore, opportunities for young people have been squeezed by either a contraction in the supply of suitable housing or by their inability to afford its cost.

The second set of factors concerns changes in family structures and encompasses the growth in the numbers of lone parents, higher divorce and remarriage rates, and increasing number of households in which the parent(s) may be unable or unwilling to support young people during extended transitions. During the same period that the family dependency of young people increased both in length and volume, family structures themselves have become more brittle. Since the 1960s, the number of lone-parent families has more than doubled, and there has been a fourfold increase in the number of divorces and a threefold growth of re-marriages. In 'snapshot' terms, the overwhelming majority of children still live with two parents. Many family structures, however, change during the time children grow up and it is important to map the dynamics of family change onto static pictures of the distributions of family types. If the dynamics of family life *are* taken into account, by the time they reach the age of 16 only around 50% of young people are still living with both their married biological parents (Kiernan and Wicks, 1990; Burghes, 1994). The implications of this in terms of 'family dependency' remain worrying but unclear. Research by Jones (1995a) shows that family support was most likely to be forthcoming where parents were in employment and where families were intact.

The third set of issues concern change in the welfare and benefit systems. Research has demonstrated that in key social policy areas, reforms were introduced which seemed oblivious to major social, economic and familial trends and to the extended process of youth transition (Harris, 1989; Craig, 1991, 1998; Maclagan, 1993; Coles, 1995; Jones, 1995b). Key among these policy changes are the 1986 and 1988 Social Security Acts. The 1986 Act, implemented in 1988, replaced Supplementary Benefit with Income Support, but removed entitlement for Income Support from 16- and 17-year-olds and set a different rate than for those aged 18-25. These changes have been continued under the Jobseekers' Allowance introduced in 1996. Prior to 1988, Supplementary Benefit was based upon a distinction between householders and non-householders in calculating entitlement. The new assessments explicitly assume that the financial responsibilities and needs of young people who are unemployed and under the age of 25, differ from those of older age groups. Assessment is based on age alone rather than needs or financial obligations.

The withdrawal of benefit entitlement from 16- and 17-year-olds was done explicitly in tandem with the introduction of a 'youth training guarantee', which asserted that all in that age group not in full-time education would be guaranteed a youth training place. Some have argued that the withdrawal of benefit was also specifically designed as both a work incentive and as a means of discouraging young people from leaving the parental home (Roll, 1990; Jones, 1991). Yet research undertaken since the implementation of the Act has consistently shown both that the guarantee is not being met, and that a significant number of young people are estranged from their parents and cannot reasonably be expected to look to them for financial support (Craig, 1991; Killeen, 1992: Maclagan, 1993; Chatrik and Convery, 1998). Some attempt to remedy this was made in 1988 with the introduction of the Youth Training Bridging Allowance and Severe Hardship Payment which were intended to address the needs of what were thought to be a very small number of 'deserving' cases. Yet between 1989-92, applications for Severe Hardship Payment increased by 300% and in 1992 nearly two thirds of applications were for repeat and continuous claims (Maclagan, 1993). The procedures for claiming this benefit are extremely complex, are often administered by staff who do not appear to understand the rules (Castles, 1997), and result in only short-term weekly benefits of less than £30. Application for Severe Hardship Payment also involves young people having to provide incontrovertible evidence that they are registered with the careers service as looking for work or a training place and that they are irretrievably estranged from their parents (McManus, 1998).

Single young people have generally been accorded low priority in terms of their eligibility for social housing and legislation has underpinned this position. For example, the 1985 Housing Act continued to encourage local authorities to take no responsibility for those who are deemed to be 'intentionally homeless' (Evans, 1996) and in 1997, housing benefit rules were further tightened so that those aged under 25 are required to live in different types of accommodation compared to older age groups (see also Excell, 1998). This policy climate has convinced many young people that 'leaving home' is an extremely precarious business and that state benefits are unlikely to provide much assistance in helping them settle in secure accommodation away from the family home.

Policy changes in education, particularly higher education, have also brought about longer periods of family dependency. The gradual erosion of the maintenance grant, the introduction of student loans to meet the shortfall, and, since 1997, tuition fees for undergraduates, means that young people who benefit from higher education do so at both considerable expense to their families and the accumulation of debt to themselves. It is estimated that the average debt accumulated by undergraduates is now of the order of £10,000 (*Times Educational Supplement*, 14 August 1998). While having a degree may qualify young people to enter a more lucrative (if increasingly insecure and precarious) graduate labour market, students characteristically now embark upon such employment careers with debts and loans to pay off. The full impact of these trends will not be felt for a few years but what is clear from this discussion is that changes in the policy context, including education, labour market and benefit changes, are all pushing in the same direction – towards further extending youth transitions and requiring longer periods of dependency upon the family. In circumstances in which this is impossible, young people have become homeless and destitute.

Youth homelessness

A number of attempts have been made in recent years to estimate the size of the homeless population although widely differing estimates are as much a result of differences of definition as difficulties in researching the issue. A recent review of the evidence indicated that in the early 1980s, the homeless population was predominantly white, middle-aged and male, although youth homelessness (especially those in hostels and Bed & Breakfast accommodation) increased markedly throughout the decade (Pleace and Quilgars, 1999). The Cabinet Office SEU reported on rough sleepers as one of its first tasks, estimating that, despite a number of initiatives introduced by governments in the 1990s, 2,400 still slept rough in London alone each year, with a further 10,000 sleeping rough outside the capital at some point during the year (SEU, 1998b). The SEU report suggests that a quarter of rough sleepers were aged between 18 and 25, although it claimed that only a few rough sleepers were under the age of 18. At the beginning of the 1990s, young people, usually defined as under the age of 25, were reported to be under-represented among the 'street homeless' or 'rough sleepers', but over-represented among those living in hostels or Bed & Breakfast accommodation (Anderson et al, 1993; Hutson and Liddiard, 1994). At the time of the 1991 Census there were 18% of 16- to 24-year-olds in the general population, but 30% of single homeless people living in hostels in the same age group (Anderson et al, 1993; Pleace and Quilgars, 1999). Taking a broader definition of youth homelessness, the 1996 National Inquiry into youth homelessness concluded that, in the previous year, just short of a quarter of a million young people between the ages of 16 and 25 were homeless (Evans, 1996). The definition this Inquiry used included those who were totally without accommodation (the street homeless) but also those who only had temporary shelter, in hostels, Bed & Breakfast accommodation or a squat, and those who were insecurely housed, living with relatives or friends who were unable or unwilling to continue to accommodate them in the long term (often sleeping on settees or floors).

The last official attempt to measure youth homelessness was made by a study commissioned by the Department of Environment in 1991. This involved a survey of 1,346 people living in hostels and Bed & Breakfast accommodation, and smaller samples of people who were sleeping rough or making use of soup runs in which food was distributed to those assumed to be homeless. This was a study covering single homeless people of all ages, although young people under the age of 25 were over-represented in all three samples (Anderson et al, 1993). The research sought to identify the characteristics of the single homeless, examine why they remained homeless and what were their accommodation and support needs and preferences. Women were less likely to figure among the homeless population than men, although the CHAR (Campaign for the Homeless and Rootless) inquiry reported recent increases in the number of young women in the mid-1990s. Minority ethnic groups were also over-represented, although this finding may have been skewed, because of the areas (mainly London) where the data were collected. Minority ethnic groups represent only 5% of the UK population, yet 40% of the single homeless living in hostels were from minority ethnic groups and under the age of 25. Those who had been 'looked after' and those who had been in custody were also heavily over-represented. Although less than 1% of the age cohort, those leaving care represented around a third of all those homeless and living in hostels or Bed & Breakfast. Among those aged 16 and 17, 39% had previously lived in a children's home and 32% had experienced foster care, with 18% and 11% respectively in the 18-24 age group. A third of all 16- to 24-year olds who were homeless also reported that they had been either in prison or a young offenders' institution, and a further 6% had been in a drugs or alcohol unit. Another significant group were those who reported that they had left home because of conflict with parents (14%), relationship breakdowns (6%), violence or abuse (3%) or because they experienced harassment or felt insecure in their last home (5%). Only 1% wanted to return home, with the vast majority (95%) wanting to find a house or a flat in which to live independently. Yet given their experience of unemployment and their entitlement to benefit, this seemed an unlikely prospect.

The vast majority of the single homeless are unemployed, dependent upon benefits, and in poverty (Pleace and Quilgars, 1999). The 1991 Department of the Environment survey found that only 12% of the sample had been in work the previous week. Forty-four per cent of 16- and 17-year-olds and 60% of those aged between 18 and 24 were receiving Income Support, giving them median incomes of £31 and £40 respectively. Perhaps understandably, most recognised that they not only needed access to adequate and secure accommodation, but help and support with budgeting and money management. However, begging was not reported to be a source of income for these groups except for a small minority of the younger age group who were sleeping rough.

Care leavers and running away from care

The younger age group is, however, a distinct and highly vulnerable group. Within it recent studies have commented on the disproportionate number of people within the population of young people 'looked after' by local authorities who become homeless, including young people who run away before the age of 18. These studies are important in that they point to an important sub-group among the homeless, who may not remain homeless for long, but when they do, have no access to an income either through employment or through welfare support. Newman (1989) estimated that there were nearly 100,000 running away incidents per year, close to the estimate of 102,000 made in 1990 by Abrahams and Mungall (1992). Surveys of general school populations estimate that one in seven young people under the age of 16 had run away from home and stayed out overnight at least once (Rees, 1993). Abrahams and Mungall also claimed that much recorded running away was concentrated within the group of young people 'looked after', with nearly a third of all runaway young people doing so from 'substitute' care. Within this latter group, the vast majority were running away from residential care and, as Wade et al (1998) concluded, more likely to run away repeatedly, stay away for longer, start running away at an earlier age and be picked up by the police.

Running away was also associated with having criminal convictions (Sinclair and Gibbs, 1998). Research by Wade et al concluded that girls were as likely to run away as boys and that the peak ages for running away from care were between 13 and 15, although there was a considerable minority who ran away before this age. This research cast doubt on previous findings that there is a preponderance of black (mainly African-Caribbean) children running away from care, although bullying (including incidents of racist abuse) were noted as important in some cases. Young people defined as having emotional and behavioural difficulties were also found to go missing more often, at an earlier age, stay away for longer, be more likely to be excluded from school, have past convictions and return reluctantly, than other runaways. All this suggests that there is a sizeable, if transitory, population of very young homeless who have no known means of financial support: it is highly likely that these will be found among those who beg at some stage in their lives.

Strategies of survival in a risk society

As the transitions to adulthood have become more protracted and less secure, many young people develop their own strategies of survival. Research on such strategies has been unsystematic although there is a growing interest in 'alternative careers', sometimes involving the informal economy of undeclared earnings, sometimes involving crime, occasionally involving forays into self-employment, and often involving the use and sale of illegal drugs (MacDonald and Coffield, 1991; MacDonald, 1994; Craine and Coles, 1995; Craine, 1997; Parker et al, 1998). MacDonald and Coffield (1991), in their study of young people's use of enterprise initiatives, indicate that very few young people did so with any degree of economic success. The majority either (barely) survived through working extremely long hours in precarious circumstances, or failed disastrously, often accruing very large debts. In his study of coping with youth unemployment in the 1980s, Craine (1997) documents how some developed quite lucrative careers involving the informal economy, drug-dealing, benefit fraud and sometimes quite spectacular and undetected crime. When faced by the collapse – or blocking – of legitimate routes through youth transitions, young people do, therefore, develop their own survival strategies: begging, again, is clearly one of these survival strategies.

Parker et al, in trying to explain the rapid expansion of recreational drug use in the 1990s, also see part of the explanation as lying in the changing nature of youth transitions.

> Rapid social changes in so many facets of everyday life have conspired to make growing up today 'feel' far less secure and more uncertain for far longer.... The unprecedented increase in recreational drug use is deeply embedded in these and other processes since such drug use is both about risk taking but also about using 'time out' to self-medicate the impact of the stresses and strains of both success and failure in 'modern' times. (Parker et al, 1998, pp 151-2)

Their work on drug use also indicates that in making choices young people make complex 'cost-benefit' analyses in which patterns of behaviour are considered to be worth the risk and the cost, and others completely unacceptable. They argue that, while the widespread use of 'recreational drugs' is rapidly becoming 'normalised' and acceptable to young people, injecting drugs or using heroin are not.

> **Despite their apparent sophistication about their own drugs of choice, 1990s adolescents maintain a fairly stereotypical imaging of hard drug users as dangerous, diseased, dishevelled injecting 'junkies' and 'saddos' who commit vast amounts of crime to fund their habit. (Parket et al, 1998, pp 151-2)**

Part of the 'costs' of drug use were seen as creating intolerable conflict with parents. In their study of young people, health and family life at the beginning of the 1990s, Brannen et al (1994) commented on the fact that, despite many parents themselves being young in the alleged permissive eras of the 1960s and 1970s, they were completely and universally opposed to any drug use. Parker et al suggest that, in the late 1990s, many parents are more tolerant of young people using the most widespread drug of young people's choice, cannabis. Yet their attitude to young people using other 'recreational drugs' in widespread circulation, such as LSD amphetamines and Ecstasy, was still very negative with many young people hiding such use from parents because of a fear of the consequences. The growing 'normalisation' of drug use by young people is, therefore, still a major cause of family friction and youth homelessness. Underlying the connection between drug use and begging, therefore, lie not only the supposedly simple economic or hedonistic motives of the young people who beg for money to buy drugs, but also more complex indirect factors mediated through the homelessness and poverty that can stem from family conflict over drugs.

Carlen (1997), in her study of the young homeless, also reported similar 'mental boundaries' of what young homeless people think to be acceptable. She discusses a variety of strategies of 'survivalism', involving increasing risky activities such as "begging, busking, prostitution, drug taking, drug dealing, more systematic and serious crime, and bouts of public drunkenness with all the attendant violent and police interventions" (Carlen, 1997, p 120). Many of these survival strategies involve huge personal risks. One female street homeless respondent reported rape. Those who made use of hostels reported attacks, abuse and the theft of personal property. Those who resorted to begging described violence and harassment. Some of Carlen's respondents reported that robbery or burglary might be considered as a necessary evil to which young people will resort in desperate situations.

Nevertheless, many regard begging as beneath them and something they will not even contemplate. Embarrassment, fear and pride were given as reasons either why it had never been resorted to or why it had been eventually rejected as a strategy for raising money. Yet 44 of her 100 respondents did report that at some stage they had been driven to begging, although the amounts raised were between £15 and £20 per day, and for some 'enough money for a bag of chips' rather than an alternative income which could compensate for the lack of a job or the lack of a home. Interestingly, and despite the fact that some research (see Chapter Six in this volume) indicates that a few young people may use income from begging to fuel expensive drug habits, many of Carlen's respondents "ruminated on the propriety of spending money from begging on drugs or drink". The relationship between the growth of drug use and begging is therefore likely to be complex, with drug use being an important source of family friction and homelessness, rather than begging apparently being regarded by young people as an easy or acceptable source of income to fund drug habits.

Conclusions and policy implications

This chapter has focused on young people and the changing world in which they are growing up in. It has examined a number of trends in education, the labour market, family life and examined how these have impacted upon social and economic inequalities; and the growth in the number of young people who are in poverty and socially excluded. It has attempted to estimate the size of a population of young people who are at risk of long-term unemployment and homelessness. It has also examined the social policy context which in many ways has exacerbated the processes of exclusion, and provided little by way of an official safety net when young people find themselves with no alternative means of support.

Following the election of a new government in 1997, there are signs that a number of youth issues described in this chapter have started to be taken seriously. The SEU especially has produced reports on homelessness, educational disaffection and the spatial concentrations of disadvantage and in 1999 is due to report on teenage pregnancy and 'status zero' 16- and 17-year-olds (SEU, 1998a, 1998b, 1998c, 1999). The unit has repeatedly recognised that the 'joined-up' problems it has addressed require 'joined-up' solutions, requiring multiagency partnerships and more 'holistic' interventions. At a local level, the same vocabulary is being adopted by statutory agencies and the voluntary sector and a number of promising locally-based initiatives can be identified (Coles, 2000). The Department of Health has been prompted to promise a fundamental and far reaching review of the care system and the scandalous lack of provision and support for young people leaving care (Utting, 1997; DoH, 1999). Clearly, if this concern is to have an impact, all the issues surrounding youth poverty need adequately to be addressed, including housing provision, adequate and suitable education and training and support, more general and generic support for young people 'at risk', and a benefit entitlement for those who fall through the net (Coles, 2000: forthcoming; COYPSS, 1999).

We have also examined a range of different ways in which young people have been developing alternative strategies of survival as they face youth transitions which are more protracted and filled with risk and uncertainty. Among these, begging is only one of a range of alternatives and for many young people, even the poor and socially excluded, it is still regarded as something to which they will not resort. Nevertheless, it is salutary to find that some of the other alternatives may prove even more threatening to a safer society, and that, regardless of their professed attitudes towards begging, some – and an increasing number of – young people are forced to engage in it or, at the very least, perceive it as a rational strategy for survival in the circumstances in which they find themselves. These circumstances are likely to involve some combination of periods in institutional care, family breakdown, low educational achievement, poor work or training prospects and very limited housing options. Welfare and employment reform – not least the restoration of adequate social assistance arrangements, guaranteed good quality training and employment, and appropriate, affordable and, where relevant, supported housing – has a large part to play in changing the circumstances which drive young people, however unwillingly, to beg.

References

Abrahams, C and Mungall, R. (1992) *Runaways: Exploding the myths*, London: NCH – Action for Children.

Anderson, I., Kemp, P. and Quilgars, D. (1993) *Single homeless people*, London: HMSO.

Ashton, D.N., Maguire, M. and Spilsbury, M. (1988) 'Local labour markets and their impact upon youths', in B. Coles (ed) *Young careers: Youth unemployment and the new vocationalism*, Buckingham: Open University Press.

Ashton, D.N., Maguire, M. and Spilsbury, M. (1990) *Restructuring the labour market: The implications for youth*, London: Macmillan.

Baldwin, D. (1998) *Growing up in and out of care: An ethnographic approach to young people's transitions to adulthood*, Unpublished DPhil thesis, University of York.

Baldwin, D., Coles, B. and Mitchell, W. (1997) 'The formation of an underclass or disparate processes of social exclusion? Evidence from two groupings', in R. MacDonald (ed) *Youth, the 'underclass' and social exclusion*, London: Routledge.

Banks, M., Bates, I., Breakwell, G., Byner, J., Emler, N., Jamieson, L. and Roberts, K. (1992) *Careers and identities*, Buckingham: Open University Press.

Bates, I. and Riseborough, G. (1993) *Youth and inequality*, Buckingham: Open University Press.

Biehal, N., Clayton, J., Stein, M.C. and Wade, J. (1995) *Moving on: Young people and leaving care schemes*, London: HMSO.

Brannen, J., Dodd, K., Oakley, A. and Storey, P. (1994) *Young people, health and family life*, Buckingham: Open University Press.

Broad, R. (1998) *Leaving care: The results of a national survey*, Brasted: Royal Philanthropic Society.

Burghes, L. (1994) *Lone parenthood and family disruption: The outcomes for children*, London: Family Policy Studies Centre.

Carlen, P. (1997) *Jigsaw: A political criminology of youth homelessness*, Buckingham: Open University Press.

Castles, J. (1997) *16 and 17 year olds. Do the government's existing policies surrounding employment, training, benefits and housing meet the needs of those claiming Severe Hardship*, Unpublished MA dissertation, Department of Social Policy, University of York.

Catan, L. (1998) 'Review of Bynner et al (1997)', *Journal of Youth Studies*, vol 1, no 3, pp 349-51.

Chatrik, B. and Convery, P. (1998) 'Nine out of ten jobless under 18s without an income', *Working Brief*, No 93, May, London: Unemployment Unit–Youthaid.

Coles, B. (ed) (1988) *Young careers: Youth unemployment and the new vocationalism*, Buckingham: Open University Press.

Coles, B. (1995) *Youth and social policy: Youth citizenship and young careers*, London: UCL Press.

Coles, B. (2000) *Youth policy and youth interventions: The new agenda and new beginnings*, Ilford: Barnardo's.

Connolly, M., Roberts, K., Ben-Tovim, G. and Torkington, P. (1991) *Black youth in Liverpool*, Culemborg: Italy, Giordano Bruno.

COYPSS (Coalition on Young People and Social Security) (1999) *Sort it out! Reforming the benefit system for 16 and 17 year olds*, London: COYPSS.

Craig, G. (1991) *Fit for nothing? Young people, benefits and youth training*, London: The Children's Society.

Craig, G. (1998) 'The privatisation of human misery', *Critical Social Policy*, vol 18, no 1, pp 51-76.

Craig, G. (1999) '"Race", poverty and social security', in J. Ditch (ed) *Poverty and social security*, London, Routledge.

Craine, S. (1997) 'The 'Black Magic roundabout': cyclical transitions, social exclusion and alternative careers', in R. MacDonald (ed) *Youth, the 'underclass' and social exclusion*, London: Routledge.

Craine, S. and Coles, B. (1995) 'Alternative careers: youth transitions and young people's involvement in crime', *Youth and Policy*, no 48, pp 6-27.

CSO (Central Statistical Office) (1997) *Regional trends*, London: HMSO.

DoH (Department of Health) (1999) *The government's response to the Children's Safeguard Review*, London: The Stationery Office.

Evans, A. (1996) *We don't choose to be homeless: A report of the National Inquiry into Homelessness*, London: CHAR.

Excell, R. (1998) 'Benefits discriminate against young people', *Working Brief*, No 98, October, London: Unemployment Unit–Youthaid.

Furlong, A. (1992) *Growing up in a classless society? School to work transitions*, Edinburgh: University of Edinburgh Press.

Furlong, A. and Cartmel, F. (1997) *Young people and social change: Individualization and risk in late modernity*, Buckingham: Open University Press.

Garnett, L. (1992) *Leaving care and after*, London: National Children's Bureau.

Griffin, C. (1985) *Typical girls: Young women from school to the job market*, London: Routledge and Kegan Paul.

Hall, J. (1996) *Status zero: A young person's road to homelessness*, London: The DePaul Trust.

Harris, N.S. (1989) *Social security for young people*, Aldershot: Avebury.

Hutson, S. and Liddiard, M. (1994) *Youth homelessness*, Basingstoke: Macmillan.

Jones, G. (1991) 'The cost of living in the parental home', *Youth and Policy*, no 32, pp 19-29.

Jones, G. (1995a) *Family support for young people*, London: Family Policy Studies Centre.

Jones, G. (1995b) *Leaving home*, Buckingham: Open University Press.

Jones, G. and Wallace, C. (1992) *Youth, family and citizenship*, Milton Keynes: Open University Press.

Kiernan, K. and Wicks, M. (1990) *Family change and future policy*, York: Joseph Rowntree Memorial Trust/Family Policy Studies Centre.

Killeen, D. (1992) 'Leaving home: housing and income – social policy on leaving home', in J. Coleman and C. Warren-Adamson (eds) *Youth policy in the 1990s: The way forward*, London: Routledge and Kegan Paul.

MacDonald, R. (1994) 'Fiddly jobs, undeclared working and the "something for nothing" society', *Work, Employment and Society*, vol 8, no 4, pp 507-30.

MacDonald, R. and Coffield, F. (1991) *Risky business? Youth and the enterprise culture*, Basingstoke: The Falmer Press.

Maclagan, I. (1993) *Four years severe hardship: Young people and the benefits gap*, London: COPYSS.

McManus, J. (1998) 'Care leavers need more help', *Working Brief*, no 98, October, London: Unemployment Unit–Youthaid.

Modood, T., Berthoud, R., Lakey, J., Nazran, J., Smith, P., Virdee, S. and Beishon, S. (1998) *Ethnic minorities in Britain*, London: Policy Studies Institute.

Morrow, G. and Richards, M. (1996) *Transitions to adulthood: A family matter*, York: Joseph Rowntree Foundation.

Newman, C. (1989) *Young runaways: Findings from Britain's first safe house*, London: The Children's Society.

Parker, H. Aldridge, J. and Measham, F. (1998) *Illegal leisure: The normalisation of adolescent recreational drug use*, London: Routledge.

Pierce, N. and Hillman, J. (1998) *Wasted youth*, London: Institute of Public Policy Research.

Pleace, N. and Quilgars, D. (1999) 'Youth homelessness', in J. Rugg (ed) *Young people, housing and social policy*, London: Routledge.

Rees, G. (1993) *Hidden truths: Young people's experiences of running away*, London: The Children's Society.

Roberts, K. (1984) *School leavers and their prospects: Youth and the labour market in the 1980s*, Milton Keynes: Open University Press.

Roberts, K. (1993) 'Career trajectories and the mirage of increased social mobility', in I .Bates and G. Riseborough (eds) *Youth and inequality*, Buckingham: Open University Press.

Roberts, K. (1995) *Youth and employment in modern Britain*, Oxford: Oxford University Press.

Roll, J. (1990) *Young people: Growing up in the welfare state*, London: Family Policy Studies Centre.

Seavers, J. and Coles, B. (1998) *Living at home: The implications of extended youth transitions*, York: Centre for Housing Policy, University of York.

Select Committee on Education and Employment (1998) *Disaffected youth*, Fifth Report, HC 498-1 and II, London: The Stationery Office.

SEU (Social Exclusion Unit) (1998a) *Truancy and school exclusions*, Cm 3957, London: The Stationery Office.

SEU (1998b) *Rough sleeping*, London: SEU.

SEU (1998c) *Bringing Britain together: A national strategy for neighbourhood renewal*, Cm 4045, London: The Stationery Office.

SEU (1999) *16-18 year-olds not in education, training or employment*, Consultation Letter, London: SEU.

Sinclair, I. and Gibbs, I. (1998) *Children's homes: A study of diversity*, Chichester: John Wiley.

Skeggs, B. (1990) 'Gender reproduction and further education: domestic apprenticeships', in D. Gleeson (ed) *Training and its alternatives*, Milton Keynes: Open University Press.

Skeggs, B. (1997) *Formations of class and gender*, London: Sage Publications.

Stein, M. and Carey, M. (1986) *Leaving care*, London: Blackwell.

Utting, W. (1997) *People like us: The report of the safeguards for children living away from home*, London: The Stationery Office.

Wade, J., Biehal, N. with Claydon, J. and Stein, M. (1998) *Going missing: Young people absent from care*, Chichester: John Wiley.

Wallace, C. (1987) *For richer, for poorer: Growing up in and out of work*, London: Tavistock.

Williamson, H. (1997) 'Status zero, youth and the "underclass": some considerations', in R. MacDonald (ed) *Youth, the 'underclass' and social exclusion*, London: Routledge.

SIX

Easy pickings or hard profession? Begging as an economic activity

Hartley Dean and Margaret Melrose

[A]s to outlandish and strange beggars they ought not to be borne with ... for all the great rogueries ... are done by these. (Martin Luther, *Liber Vagatorum*, 1528)

[T]he beggar who suns himself by the side of the highway, possesses that security which kings are fighting for. (Adam Smith, *A theory of moral sentiments*, 1757)

A beggar, looked at realistically, is simply a businessman, getting his living, like other businessmen, in the way that comes to hand. He has not, more than most modern people, sold his honour; he has merely made the mistake of choosing a trade at which it is impossible to grow rich. (George Orwell, *Down and out in Paris and London*, 1933)

"When I was a kid I run away from the children's home, 'cos I didn't like it, and er, didn't have no money, so I had to beg for food and stuff like that, and er, then I got into drugs, like, so I had to start begging for drugs; 'cos ... when I got like old enough the DHSS didn't want to know me [or] give me money 'cos I was homeless.... I've been on the streets since I was about 13.... I hate it ... it's not nice waking up in the morning cold and all that.... [A]ll my rights have been tooken away from me really ... 'cos of the way people treat you. Like, they sort of sweep you under the carpet." (A 36-year-old London beggar, 1997)

Begging is a perennial phenomenon, capable of a variety of competing interpretations. The first three of the epigraphs above, separated in provenance by approximately 200-year intervals, give expression to three quite different mythologies about the nature of beggars and begging: the

fourth reflects contemporary reality. Although begging has lately returned
to the agenda as a political issue (see Chapter Two in this volume), from
a policy perspective little research has been devoted to the contemporary
manifestation of the phenomenon, except in so far that begging is
associated with homelessness (for example, Murdoch, 1994). This is
understandable in the late modern context: the temporo-spatial revolution
that shrinks the globe we inhabit (Giddens, 1990) can dislocate the sense
of 'home' (Walter, 1979), bringing a new dimension to the meaning of
home*less*ness and new fears regarding the spaces occupied by people who
are literally homeless (Wardhaugh, 1996, and Chapter Seven in this
volume). Globalisation, however, is fundamentally an economic process.
Its technological and cultural aspects are underpinned by a massive
expansion in the circulation of capital and a radical restructuring of labour
markets. It is global economic forces which are implicated in the increasing
social inequality and exclusion that are evident at the local level within
'developed' Western societies (Jordan, 1996, and Chapter Four in this
volume) and in the growing significance of diverse forms of informal
economic activity, ranging from casualised or illegal forms of employment
and entrepreneurship at one end of the spectrum (see, for example,
Bourgois, 1996), to street-level economic activity, including begging, at
the other.

Begging, therefore, should be understood as a specific form of economic
activity occurring within particular historical circumstances and local
contexts. This chapter reports the findings of a small-scale pilot study
involving interviews with beggars in England and Scotland, conducted
in 1997. The specific methods of the study and some of their implications
are separately discussed later in this book (in Chapter Nine). Here we
describe the people who took part in the study, the nature of their
economic activity and the basis of their social exclusion. We shall conclude
with some discussion of the policy implications.

The sample

No claims can be made for the representativeness of the sample, but it
consisted of 19 men, aged from 21 to 47. More than a third of the sample
(eight participants) were aged under 26. Two of the participants were
from minority ethnic groups (one African-Caribbean, the other defined
himself as 'mixed race'); the remaining participants were white. Of the 19
interviews, 14 were conducted in England (11 in London, one in Luton

and two in York) and five in Scotland (Edinburgh). It should be noted that begging remains a criminal offence in England, but not in Scotland.

A majority of the sample (11 participants) had been begging for more than five years: for them begging was not a transitory activity. However, a substantial minority (eight) combined begging with other economic activity, including *Big Issue* selling, busking or casual employment. A substantial minority (eight) were claiming social security benefits and begging, though a majority who were entitled to claim benefits, were not doing so: the reasons for this will be discussed below. Nonetheless, most participants were combining income from begging with income from other sources. Less than half the sample (nine participants) were actually sleeping rough, seven were staying in hostels or with friends and three had accommodation of their own. Not all beggars are homeless, but, as we shall see, access to housing remained a critical issue for most of the sample.

Almost half the sample (nine participants) had previously been in some sort of institutional care, either within the childcare system, mental hospital or prison, and all but five made specific reference to a troubled family background. Most participants had had experience of the criminal justice system, including 14 who had been either arrested, cautioned or convicted for non-begging related offences, such as shop-lifting. A majority of the sample (14 participants) had previously worked, including six who had had permanent jobs. Almost half the sample (nine participants) admitted spending some or all of their income from begging on drugs or alcohol and a majority (13) admitted current or past involvement with drugs and/or alcohol. Experiences of dysfunctional families, of institutional care and/or brushes with the law, therefore, figured significantly within the narratives which were disclosed. Such narratives were characteristically chaotic: they told of lives which were at best unhappy and at worst traumatic. The cost of sustaining a drug or alcohol habit was cited or appeared to be a significant factor dictating the need for some participants to supplement income from other sources (including social security and/or casual employment) through begging.

The begging process

The study deliberately targeted only those people who had been actually observed 'begging', which we defined as soliciting a voluntary unilateral gift in a public place. Generally, the approach to begging adopted by the participants was essentially passive, even in Edinburgh where beggars need not in theory fear the legal consequences of a more active or conspicuous approach. All begged from a sitting position, some silently, with a hat placed in front of them or with a sign, usually saying 'homeless and hungry, please help'; others, more vocally, asking passers-by if they could 'spare any change'. Several participants said they would vary their technique, depending on the circumstances or their mood, and virtually all emphasised the importance of being 'polite' to passers-by. Participants were, by and large, conscious of the offence which they might cause and sought to minimise this by being as unobtrusive or as obsequious as possible (cf Chapter Eight in this volume). Only rarely did participants describe a more up-beat approach:

> "I use a bit of imagination, ha ha. I've always been a bit of a showman. Depends what mood I'm in. Sometimes I might be really sad, so it's quite hard. So I might not say anything. I mean, just sit like that. *[Cups his hands in front of him in a theatrically supplicatory posture.]* But if I'm really happy I'll say 'Hey! Man! Look, you can get some money in the hat now! Woah', and 'Get the money in the hat now!'. Have real good fun you know."

Experience indicates that there are those who sometimes beg by approaching people on the street or in tube trains, but, although a couple of the participants in the study said they had on occasions tried such an approach (when they had been drunk, for example), most eschewed it as risky and/or ineffectual.

Most participants (12) chose their begging pitches, in part at least, for the numbers of passers-by that they could normally expect (main streets, outside supermarkets, etc), although a few (five) chose quieter but established pitches at which they were known by the regular inhabitants.

Seven participants had at some time been arrested or charged specifically for begging and most, including those from Edinburgh, reported being questioned or moved on by the police. Although begging is not a criminal offence in Scotland, at the time of the study the *Scotsman* newspaper had initiated a campaign to persuade local authorities to pass by-laws prohibiting begging. Of those who discussed the legality of begging, almost half our participants (six out of 13) were either confused or ignorant on the subject. One of the participants interviewed in York confirmed our suspicion that the police tend to be especially vigilant in tourist locations (see also Chapter Twelve in this volume):

> "I've had quite a lot [of trouble with the police], because people,
> people like shop owners ring 'em up and stuff like that you know,
> give me fines and stuff for begging.... I got a £160 fine not so
> long back. I were due in court on [date] and I didn't turn up, so
> the police, they'll probably 'ave a warrant out for me soon
> anyway."

Estimates of the amount of money obtained by begging varied enormously.
A couple of participants were very vague (one said "I don't count it"),
but of the 16 who offered an estimate of their total income from all
sources, half put this at less than £100 per week and half at more than
£100 per week. Participants with a substantial heroin habit needed to
make £60 a day or more to feed their addiction. When it was put to
participants who claimed to make just £10 a day from begging that
other people claimed to be getting several times as much, the suggestion
was greeted with derision: we were assured this was not possible and that
we had been absurdly misled. Conversely, however, when participants
who claimed they had made as much as £120 in a day were told that
other people were making a great deal less, they were sceptical, asserting
that the people we had spoken to couldn't have been very good at begging.
Plainly, it is impossible to verify the data, but the evidence probably does
suggest a huge variation in 'takings'. What is more, participants did not
necessarily set out to maximise their takings: a number (nine) would beg
on any one day only for so long as it took to reach a certain takings
target, and at least one acknowledged that his particular method of begging
was not necessarily the most effective.

A number of participants (five) referred to begging as a 'job' or as
'work', or to their takings as 'earnings':

> "I work every day. I can't stand sitting at home.... Tell you
> what, it's a job, it's a job. I'm telling you, there's as many ins and
> outs involved in begging and busking and street working as there
> is in any other job. Probably more in fact. Some people say 'Get
> yourself a job!', but I always tell them that they should try it
> themselves ... it can be a very distressing job."

Some participants even referred to the passers-by who gave them money
as their 'customers' and stressed the importance of both affording 'respect'
to their customers and winning it from them in return. The dominant
discourse of the market transaction can be applied by beggars, apparently

without conscious irony, to defend the nature of their activity (cf Jordan, 1993).

Almost half the sample (nine participants) reported or claimed to have had health problems. In some instances, these were a consequence of substance abuse. In the worst such case, the participant would not seek medical help because there was an arrest warrant out for him and he was being sought by the police, although he fully expected that he would die from liver failure within a year or so. In many ways, however, it was surprising that so many of the participants, in spite of their life-styles, stayed as fit as they appeared to be. Most said they did not go hungry, but inevitably, some of them were not obtaining a satisfactory diet:

> "I don't really eat healthy food or owt like that, you know what I mean. It's mostly junk food. I do get enough though. I reckon I do ... but some days, some days I'll just like, I just won't feel like eating at all, you know what I mean. I'll go a whole day without eating, but the next day I'll make up for it like."

A majority of the sample (13 participants) had been subject to violence or assault while begging. Such incidents included systematic beatings by vigilantes, casual violence from passers-by (characteristically, young, male and drunk), and abusive behaviour (spitting, the throwing of cigarette ends, the kicking over of the participant's hat or board).

> "I get attacked about once a week. Yeah, pushed or someone tries to kick you.... Only about once a week, it's not often, [but] sometimes as many as two or three times."

> "I suppose [name] would have got abuse – that's the girl I beg with, she'd have got abuse at least once a day anyway. At the weekends it was terrible, the abuse, 'cos they were all drunk and loud and jumping about. I don't know, they're revolting."

Two participants reported significant injuries from such attacks and another claimed he had known of beggars who had been killed. However, as several participants explained, violence, intimidation and theft could also be perpetrated on beggars by other beggars and street-people. Several participants expressed their sense of vulnerability and two explained how they had on occasions been approached by people who would demand that they hand over their session's takings. In Edinburgh, one participant described the practice as the 'taxing' of beggars. 'Taxing' has been observed – in the recent past, at least – to have been rife on the streets of London (see Fooks and Pantazis, 1999).

Most participants begged alone. Only five reported ever having worked with a partner, and none claimed to have worked as part of an organised group or team. Anecdotal evidence suggests there maybe, both in London and Edinburgh, communities or groups of street people who gather within a particular vicinity, but it has not been possible to unearth any evidence that such communities are organised for economic purposes. In fact, the evidence suggests it is unlikely. Most participants (15) acknowledged having contact with other beggars, but they were as likely to describe these relationships as competitive or hostile as cooperative or supportive. A few participants clearly wished to present a romantic image of a self-supportive street community, but then contradicted or undermined such imagery by their own accounts. For example, disputes over the 'ownership' of or the rights to beg at a particular pitch are clearly commonplace.

> **"I try and keep myself to myself. That way you don't get pulled into their rows and arguments, or end up getting stabbed and put in the hospital, which has happened to quite a few people."**

As a means of subsistence, it would seem, begging is a potentially hazardous activity situated within highly competitive and predatory social relations.

Social exclusion

Begging is conducted beyond the norms of formal economic activity, but is it a *socially* excluded or excluding form of behaviour? Begging is, in economic terms, a marginalised activity, but are beggars normatively excluded from the values, prejudices and aspirations of other citizens?; and what is the objective basis of their alienation from social relations?

Normative exclusion

Participants were asked whether they begged out of choice. Most (12) said no, and only two unequivocally said yes; those who were more equivocal would emphasise that, though they had decided to beg out of expediency, it was not, as it were, a life-style choice. In one sense, particularly for those with an addiction, choice was an irrelevance, or else the alternatives were even less desirable:

> **"Like you don't really plan ahead. You just think of the day. You live for the day. See yourself all right. Stop yourself from rattling.... But like it's better begging than going out and mugging old grannies and robbing houses and that, and shop-lifting, definitely."**

A majority of the sample (13 participants) admitted that they felt bad about begging and, while others gave more equivocal replies, only one participant professed indifference. Characteristically, participants acknowledged that they felt ashamed to be begging; they spoke of their loss of pride and dignity. Even those who sought to defend begging as being in some way honourable, would tend to contradict themselves and confess that they wished they did not have to beg. For example, one man who insisted that, as a beggar, he 'worked hard', later said "I feel disgraceful when I'm sitting there. I just wish I had the same as everybody else". Another – one of those who claimed he was begging out of choice – later declared "I've got to get out of this begging trap, because ... once you're in, it's very hard to get out".

In spite of the fact that none of the participants unequivocally or consistently celebrated their status as beggars, a substantial minority (nine) reported that, at least some of the time, they felt alright about life. In some instances, this reflected some optimism on the participants' part that they might not have to endure their present predicament for ever. In others, it reflected a sense of rueful resignation and an acknowledgement, for example, that:

> **"I don't think I could handle the responsibility of my own house – all the responsibility that goes with it. I can't handle that. So, sometimes I think to myself that I'm better off. I've no one to worry about and all that – no one but myself, no bairns, no wife, no kids, nothing like that."**

This was not the dominant view, however, and in no way diminishes the reality that most participants said they felt 'down' or bad in themselves. As one poignantly confessed, "I've wasted my youth doing this".

To determine the sense in which, as beggars, these participants regarded themselves nonetheless as citizens, they were asked whether they thought of themselves as having rights as members of society. Over half the sample (12 participants) felt that they did or that they should have some sort of rights, though some felt such rights as they had were denied to them or that "they never come in any use". Asked what kind of entitlements they felt they were not getting, the most commonly mentioned entitlement was housing: in terms of social rights, housing appeared to be a greater priority than cash benefits. Others spoke of the right to work:

> **"I should have the rights to be able to go and get a job tomorrow if I want a job, or if I could find a job, then I should be allowed to work. Last week I tried to get a job, and he wouldn't let me have it because of how I look. Now that is, this is what we're talking about as rights."**

However, several participants also claimed that they were denied their basic civil rights, 'freedom from harassment' or 'protection from the dangers of society'. Some complained, in particular, about the failure of the police to protect them from violence. Participants related stories of how police had refused to intervene on their behalf or had sided with their assailants: "by and large the police will take the view that you've encouraged them or you shouldn't have been doing what you were doing". Other research findings suggest that, even where specialised police homeless units have been established to protect people living on the streets, their interventions tend in practice to criminalise rather than protect (Fooks and Pantazis, 1999). Emphasising the uniquely marginalised status of the beggar, one participant suggested – "people who are thieves and drug dealers, they get more rights than us". Other participants recounted how, even off the streets within hostels for the homeless, they were vulnerable to the theft of their possessions.

Some participants were politically quite well informed, though disillusioned about the relevance of the democratic process to the daily reality of their lives: as one said, "I wouldn't vote for any of [them]. I'm not allowed to vote anyway 'cos I'm homeless". Echoing an almost Blairite sentiment, one participant admitted, "I don't suppose I give anything to society, so I haven't got any rights from it". Another said, "Society don't owe me nothing". Turning from rights to responsibilities, participants were asked not only about the extent to which they were begging out of choice, but also who or what might be to blame for the fact that they were begging. Although subject in all but two instances to some kind of qualification, seven participants acknowledged that they had, in a sense, 'chosen' to beg, and 10 acknowledged that they were themselves in some measure to blame. While some participants blamed their circumstances upon some particular life event, comparatively few (five) directly blamed the government. It must be stressed that several participants gave confused and internally contradictory accounts. Certain participants at certain moments were prepared to extol the advantages of begging and the independence it gave them:

> "[B]ecause where I was came from originally [children's home and subsequently prison] we've always been told what to do, where to go, when to wash, what to wear, and it's like you break out from that authority, and you do something and it makes you in control.... If you're thieving or selling drugs obviously you're heading to hell man, you're just going to pfff, you know. You've got to understand that whole circle of life.... [W]ell I have done ... when I started [begging] ... I know I'm in control, to put food in my mouth, to get myself a few quid, and I'm not hurting nobody by it.... I know I can get by. You know, I don't cry, or, or run to anyone."

However, the fragility of that independence and the uncongenial nature of their existence was all too evident to participants: brave statements such as this were often followed by expressions of utter despair. As one who acknowledged that he had 'chosen' to beg said, "it's the punishment that fits the crime". No amount of self-justification could conceal the extent to which "[b]eggars are the lowest of the low. You can'y get away from the fact". Yet it remains the case that the (albeit narrow) majority of our participants did not cast themselves as victims, but as independent actors. One participant bleakly confessed "I've mucked it all myself through drink and drugs" then struggled to answer our question about 'choice':

> "Well I haven't got any choices, just to beg or hand myself in and go to prison. I don't know why, but I don't fancy it. I have to beg. You don't have to. You don't have to. People don't have to beg, but when your circumstances are without [*sic*] an' if you don't beg you're not going to survive, you'd drop dead somewhere."

Even those who blamed government policies for their plight might also express their desire for independence and dignity: "if I could choose I'd love to have a job, I'd love to have a home.... [J]ust 'cos you're on the streets it doesn't mean to say you're not – you're still human aren't you".

In fact, participants' aspirations for the future were, by and large, strikingly conventional. Over half (12 participants) said they would ideally have liked a job, and/or a home, and/or a family, although around a quarter (five) confessed they just didn't know what they wanted for the future. In practice, when asked what they thought they would be doing or expected to be doing in a year's time, fully half (10) said they didn't know, that they preferred not to think about it or that they would be doing the same as they were doing now. Younger participants were more likely than the older participants to expect begging to be a transitory phase, but few of them recounted coherent plans for getting out of begging and were generally pessimistic about their prospects. One participant acknowledged, "I don't want to have a crummy job that's only paying £3 an hour, because like ... at the moment ... maybe I'm not ambitious", but others voiced an assertion – an often tenuous article of faith – that what they hoped for was a 'proper job'.

One of the most strongly expressed yearnings among participants within the sample came from those who sought to 'settle down' in a permanent (heterosexual and characteristically patriarchal) relationship. This was sometimes expressed in what were, in the particular circumstances, improbably idealised or romanticised terms:

> "I'd like very much if tomorrow I could wake up, snap my fingers, have a really good job, open up a bank account, save up as much as I could, ... get married, have a proper wedding and start a normal life.... In fact I'd like to even, maybe, at some point, even start my own business."

> "[W]hat I would ideally in my dream is like, is to buy a plot of land, out in the country somewhere, or quite a few acres of land, so that I could plop myself in the middle with a caravan – decent enough to sort of live in with sort of maybe a family or whatever. Get a little farm going. Say it's a nature reserve. End of story. Put a big fence around it. Tell people to get lost if I don't want them on the land."

> "I'd rather be like in my own house with a wife and bairn and that and a job."

"I mean the perfect day for me would be to wake up at seven
o'clock, get a shower, get some breakfast, put on me working
clothes, give me girlfriend a kiss, go to work, come home from
work, have something to eat and spend the night watching telly
with me girlfriend."

"I feel very cheated.... I'm having the piss taken out of me
every day.... I wouldn't mind if I had a girlfriend, a mate to be
with. Just for her – to be with, you know."

If the participants' values and aspirations tended to coincide with those
of the social mainstream, then so in some ways did their prejudices towards
'others' (cf Dean and Taylor-Gooby, 1992). In the course of the interviews,
more than half (12 participants) made hostile or disparaging references
either about people who were not 'genuine' or 'true' beggars, or about
the preferential treatment alleged to be received by 'foreigners'. There
was a measure of implied or even express resentment of people (sometime
referred to as 'casuals') who were thought to be begging when they
didn't need to and, in a couple of instances, explicitly racist remarks were
made about minority ethnic groups who were believed to be taking
homes and jobs away from people living on the street. Paradoxically, it
seems, even those who themselves are living beyond the margins of 'polite'
society can share in its intolerance of those whom they cast as undeserving.

Objective alienation

In spite of the attitudes which they might share with mainstream society,
the beggars in our study plainly were practically and 'socially' excluded
in more than a purely symbolic sense. The conventional notion of social
exclusion is classically Durkheimian in provenance (Levitas, 1996), and
rests on the notion that certain minorities may be 'alienated' from society:
exclusion in this sense represents not so much the opposite of social
inclusion, as a (potentially remediable) failure of social integration. There
is, however, in the Marxist sociological tradition, an alternative concept
of 'alienation' which sees the consequences of capitalism itself in terms of
the self-alienation of the members of civil society from their own 'social
humanity' (for example, Marx, 1845): upon such an analysis we are all of
us universally excluded from the realisation of our social potential.

Though fully mindful of the contested nature of the concept of social exclusion, we were aware of some subtle differences between the participants in our study in relation to the nature of their exclusion. Certain of those differences stemmed from the basis upon which they were distanced or alienated from the society that surrounded them. Others related to the degree to which they were in control of their lives; to which as actors they were relatively autonomous or passive agents.

Some participants were alienated from society in a neo-Durkheimian sense. In entering begging they had in some way stepped beyond conformity and become 'outsiders'. Thus one participant, a former heroin addict, now on a methadone programme but apparently sleeping rough, sought to describe the obstacles in his path if he wanted "to become a member of society": he was conscious that social inclusion entails integration. Others were alienated in a more inherent sense. It was as if they did not or could not engage with conformity and were 'strangers'; strangers not only in the sense of being generally self-alienated – as Marx might have implied – but in the particular sense of being beyond the pale of civil society itself. One of the participants, who in earlier life had suffered brain damage in a fight and was subject to episodes of bizarre (and suicidal) behaviour, defined this perfectly for us when he said, "I hate scrounging, but sometimes it's got to be done. I can't help that I'm a stranger, you know".

Of the 19 participants in our sample, we felt that nine could be described as 'outsiders'. Most of these (seven) had little control over their lives: they were *entrapped*, as it were, usually as a direct or indirect consequence of drug or alcohol addiction. Two of these participants, however, did seem at the time they were interviewed to have some degree of control over their lives: both had travelled quite extensively and, in spite of their precarious circumstances, each exhibited something of the *adventurer*. The other 10 participants could be described as 'strangers'. Of these, four had little control over their lives: they had each been the victim of some *tragic* circumstance (such as a catastrophic injury or bereavement) which left them unable to cope. Six of these participants, however, did seem to exercise some degree of control over their lives and presented as in some ways quite *enigmatic*: they were characteristically self-sufficient, but either oddly secretive or somehow socially disengaged.

The taxonomy described is illustrated in Figure 6.1, in which the vertical axis represents the difference between 'outsiders' and 'strangers' and the horizontal axis represents a continuum between relative autonomy and passivity. This analysis, however, should be regarded with considerable caution, not least because the categories created are no more than ideal

Figure 6.1: A tentative taxonomy of beggars

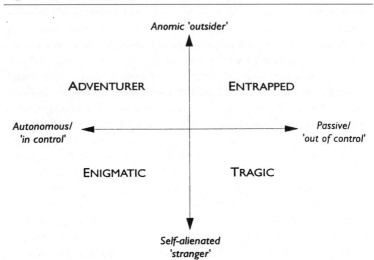

types and tend in practice to overlap with one another. The classifications were derived from discursive data obtained at a particular moment in time and there can be little doubt that the objective circumstances of beggars can change rapidly from day to day. When one of the participants in our study was observed again some weeks later, he had entirely changed his demeanour: he had lost the element of controlled self-assurance which had previously marked him out as an 'adventurer' beggar and appeared to be in a state of extreme intoxication and distress. Nonetheless, these findings do serve to illustrate that – even in the paradigm case of the beggar – the dynamics of what may be called 'social exclusion' are complex and that the concept itself needs to be addressed critically.

Policy implications

Lack of time and resources meant that we could not develop our study more fully to explore the range of matters which began to emerge from our interviews, or to expand our sample to include representatives of all the different social groups that seem to engage in begging. Despite this, the diversity of the sample that was achieved and the high quality of the discursive data that were obtained provided a rich and informative picture. This enables us to pick out a number of policy-related issues.

First, although not all beggars are failing to claim their entitlements to social security benefits, it is clear that the inaccessibility and opaqueness of the social security system is a factor for some. Some participants rendered lengthy and confused accounts of their attempts to claim benefits and, as one put it, "it's not worth the hassle". The increasingly deterrent nature of the social security system remains such that even ostensibly intelligent and resourceful participants could not muster the will to establish or re-establish benefits claims, while those who seemed most vulnerable found the system bewildering and insensitive to their needs. One participant, with a long history of what would seem to have been severe (and inadequately treated) clinical depression, explained:

> "... if you've gone through what I've gone through ... then you start to understand what it feels like when you try and get benefits. *[Imitating]* 'Where was your last work? Why did you leave your last work? Oh, you're suspended for so many months'. And then they turn round and say, 'Right, go on this Job Start, Restart, or erm Job Seekers, whatever'. And you're like [saying] 'But, why?' And you say 'Why?' *[Imitating]* 'If you don't, we'll dock yer benefit'. And they can actually deduct yer benefit ... which means if you don't do Jobseekers you get zilch, basically."

The explicit intention behind the introduction of Jobseekers' Allowance and, more recently, the New Deal 'single gateway' claims procedures, is to increase work incentives. The consequence is that those who will not seek formal work will be driven off benefit and may survive by other means, such as through crime, informal work or street-level economic activity. The concern raised by our findings is that several of our participants, though they would require an enormous amount of support if they were to be assisted into the legitimate labour force, were being entirely rebuffed by the social security system. Many wanted work very badly, though few were employable in their present condition. Some of these were even engaged in entirely unassisted and self-evidently futile attempts at job search.

Second, although not all beggars are homeless, housing is a critical and consuming issue for many. So far as statutory provision goes, the 'priority need' criterion under UK homelessness legislation – by which most childless adults are excluded from assistance – remains a source of resentment for some:

> "[W]hat they see it as is, erm, a woman with kids needs a house more than somebody like me.... Even though she's got a place, her needs are greater than mine, you know what I mean. Just – its pretty stupid really, but that's the way it goes."

> "If you're a lassie, you're pregnant, you've got a bairn, nay problem. And they say they're no' biased! And they say they don't discriminate, which is rubbish."

The right to a home has never been universally guaranteed, but to the extent that the 'priority need' provisions are supposed to assure protection even for childless adults if they are 'vulnerable', our findings raise yet again concerns that single men with substantial personal difficulties are not getting the assistance they need.

So far as voluntary sector provision for homeless people is concerned, some participants complained, as we have seen, about the failure of such institutions to guarantee the protection of belongings, but also about the level of the charges levied by such hostels through the social security system. The more cynical participants felt that some of the homelessness charities are making an 'industry' out of homelessness: as one put it, "there are people living off the back of homeless people". Undoubtedly, homeless individuals who live by begging are likely to be those that are most disaffected by such provision as is available, but our findings do indicate that, for some single homeless people, provision falls substantially short of their needs and expectations.

Third, and closely related to the issue of independent sector provision for homeless people, is the role of such initiatives as *The Big Issue*, and the capacity of community level enterprise (see Bird, 1997) to provide pathways out of begging. Several participants drew comparisons between begging and selling *The Big Issue*. Opinions were radically divided, not only about how remunerative *Big Issue* selling can be, but about the status of *Big Issue* vendors. Some participants claimed they could get more money selling *The Big Issue* than by begging; others believed it was much less. Some participants believed that *Big Issue* selling afforded a greater sense of self-respect, others bemoaned the numbers of *Big Issue* sellers, their competitiveness and/or the fact that so many of them were not 'genuinely' homeless or even necessarily impecunious. Certainly, *The Big Issue* represents a creative idea, but the evidence would suggest that it by no means meets the needs of all those who are homeless on the street and that it may be developing a form of street-level economic activity that merely runs parallel with begging.

Fourth, the prevalence within our sample of people with experience of being looked after by local authorities and/or who were currently addicted to drugs re-emphasises familiar issues concerning the quality of the assistance that is given to young people when they leave local authority 'care' (Biehal et al, 1995; Banardo's, 1996) and the scope and effectiveness of current drug treatment programmes (Dorn and South, 1987).

The pilot study described in this paper illustrates the intransigent complexity of the policy issues raised by contemporary begging and the futility of any kind of 'zero-tolerance' approach to the elimination of begging (Blair, 1997, and see Chapter Thirteen in this volume). It also demonstrates the need for further more extensive research and analysis. To unravel the ambiguous nature of begging as a phenomenon, it is necessary to understand the sheer diversity of the people who are engaged in it. To the extent that begging is a social policy issue, it is because, while so many beggars are self-evidently not the rogues so feared by Martin Luther, neither do they enjoy the freedom and security which Adam Smith supposed. Begging may be understood, if not quite as a 'business' in Orwell's ironic sense, as an economic activity. It is a hazardous and precarious form of economic activity engaged in by and large by vulnerable and socially damaged people. Beggars have much to tell us about the limits and the limitations of social policy.

Note

The study reported in this chapter was internally funded at the University of Luton. The authors are grateful to Keir Gale who, having undertaken much of the preparatory work for the study, was unable to complete it. The authors are also grateful to Gary Craig and Michael Adler for assistance during the fieldwork.

References

Barnado's (1996) *The failure of social policy to meet the needs of young people leaving care*, London: Barnado's.

Biehal, N., Clayton, J., Stein, M. and Wade, J. (1995) *Moving on: Young people and leaving care schemes*, London: HMSO.

Bird, J. (1997) 'Let's do business for the underclass', *The Guardian*, 29 November.

Blair, T. (1997) Interview in *The Big Issue*, 6-12 January.

Bourgois, P. (1996) *In search of respect: Selling crack in El Barrio*, New York, NY: Cambridge University Press.

Dean, H. and Taylor-Gooby, P. (1992) *Dependency culture: The explosion of a myth*, Hemel Hempstead: Harvester Wheatsheaf.

Dorn, N. and South, N. (1987) *A land fit for heroin? Drug policies, prevention and practice*, Basingstoke: Macmillan.

Fooks, G. and Pantazis, C. (1999) 'Criminalisation of homelessness, begging and street living', in P. Kennett and A. Marsh (eds) *Homelessness: Exploring the new terrain*, Bristol: The Policy Press.

Giddens, A. (1990) *The consequences of modernity*, Cambridge: Polity Press.

Jordan, B. (1993) 'Framing claims and the weapons of the weak', in G. Drover and P. Kerans (eds) *New approaches to welfare theory*, Aldershot: Edward Elgar.

Jordan, B. (1996) *A theory of poverty and social exclusion*, Cambridge: Polity Press.

Levitas, R. (1996) 'The concept of social exclusion and the new Durkheimian hegemony', *Critical Social Policy*, vol 14, no 2, pp 5-20.

Marx, K. (1845) 'Theses on Feuerbach', in *Marx-Engels Gesamtausgabe*, Volume 1, Section 5 [translated extract in T. Bottomore and M. Rubel (1963) *Karl Marx: Selected writings in sociology and social philosophy*, Harmondsworth: Penguin].

Murdoch, A. (1994) *We are human too: A study of people who beg*, London: Crisis.

Walter, T. (1979) *A long way from home: A sociological exploration of contemporary idolatory*, Exeter: Paternoster Press.

Wardaugh, J. (1996) 'Homeless in Chinatown: deviance and social control in cardboard city', *Sociology*, vol 30, no 4, pp 701-16.

SEVEN

Begging in time and space: 'shadow work' and the rural context

Julia Wardhaugh and Jane Jones

The aim of this chapter is to explore begging and the related occupations of busking and *Big Issue* selling as marginal economic activities that are conducted in time and space. Temporal and spatial activities have been addressed in relation to marginal – primarily homeless – street populations (see, for example, Duncan, 1983; Murray, 1984), but this chapter is distinctive both in its attempt to focus on economic dimensions of the temporal and spatial structuring of street life, and in its adoption of 'the rural' as a spatial focus and site of sociological enquiry in relation to the question of begging as an economic activity. Studies of homelessness and related phenomena such as begging have long been predominantly urban in focus, although more recently there has been a growing body of work on rural homelessness (Button, 1992; Lambert et al, 1992; Ford et al, 1997; Jones, 1997). Recent work by post-modern critical geographers has begun to deconstruct the binary divide between country and city, to address the complexity and diversity of rural culture and society, and to develop a focus on the marginalised rural 'other' (Philo, 1992; Soja, 1997; Milbourne, 1997).

The question of defining rurality is both complex and contested: objective measures such as population density and economic activity are counterposed against such sociocultural factors as community and identity (Halfacree, 1993; Cloke et al, 1997). For the purposes of this study we have adopted a working definition of rurality. Our concern has been primarily to contrast North Wales as a rural region with urban-based studies of begging[1]. This is not to deny the existence of urban centres within the region, but is simply to begin by asking the question whether economic, social and cultural life is qualitatively different in rural and urban areas. At the same time, we recognise degrees of rurality, and therefore, while we define the region as a whole as rural, we distinguish between 'semi-rural' areas such as the coastal towns, and the 'deeply-rural' villages and hamlets of the valleys of Snowdonia.

Our approach is necessarily exploratory, given the dearth of studies on begging and other marginal economic activities in rural areas, and our sample is small, reflecting the scattered nature of the population of North Wales in general and of deviant sub-groups in particular[2]. Nevertheless, the qualitative data are rich and allow us to raise a number of theoretical, empirical and methodological questions, and thus to stimulate wider debate and research. Our analysis centres around begging and related activities as examples of shadow work, and we define 'shadow work' as illegitimate or quasi-legitimate subsistence activities engaged in by street people such as beggars and the homeless (Illich, 1981; Snow and Anderson, 1993). Such activities fall outside the legitimate systems of employment and welfare, but nevertheless include some involvement in the market system. Beggars, for example, appear to offer no goods or services in exchange for money, but nevertheless utilise capitalist concepts in their talk of customers or clients, and in their awareness of temporal fluctuations that affect their market place (cf Chapter Six in this volume).

We go on to relate this core concern with begging as a shadow work activity to questions of time and space: what are the daily, weekly and seasonal rhythms experienced by the rural beggar? To what extent do they employ cyclical as opposed to linear concepts of time? What happens when subsistence economic activities require marginal people to enter into prime space, and which exclusionary tactics, if any, are employed by the settled population? How do beggars, buskers and *Big Issue* sellers formulate mental maps and develop a sense of place (Turner, 1974, 1979; Massey 1992)?

The empirical study on which this chapter is based took place in the semi-rural coastal strip of the counties of Gwynedd and Conwy, with their combined population of around 200,000 people. However, our geographical focus was potentially wider, encompassing the whole of the North Wales region, from Holyhead in the west and Wrexham in the east, and from the northern coastal towns such as Colwyn Bay and Llandudno, to the market towns of Dolgellau and Bala in the southern part of the region. However, early exploratory visits to towns and villages in the Conwy and Ogwen valleys suggested that begging was either absent or hidden within such places. Anecdotal evidence suggested that itinerant beggars such as Irish travellers were present in and around places of transit such as the port of Holyhead, but it was beyond the scope of this study to investigate such highly spatially dispersed forms of begging as an economic activity (see Beier, 1985, for an historical account of begging and vagrancy in North Wales).

The fieldwork on which this chapter is based was thus confined to highly visible forms of begging and related economic activities such as busking and selling *The Big Issue*, for two major reasons. First, the visibility of street-level economic activities makes gaining access a relatively easy process, and second, public, political and social concern is focused overwhelmingly on the illegitimate and quasi-legitimate economic enterprises undertaken in public places by street people. Six young people aged 20-30 years were interviewed: direct contact was made with two non-homeless buskers on the streets of Llandudno (the 'Queen of Welsh resorts'); and access to four homeless people in the university and cathedral city of Bangor was negotiated with a local voluntary agency based in nearby Caernarfon.

The question of defining begging is contentious, although in economic terms it is fairly straightforward to describe it as a subsistence form of activity, involving the soliciting of donations from the public. Socially, however, begging is not only a highly marginal and stigmatised activity, but one that leads to the ascription of a deviant 'master status' to the one who begs. That is, the identity of beggar becomes of primary importance, eclipsing any other possible identities. It is not possible to be a person who simply *does* begging: rather one *becomes* a beggar (Goffman, 1959). The process of stigmatisation is likely to deter individuals from voluntarily embracing the spoiled identity of the beggar. Other marginal economic activities such as busking or *Big Issue* vending, while certainly stigmatised, nevertheless carry with them at least some positive connotations, such as those associated with working in order to earn a living. The process of being badged in order to sell *The Big Issue* confers a legitimate status on the individual, and largely removes them from police attention, while busking, although technically illegal unless a street entertainment licence has been obtained, also seems to be less subject to police regulation.

This continuum of legality to illegality is an important consideration for people making their living on the streets as they are constantly subject to the public and the official gaze, and their livelihoods may be severely affected by unwanted attention. Equally important in the election of identities other than 'beggar', however, is the question of personal dignity, with everyone in this study adopting varying strategies to enhance their sense of personal worth (see, also, Wardhaugh, 1996 for a discussion of these issues in relation to beggars and *Big Issue* vendors in Manchester). Ironically, and despite their best efforts, public perceptions of the North

Walian street-people tended to conflate various marginal street occupations into one, labelling buskers and *Big Issue* vendors as both beggars and homeless people. For example, letters have appeared in the local newspaper from members of the public, complaining that *Big Issue* vendors are nothing more than "beggars in disguise" (*Bangor Chronicle*, August 1998). The key factor here seems to be a respectable-disreputable divide, as other people on the street such as newspaper vendors and charity collectors escape these processes of labelling and stigmatisation (but see Chapter Eleven in this volume).

Begging as an economic activity

Despite the sensational media reports of the early 1990s which claimed that 'bogus beggars' were able to earn more than those in many respectable professions, the nature of begging as a stigmatised activity means that people tend to engage in it as an economic activity of last resort (Murdoch, 1994). As we have noted, many prefer to identify themselves as buskers or vendors, and indeed it is true that there may be few who engage solely in begging, rather than in a range of subsistence activities. In the same way as for the mainstream population, decisions concerning occupation are affected by questions of status, convenience, sociability and location as well as purely economic considerations. Ellie[3], for example, found she could make the same money busking as she did while begging, but preferred busking as a less troublesome occupation, believing that identifying as a busker allowed her to distance herself from some of the negative connotations attached to begging:

> "There's another thing about begging, busking, whatever, everyone has a go at us about it, taking money off people ... that's why I like busking, 'cause I'm not saying anything, I'm just playing my music, so if anyone comes at me ... I can just say 'I'm not begging. I'm just playing my music to you, you don't have to drop me money, I'm getting pleasure out of it myself'."

For others, their attempts to distance themselves from the stigma of begging and to establish themselves as respectably employed met with limited success:

> "It's all right selling *The Big Issue*. You can class it as a job, though other people don't. A bloke told me I was spending all my f***ing money on beer, and I thought 'why not? I do a job'."
> [Dill]

Whatever the kind of face-saving or identity work engaged in by those earning their living on the streets, economic factors remained a pressing and often urgent consideration (Goffman, 1971; Snow and Anderson, 1993; and see Chapter Eight in the volume). Persistent themes among those interviewed were those of 'getting by', 'making a living' and simply having enough to eat, and in this respect, begging was often combined with other activities in order to make sufficient money. Jamie, for example, having been robbed of his money on the street, resorted to a combination of begging and *Big Issue* selling, and was delighted with his earnings of £15 for a day's work:

> "So I just scrounged a couple of pounds off the street, begged a couple of pounds, went and got some *Issues* and sold them, went and got some more and sold them. Went back and forth, back and forth, made more and more and more. It gets you by, kind of feeds you. I've sold 30 already today ... the most I've sold in one day, so I'm like that [*rubs hands together and smiles*]."

For a minority of those working, although not necessarily living, on the streets, economic factors may be less important than other values. Lisanne described herself as a pavement artist, someone more interested in aesthetic ideals than monetary gain. Living with her partner in a bedsitting room in a hamlet in the Conwy valley, she was currently claiming benefits as well as making £70 or £80 per week with her street art; her ultimate aim was to be economically self-sufficient and to follow the travelling life:

> "We sign on and we wanna stop signing on and just support ourselves, 'cause they just give you a horrible time. And you just sign on for the fact of having a house, and I don't want either of them."

Begging in time and space

Cyclical and linear concepts of time

If it is true that time is inherently social, then it allows us to see that how we understand time is necessarily related to how we use time and vice versa (Durkheim, 1965). Particular cultures will utilise the marking of time in conjunction with other necessary reference points that make up the intrinsic patterns of their own distinctive cultural life-styles:

> **[S]ystems of time reckoning reflect the social activities of the group.... [T]ime reckoning is basically dependent upon the organisation and functions of the group. The mode of life determines which phenomena shall represent the beginning and close of seasons, months or other time units. (Sorokin and Merton, 1937, pp 620-1)**

It has been fairly well-established that, for those subsisting and living on the streets, time takes on a cyclical rather than linear quality. Murray, for example, recognises this concept of social time, and goes on to develop a framework based on "images of time present in a society" (1984, p 54). This framework allows for an understanding of social action that can be situated within a particular time image, one that in turn reflects a past, present or future orientation. Two of the most pertinent of these time images are the cyclical image and the linear image. Cyclical time images can be associated with both pre-agrarian and agrarian traditional societies, societies where daily sustenance and indeed all economic considerations (for example, trading and selling at local markets) would be dependent upon successful yields from fishing, hunting, livestock and harvesting (Blondel, 1992). Of crucial importance for survival, therefore, would be a necessary concern with the marking of time cycles, cycles that are repetitions of past patterns, and that are set within a framework of diurnal and seasonal patterns. In contrast, linear time has been associated with modern and post- or late-modern societies, with their urban capitalist economies and westernised cultural life-styles. This linear conception of time inevitably allows for perceptions of a forward progression, both in terms of the life progression of the individual, and as a kind of evolutionary orientation to the next stage in the development of a globalised Western society (Murray, 1984; Massey, 1994).

However, some marginal populations experience cyclical (pre-modern) time rhythms within the dominant linear temporal framework characteristic of modern or post-modern societies. Murray found that street homeless people tended to move within a cyclical conception of time, and that this was linked to the repetitive daily routines necessary for their daily survival:

> ... cyclical time ... occurs for two reasons. First, one doesn't look to the future in terms of forging ahead, or progressing to new goals. Rather, one's primary goal is survival, a goal which must be re-achieved every day.... The second factor ... is the cyclic schedules of the institutions which affect the homeless. (Murray, 1984, p 59)

There is also a certain paradox within the question of linear versus cyclical time, in that a sense of linear progression through time, of being somewhere and moving forward into the future, is only achieved by means of the endless repetition of cycles of time. It is the sense of purposefulness and activity encapsulated within the completion of daily, weekly and seasonal routines that locates the individual within a framework of time. Thus, cyclical and linear time can be said to be interdependent, rather than mutually exclusive concepts. This interdependency of concepts of time can create a contradictory context within a person's particular conception and usage of time within a given culture or sub-culture. For example, although cyclical temporal patterns were clearly evident in the life-styles of the homeless people interviewed for this study, there were some interesting variations in their conceptions of time.

Jamie found that the discipline of engaging in regular employment as a *Big Issue* vendor, provided a welcome structure to his otherwise aimless days and nights:

> "Before I sold the *Issue* I went about in a trance. Just sat about and walked about. Pissed off walking about, so I'd sit about. Pissed off sitting about so I'd walk about. Absolutely nothing to do. Maybe have a couple of cans, blank out the day a wee bit. Feel a bit happier."

In contrast, Lisanne discovered that the order imposed on her life by her subsistence strategy led to an unwelcome inclusion in the linear temporal existence shared by most of the employed population of Western societies:

> "I'm desperate to get away, just the whole routine of doing this
> kind of stuff [pavement art] in the same place, it gets so tedious,
> boring. You might as well be doing it and move about. The fact
> of having a house and tying yourself down defeats the object,
> you don't really want that."

A season for everything

While participation in shadow work in the form of begging, busking
and selling *The Big Issue* clearly provides a degree of temporal structure,
nevertheless, these occupations are characteristic of life-styles that can
largely be understood within a cyclical conception of time, driven for
the most part by the need for physical survival. These physical needs
provide the impetus to structure one's time patterns in order to maximise
any economic gain. By the same token, the adoption of particular time
patterns in terms of a daily survival strategy, means that there can be little
hope of ever moving on from circumscribed economic and social positions.
In effect, the survival strategies adopted by street-people often serve to
exacerbate their marginal position, in the sense that a necessary primary
focus on daily survival keeps them trapped within a repetitious, cyclical
life-style:

> "I sell every day. I have to. If I make £20 before 12 or 2 o'clock
> I'll finish then. I set an average of what I need for the day, for
> food, what I drink, or if I've got a fine to pay. Twenty, thirty
> pounds a day. Sometimes I can only make a fiver, which is even
> worse, 'cause I've not got enough for the next day's *Issues*, so that
> means I'm only going to make a fiver the next day, whereas if I
> make £20 one day I can use £10 for food and whatever, and
> £10 to buy 20 *Issues* next morning." [Dill]

Other studies of begging have made similar findings. Murdoch, for
example, found that life on the homelessness circuit was quite different
from that experienced by those with a home and a job:"although begging
emerged as being intrinsically linked to homelessness it was generally
seen as a means of day-to-day survival, rather than a route out of
homelessness" (1994, p 19).

Whatever their occupation, it seems clear that all those working on
the streets need to develop a clear sense of temporal patterns if they are to

earn a living: their working days are often as highly organised as those employed within the formal sector, and indeed shadow workers often appear to be acutely sensitive to subtle changes in the rhythms of daily life. Each of the people interviewed had a clear sense of the structure of their working day: the buskers in Llandudno worked largely in the afternoons, finding the last shopping hour of the day to be particularly productive; *The Big Issue* vendors frequently worked long hours, six days a week, keeping to usual shop and office hours, while it was begging that was the occupation most amenable to 'flexitime'. Jamie, for example, often worked evenings as well as afternoons:

> "It's better about this time of day [2pm] and say four to six, and then say 8 o'clock to 11 o'clock, that's no' a bad time. Like a guy last night gave me £15 to get a bed for the night, something hot to eat. I'd had a lot of verbal from people earlier on, and then this guy hit us with £15, I think it's a pretty cool place, Bangor."

Ellie had a sophisticated understanding of the nature of the many towns in which she had worked, and classified them according to their use of daily time. Asked about the best time for busking, she replied:

> "It depends on the place, some towns are morning towns and some are afternoon towns, people have different routines. Generally, Bangor is an afternoon town, people come out more in the afternoon, and that's when you get more money."

Beggars, buskers and *Big Issue* vendors also tended to follow weekly routines, with varying degrees of flexibility. All said that they worked five or six days per week, with everyone having at least one rest day which varied according to place: the people in Llandudno worked on Sundays because this was often the busiest day of the week in this popular tourist town, while the consensus was that there was little point in working in Bangor, with its Sunday closing of shops. For some, their weekly routine was imposed by their nature of their employment: Ronny, for example, was allowed to sell *The Big Issue* outside the prime site of Safeways only on Mondays and Fridays, and spent the rest of the week working outside WHSmiths. For those with two or more occupations, their calculations were more complex: Ellie found that Mondays were best for selling *The Big Issue*, for the simple reason that it was newly-issued on Sundays, but that Wednesdays were the best day for busking: "I don't know why, I can't think of the psychology behind it".

Finally, shadow workers are subject to seasonal variations that affect the nature of their employment. Contrary to the experience of many people employed in a rural area heavily dependent on the tourist industry, shadow workers found that winter was on the whole better than summer for making a living on the street. In Bangor a major factor was the disappearance of most of the students in the summer months, when some 7,000 people disappear from a city with a permanent population of some 17,000. In this case, therefore, the available number of potential customers was clearly a significant factor. However, income is not necessarily solely dependent on numbers but may equally be influenced by the nature of interactions between beggars, buskers and vendors and their clients:

> **"I've mixed views on whether it's better in the summer. In the winter you get people looking at you and they feel the cold, and subconsciously they'll think 'that person's sleeping out tonight'....
> In the summer it depends on the mood of the day, if it's sunny like today, they're happy and people give you money, and then, you're in a better mood yourself."**

Marginal people in prime places

> **... the legal exclusion of homeless people from public space (or at least the legal exclusion of behaviours that make it possible for homeless people to survive) has increased in strength during the late 1980s and early 1990s.... (Mitchell, 1997, p 314)**

Social space has traditionally been negotiated at the level of a public–private spatiality, with the private 'home' being a supposed 'place of safety' where one can retreat from everyday life spent in public space. However, this separation of space into a public–private divide may be less relevant to an analysis of street-people such as the homeless, in that if being homeless signifies having no home of one's own, then the only space left within this binary divide is public space. Furthermore, home signifies a place where at a physical level survival functions such as eating and sleeping may take place, and where a social and bureaucratic identity may be maintained by the simple expedient of having an address for correspondence, thus allowing for economic participation in the employment or welfare systems.

This raises the question of whether, and if so, how these physical and economic functions can be achieved by those solely occupying public space. Street-people, including beggars and the homeless, engage in a constant negotiation and renegotiation of public space. For example, an individual may be able to sleep on a park bench, in a graveyard, or in a shop doorway until moved on to the next space; or they may have to participate in shadow work of one sort or another within the confines of a legalised definitional framework that impinges on the use of public space:

> **Begging is an offence under the 1824 Vagrancy Act, which condemns 'every person wandering abroad, or placing himself or herself in any public place, street, highway, court or passage, to beg or gather alms'. People who are begging can also be arrested on other grounds such as feigning poverty to obtain money (the 1968 Theft Act) or for disorderly and threatening behaviour (1968 Public Order Act). (Murdoch, 1994, p 37)**

For street homeless people, then, all space is public space in that they have no private space to which to retreat. Not all beggars are homeless, but their work on the streets orients them towards the use of public space. Along with the homeless, they are constructed and represented as street-people, as those with few rights to private space yet with limited access to public places.

A more useful classification with regard to marginal street populations may be prime versus marginal space (Duncan, 1983; Snow and Anderson, 1993). If we can understand prime and marginal space, not as polar extremes but as two markers on a continuum, where the actual positioning of a specific space along this continuum is subject to its practical and symbolic value and usage, then we may begin to understand the fluid nature of social space. Furthermore, this fluidity acts as a defining factor for street-people who have constantly to negotiate and renegotiate their own usage of space according to the varying nature of spaces and places at a particular point in time:

> **A culture includes the 'maps of meaning' which make things intelligible to its members. These 'maps of meaning' are not simply carried around in the head, they are objectified in the**

> **patterns of social organisation and relationships through which
> the individual becomes a 'social individual'. (Clarke et al, 1976,
> p 10)**

Prime spaces include areas that are used by citizens for residential, commercial and recreational use, while marginal spaces are typically those areas that are abandoned or undervalued by users of prime space: examples include derelict areas, waste ground and back alleys. As already discussed, usage or non-usage of an area can quickly change, as in the case of the once abandoned dockland areas of our cities which now provide residential, housing and commercial premises for 'selected' customers. For marginal street-people there is often no place to go within prime space, as this is a space wherein they will always be within public view.

Street homelessness and marginal street occupations become conflated with dangerousness when they become visible, and it is this visibility that represents a threat to the security and sense of place enjoyed by settled citizens. Thus, it is not marginality per se that is dangerous; rather, it is the visible presence of marginal people within prime space that represents a threat to a sense of public order and orderliness (Wardhaugh, 1996). Therefore, in order to aid their economic survival and to conduct basic bodily functions, street people must seek out those marginal places where they can take cover and remain 'hidden' (and thus forgotten). However, the pursuit of economic survival requires them to enter, at least temporarily, into prime space, and so they are faced simultaneously with the need to use and to avoid public space.

Many can survive in the larger towns and cities by occupying marginal, interstitial places within general prime space, as in the case of those who subsist largely within the venues on the homelessness circuit in places such as Manchester's Chinatown (Taylor et al, 1996; Wardhaugh, 1996). In smaller towns and villages, however, there are quite simply insufficient hidden or marginal places into which deviant populations can disappear, and for the economically active shadow workers in particular, there are few places to hide. Shadow work in rural areas necessarily takes place in full public view, and there is little chance of anonymity: buskers, beggars and vendors are relatively few in number and are therefore highly visible, particularly within fairly traditional and conservative small communities. Is it possible, then, to make a living yet stay out of trouble?

So far in this discussion, we have emphasised the similarities between the three economic activities of begging, busking and *Big Issue* vending, but in terms of potential conflicts within prime space, significant differences begin to emerge. All three groups were careful to negotiate their relationships with their 'customers', and none were reckless as to the potential for trouble in a society that tends to classify all of them as troublesome down-and-outs. For those working but not living on the streets the prospects were relatively good, with the buskers in Llandudno, for example, being largely successful in avoiding conflict with shopkeepers, security guards and the police. However, the beggars and *Big Issue* vendors living in and around Bangor found it impossible to disappear from the streets, on which they had to live and subsist for 24 hours each day.

John and Lisanne, on the whole, enjoyed busking on the streets of Llandudno: as natives of the town they possessed a detailed local knowledge that enabled them to successfully negotiate potential hazards, and they were able to return each evening to their home in the Conwy valley. They had clear mental maps of their town, carefully choosing their regular pitches outside the big stores: "everyone goes to Marks and Spencer ... so if you stand outside you usually make a lot of money" (John), and "I have a set pitch, I usually do it by Millet's ... different people have different preferred places. By Millet's there's quite a bit of room and it's sheltered by the veranda" (Lisanne). Each went on to relate several anecdotes about friends or acquaintances who had been moved on for busking or begging on the town's promenade and pier: prime tourist locations. This local legend, rather than direct experience, was sufficient to deter them from using such places for their work:

> "I have thought about doing it [busking] on the prom, but it's a
> bit weird 'cause I'd probably get moved on straight away, with
> the security guards. 'Cause like in Mostyn Street there's no
> security guards, each bit of pavement is owned by that particular
> shop. But by the time you get onto the prom, it's governed by
> Leisure Island and it's really strict." [John]

Similarly, simple knowledge of the likely responses to buskers or beggars on the part of large entrepreneurial concerns in the town's retail park and shopping mall was sufficient to deter any attempt to engage in informal economic activities in such locations, thus serving to create de facto exclusion zones.

Although Bangor has a similar population size, it is a much smaller and more compact town than Llandudno: with only one major shopping street, there are few places that marginal people can claim as their own. The only substantial shared public space outside of the shopping mall (which, in common with many towns and cities is out of bounds to street-people), are the gardens around the Cathedral. Marginal street-people share this space with local residents, students and visitors, but for them it is their only venue for meeting with others, eating and drinking, carrying on their trades, and (often) sleeping at night. While conducting the interviews in Cathedral Gardens, one of us observed the police questioning the street-people sitting in the Gardens, and noted that they came close to making an arrest. Cathedral administrators had made complaints about the street-people and wished to see them excluded from the Gardens, on the grounds of creating a public nuisance; they had also successfully requested that Thresher's wine shop should ban them from their premises. Such spatial exclusions of marginal populations are hardly unusual, but have a particular impact in small towns serving rural areas, in that there is often, quite simply, nowhere else to go (see Davis, 1990 for a classic analysis of the carceral city; also Chapter Twelve in this volume).

Furthermore, some shadow workers are more spatially constrained than others: in theory at least, beggars can move on elsewhere, although we have already noted the limited number of towns in which begging takes place in rural North Wales. *Big Issue* vendors, in contrast, are only authorised to sell their product in specific locations. Dill, for example, was licensed to sell outside Thresher's, and although he was satisfied with the brisk business that went with this prime pitch in the middle of the High Street, he faced the dilemma that pursuing his trade brought him directly into the centre of contested space. Thus, although he was participating in the legitimate economic practice of being a street vendor with a licence, he was nevertheless classified primarily as a homeless person. Paradoxically, possession of a *Big Issue* badge does confer a legitimate economic status at the same time as it signifies homelessness and therefore a marginal social identity. As we have already discussed, it is the visibility of street people that presents a direct challenge to the 'normal' use of prime space by 'respectable' citizens. We would argue that such a challenge is particularly evident within a rural context, given that the presence of beggars and other street-people (whether economically legitimate or not) conflicts with the image and myth of the 'rural idyll' (Philo, 1992; Soja, 1997). Such myths are important in the marketing of North Wales as a tourist destination, and they also serve to obscure the economically underdeveloped nature of the region (Cloke et al, 1997).

A sense of place

Along with their clear sense of the temporal and spatial ordering of the venues and locations used by them, we found that shadow workers have a highly-developed sense of place. Their mental maps operated on a number of different levels, from the detailed local knowledge of how towns are structured, to a sense of the nature of other rural and urban places, both within and outside of North Wales. Only two of the respondents had been born in North Wales, and all had attachments, of both a practical and a romantic nature, to other places. Thus, all had the option of living elsewhere, and to varying degrees had chosen to live in their present locations, whether for positive ("it's quieter here") or for negative ("it's worse elsewhere") reasons. For some, there was evidence of the influence of the myth of the 'rural idyll', in that they felt themselves to be escaping from an urban nightmare:

> **"I don't like the cities 'cause I get a load of shit, 'specially being on the streets. It's quieter here, you've got homeless people in the town [Bangor], but you haven't got any badheads. Not like in Piccadilly.... I was getting loads of hassle when I was in Manchester, and I thought 'Bangor, a small town, somewhere quiet by the sea'." [Dill]**

For others, however, this 'rural idyll' was complicated by questions of national identity, language and belonging and those not born in Wales needed to negotiate their way around the countryside in an attempt to find a space for themselves (Ching and Creed, 1997). Many felt 'at home' in Bangor, a student town with a large youth population, but were rather more uncomfortable 10 miles away in Caernarfon:

> **"I generally stay in Bangor ... you can busk in Caernarfon, but everyone's very Welsh in Caernarfon, so it's a bit dodgy if you're English and you're playing Irish tunes ... you might get someone coming along and beating you up." [Ellie]**

Those who were Welsh wryly observed the ways in which their culture was packaged and sold back to local people and tourists, by the 'charity buskers' who were able to earn more each day than any other beggar, busker or vendor on the streets:

"Have you seen the woman who dresses up in a Welsh costume? She's really nice, she gives all the money to charity, she's the perfect image of the Llandudno resort. So everyone wants her, people pay her to go and do it outside their shops, the council hire her to go and stand in the Victoria Arcade. She says she gives it all to charity, she's earning £60-70 a day, she's earning loads. But it doesn't all go there, she takes about 30-40 quid for herself, it's a bit of a con really, she's getting paid to con people." [John]

Conclusion

The occupations of begging, busking and *Big Issue* selling are marginal economic activities that entail complex social, spatial and temporal negotiations. The spatial aspects of shadow work and street life in urban areas have been fairly well-documented by sociologists and human geographers, although the temporal aspects of these phenomena have received relatively little attention. This chapter has attempted to locate our qualitative study of the economic strategies of homeless people within a spatio-temporal analytical framework, and in doing so to focus on the 'rural' as a site of social enquiry. Its two major tasks have been to integrate spatial and temporal analyses of marginal economic activities, and to do so within a rural rather than urban context. We would hope to stimulate a debate concerning the nature of social and economic life among marginal populations in rural areas, and recognise the need to finely map the socio-spatial variations within places defined as rural, as well as the more evident differences between urban and rural spaces.

Notes

[1] One of the authors has been involved in a larger study of urban youth homelessness, law breaking and criminalisation (the Three Cities Project, funded by the ESRC in 1992-95). However, it was explicitly decided that we should not compare our empirical studies of rural and urban street activity in this chapter, partly for reasons of space, but mainly because we believe that the study of begging in rural areas is so underdeveloped as an area of enquiry that it merits separate consideration. However, for

a comparison of the regulation of street people in urban and rural areas, see Wardhaugh, 1999.

[2] This chapter is based on exploratory work that is part of both authors' engagement with the larger project of developing rural criminology as a discipline. We hope to engage in debates around deviance, marginality and social control in rural areas, as well as the problem of defining rurality. Even in a strictly exploratory context, the size of the sample may appear by some standards to be unacceptably small, yet in fact it represents a significant proportion of those engaged in street-level economic activities in coastal north Wales. The relatively small and geographically-dispersed nature of deviant populations is, after all, a feature of rural society.

[3] All personal names used are pseudonyms, in order to protect confidentiality.

References

Beier, A.L. (1985) *Masterless men: The vagrancy problem in England 1560-1640*, London: Methuen.

Blondel, J. (1992) 'What are political parties for?', in A. Giddens, *Human societies: A reader*, Cambridge: Polity Press.

Button, E. (1992) *Rural housing for youth: A report on the causes and responses to youth homelessness in rural areas*, London: Centrepoint.

Ching, B. and Creed, G.W. (eds) (1997) *Knowing your place: Rural identity and cultural hierarchy*, New York, NY: Routledge.

Clarke, J., Hall, S., Jefferson, T. and Roberts, B. (1976) 'Sub-cultures, cultures and class: a theoretical overview', in S. Hall and T. Jefferson (eds) *Resistance through rituals: Youth subcultures in post war Britain*, London: Hutchinson.

Cloke, P., Goodwin, M. and Milbourne, P. (1997) *Rural Wales: Community and marginalization*, Cardiff: University of Wales Press.

Davis, M. (1990) *City of quartz: Excavating the future in Los Angeles*, London: Verso.

Duncan, J.S. (1983) 'Men without property: the tramp's classification and use of urban space' in R.W. Lake, *Readings in urban analysis: Perspective on urban form and structure*, New Brunswick, NJ: Rutgers University Press.

Durkheim, E. (1965) *The elementary forms of religious life*, New York, NY: Free Press.

Ford, J., Quilgars, D., Burrows, R. and Pleace, N. (1997) *Young people and housing*, York: Centre for Housing Policy, University of York.

Goffman, E. (1959) *The presentation of self in everyday life*, Harmondsworth: Penguin.

Goffman, E. (1971) *Relations in public: Microstudies of the public order*, London: Allen Lane.

Halfacree, K. (1993) 'Locality and representation: space, discourse and alternative definitions of the rural', *Journal of Rural Studies*, vol 9, no 1, pp 23-37.

Illich, I. (1981) *Shadow work*, Boston, MA: Marion Boyars.

Jones, M. (1997) *Rough sleepers: A rural issue?*, Swansea: Shelter Cymru.

Lambert, C., Jeffers, S., Burton, P. and Bramley, G. (1992) *Homelessness in rural areas: A report on research for the Rural Development Commission*, Bristol: SAUS Publications.

Massey, D. (1992) 'A place called home?', *New Formations*, vol 17, pp 3-15.

Massey, D. (1994) *Space, place and gender*, Cambridge: Polity Press.

Milbourne, P. (ed) (1997) *Revealing rural others: Representation, power and identity in the countryside*, London: Pinter.

Mitchell, D. (1997) 'The annihilation of space by law: the roots and implications of anti-homeless laws in the United States', *Antipode*, vol 29, no 3, pp 303-35.

Murdoch, A. (1994) *We are human too: A study of people who beg*, London: Crisis.

Murray, H. (1984) 'Time in the streets', *Human Organization*, vol 43, pp 154-61.

Philo, C. (1992) 'Neglected rural geographies: a review', *Journal of Rural Studies*, vol 8, no 2, pp 193-207.

Snow, D.A. and Anderson, L. (1993) *Down on their luck: A study of homeless street people*, Berkeley, CA: University of California Press.

Soja, E. (1997) 'Planning in/for postmodernity', in G. Benko and U. Strohmayer, *Interpreting modernity and post modernity*, Oxford: Blackwell.

Sorokin, P. and Merton, R. (1937) 'Social time: a methodological and functional analysis', *American Journal of Sociology*, no 42, pp 615-29.

Taylor, I., Evans, K. and Fraser, P. (1996) *A tale of two cities: A study in Manchester and Sheffield*, London: Routledge.

Turner, V. (1974) *Dramas, fields and metaphors*, Ithaca, NY: Cornell University Press.

Turner, V. (1979) *Process, performance and pilgrimage*, New Delhi, India: Concept.

Wardhaugh, J. (1996) '"Homeless in Chinatown": deviance and social control in Cardboard city', *Sociology*, vol 30, no 4, pp 701-16.

Wardhaugh, J. (1999) *Sub city: Young people, homelessness and crime*, Aldershot: Ashgate.

EIGHT

The face that begs: street begging scenes and selves' identity work

Andrew Travers

According to Erving Goffman, all face-to-face interactions have a spontaneous yet determined structure (Smith, 1999), and begging interactions are no exception, as this chapter will show. However, the analysis that follows[1] goes beyond Goffman's thinking, since begging interactions are not seen through a single interactionist metaphor/frame (such as the theatrical metaphor) but through three disjunct 'cartographies' (or theoretical mappings) chosen for their extra-interactional resonance.

Goffman has been criticised for relying on the reader to validate his analyses (Cioffi, 1971) but his method has its advocates (Lofland, 1980; Manning, 1980; Edmondson, 1984). The method of successive cartographies, like Goffman's, depends on reader validation. Crudely stated, it succeeds if it establishes the phenomena as warranting its analysis; that is, if it makes the reader (as sociologist) take the phenomena seriously. Howsoever, the broad scale of the cartographies used here does not retain extremely fine details of the conduct observed, and a high level of abstraction is maintained so that the concepts of self and identity do not disappear into a microanalysis. For what is aimed at is a tropical report (White, 1978) that fathoms the obvious without losing sight of its surface. This, of course, means that, though begging comes into focus as a sophisticated behavioural routine, the 'perspectives by incongruity' (through which it does so) violate ethnomethodological precepts – as did Goffman's (Watson, 1989).

The three cartographic frames that will project begging as an interaction depend on the theses:

- that the emotion of envy is an engine of Durkheimian social effervescence (Blum, 1994);
- that a softcore frame is a denial of the pornographic frame it displaces (MacCannell, 1989);

- that a 'scene' is a near-row in which interactants *collaborate* to avoid a violent closure (Frank, 1976, 1982).

The choice of these cartographic frames in its turn depends on a fieldworker intuition that they open up rather than close down begging interactions to reveal a structure to begging interactions that has significance for theories of self, of face-to-face interaction in general, and of the public performance of consumer society. The analysis as a whole can be summarised in the simple proposition: *coalescing interactants work together through their envy-activated, intersubjective selves to divide into discrete identities*. And since that proposition runs like a leitmotif through the chapter it allows street begging scenes – at the end of the chapter – to be read backwards into face-to-face interaction considered as a *sui generis* social order (Goffman, 1983a; Rawls, 1987). This, I shall contend, yields a generalisable 'law' of interaction.

Empirical studies of begging are few and far between. Gilmore (1940), Gore (1958), Misra (1971), Bamisaiye (1974), Ratnapala (1979), Shichor and Ellis (1981), Schak (1989), and Meir–Dviri and Raz (1995) provide sharp insights into begging strategies in a variety of cultures but, because they describe the strategies in terms of beggars' orientations to a taken-for-granted world, they do not probe the phenomenology of human begging behaviour. Fabrega (1971), Gmelch and Gmelch (1978), Heirling (1990), and Santos et al (1994) do concentrate on begging as an interaction between beggars and the public but not so as to develop interaction theory. Though Fabrega, Gmelch and Gmelch, and Heirling link some of their perceptions to Goffman's early face-to-face sociology, no studies of begging (which always occurs in public) approach it through Goffman's (1963, 1972) or anybody else's sociology of public places. In the substantive studies of begging to date, the emphasis is nearly always on what can be said about beggars as people who have an unusual livelihood and not on what can be said about interaction when it is the public occasion of begging. Opportunities of either opening up begging to see how it succeeds as an interaction or of opening up face-to-face interaction from the direction of its unique case of begging have not been taken. This chapter, however, takes both of these opportunities.

Elsewhere (Travers, 1994b, 1995) I have specified, in response to Mead, Goffman, Schutz and Lacan (among others), the difference between an interactional self-of-the-moment and an identity, and this difference is assumed throughout the chapter. To clarify, a self is a self because at any given instant in interaction with other selves it reads itself and can be read as the animating 'surplus' of its identity (or identities). To expand, self:

- *identifies* selves (others as well as itself) *as* identities
- or *identifies with* one or more of those identities
- or *identifies with* one or more selves: in an intersubjective cosmos.

Most importantly, the self of such thinking cannot be reducible to identity. It is akin to the 'subject' of James' (1890, p 307) and Cooley's (1902, p 170) 'self-feelings', while an identity, by contrast, is only a cultured characterisation (or caricature or biography or portrait) of self. The above account of self thus bypasses Mead's and symbolic interactionists' versions of self and identity (though it would be surprising if their versions did not also produce begging as a drama of identity work).

The sociology of public places (for example, Lofland, 1989) has been revitalised by Gardner (1995) who finds that gender is the principal but much glossed over identity issue therein. Gardner's careful analysis of women's feelings (and the pervasive identity consequences of those), when men offend women in breach of the Goffman rule of civil inattention, is a tour de force. Cahill and Eggleston (1994) also revitalise the sociology of public places in their heart-rending study of wheelchair users. Gardner's book and Cahill and Eggleston's paper draw attention, after Goffman, to painful identity problems that arise between strangers just where it may be thought – by those getting away with or condoning offences – that such problems are trivial. This chapter's analysis of begging interactions is consonant with Gardner's and Cahill and Eggleston's theoretical preoccupations and incidentally contributes to an appreciation of public places as treacherous social arenas where a relatively free association (often enough as scripted as Greek tragedy) has rules wide open to abuse (sardonic flattery in the case of beggars).

Before we go straight into the cartographies themselves, three more introductory notes are necessary:

- Whenever the phrase 'civil inattention' is used, it refers to Goffman's definition (1963, p 84):"The slightest of interpersonal rituals" by which interactants show others that they know about them but will not exploit their knowing for purposes intrusive of the other's reciprocal knowing.
- Each cartography comprises tabulated analytical forays that are not meant to exhaust the phenomena. The cartographies can be no more than 'takes' of real lives that for the protagonists are rooted in histories they cannot escape. Space is thus left for further analyses and for further extrapolations to the general case of any face-to-face interaction.

• It is Goffman's (1983a) suggestion that interactions have formal similarities that may be explored analytically (in Simmel's sense – see Smith, 1994) that warrants the extrapolation – at the end of the chapter – from begging interactions to *any* interaction[2].

First cartography: begging as a springboard to enviability

Because beggars make those people who pass them by feel glad that they are not beggars, they create in their passers-by a brief emotion of enviability. And the passer-by, feeling enviable, cannot shake off this feeling by reversing the interactional flow of energy. Enviability here is irreversible because the passer-by is designed by the beggar's show of misery to be incapable either of envying the beggar or of feeling contempt for the beggar. (Contempt would only be possible if the beggar indicated an envy of the passer-by that the identity of beggar precludes.) So the enviability that beggars provoke is 'enviability-at-a-loss'. And, if we go along with Blum (1994), we shall have to admit that enviability-at-a-loss is a gain of interactivity for social life.

Introducing Blum's cartographic frame

Blum (1994) says that society is kept alive by a Durkheimian effervescence of interactants who are each unstable composites of the need to reconcile their 'differences from' and 'unities with' others in an inevitably Weberian (1947) condition of incessant social stratification. Drawing upon Simmel (1955), Blum declares that jealousy and envy are engines of sociality, integrating separate selves at the cost of their rigidification into discrete identities. But, if they are to remain civilly self-adjusted, selves, according to Blum, must avoid a rigid intransigence that is violent in effect. Intransigence, Blum points out, is laughable when seen with detachment (Bergson, 1956), and violent if it justifies itself with a theory of social life as a field of antagonisms. Rigidity of self (including 'formulaic kindness'), then, is violent because it attacks the particularity of self. And, Blum continues, if inspired by jealousy and envy, reprisals for such attacks are an over-defence of self-worth. However, the jealous individual (who does not concern us here), in claiming the particularity of a relationship, and the envious individual, who in the name of equality claims that others should not have more than the envious self, are *excessively* self-adjusting. Envious people (and jealous people), in this view, suffer pains of rigidity as they impossibly seek complete clarity about what self means to and for the other and, thus, to and for itself.

Enviability, when unaccompanied by contempt (for provocateurs such as beggars), becomes, in Blum's construct, the humbling emotion of ontological privilege. It is at a loss for how to cope with an unwanted sense of social superiority. As a consequence, in the presence of a beggar, the person feeling enviability-at-a-loss becomes unwilling or unable to put themself on a level with beggars. At the same time, beggars themselves – by seeming to acquiesce in beggary – do not appear to envy those who, by comparison to beggars, feel enviable.

Cartography of enviability-at-a-loss in begging interactions

- *We are beneath even your contempt.* Sitting or standing in demeaning locations, beggars disadvantage themselves towards passers-by, who, upright and mobile, seem imbued with purposes beyond the begging interaction. Contriving to look up at others from below (when sitting) or from discomfort (when standing), beggars pedantically underline the message, "We are at the bottom of your social scale". Indeed, the whole beggar demeanour is like a social doorstep, compelling the passer-by to step up from it into a relative superiority assured in every case by the forward motion of the passer-by. Thus social distance between beggar and passer-by is opened wide by the beggar in a situation of instant Weberian stratification. Self-destructive of a worthier identity than that of beggar, the beggar constructs passers-by as intransigently better-off, whether or not they want to feel this way about themselves.

  Further, and crucially, contempt for the beggar is impossible, since contempt only arises in the face of another's failure to be equal to what they try to appear to be, and the beggar is a beggar precisely by managing to look as though attempts by them to socially ascend would be futile. And the beggar, by appearing to be already utterly shamed, necessarily pre-empts all contempt that would be directed at them (contempt implies parity – "If I were failing like you, I would be ashamed"). So, beneath even contempt, a beggar, by not evincing an unjustified self-respect (envy) that could be counter-attacked, uses the image of beggary to launch passers-by into enviability-at-a-loss.

- *Enviability-at-a-loss.* The upwardly-stratified passer-by is suddenly particularised from below by a beggar, and may react by giving money. But this does not release the donor from enviability. Rather, it reinforces enviability by merging it with the feeling that the donor had to act on it in the circumstances. In contrast, the non-donor acts as if there are no 'circumstances'. The non-donor stiffens his or her body with the self-consciousness of pretending that the beggar, even less than a non-person (Goffman, 1953, pp 217-30), is a thing one should *not* be expected to 'not see'. For the non-donor, his or her stiffness and self-consciousness, occurring right at the heart of an emotion (enviability) that should promote a relaxed attitude, reinforces the enviability, the more so the more it becomes conscious of itself. The non-donor's enviability is at a loss of course, since it cannot be discharged in counter-envy or contempt.

- *The malice of beggars' intransigence.* Blum says that particularisation is malicious, either because it attacks another self's worth or because it defends against that attack. Malice in the beggar is so exquisitely subtle that it is almost invisible. The beggar is firstly malicious to him or herself, by performing self-destruction into a demeaned being, and, secondly, malicious to others by breaching the requirement of civil inattention not to overtly solicit attention from strangers in public places. But the self-destruction of beggars flips other people's reciprocal selves to equal and opposite heights of self-construction that they did not choose to occupy and from which, no matter their concomitant self-disgust, they cannot descend. Lévi-Strauss (1962, p 6) registers this when he says that Calcutta beggars "debase you with their veneration". The result is unbalanced enviability, a degrading thrill of social excitation, without which, Blum notes, society ceases to be interactive and becomes too rigid to reproduce itself through its flexible components (selves).

- *Reverse-envy of beggars.* It is too much to say that beggars are *never* envied. Because of their placement, which gives them excellent surveillance opportunities, partial exemption from civil inattention rules, and some impunity in accosting strangers, beggars, like innocent Situationists (Debord, 1983), now and then may be seen as enviably free even while they incite enviability-at-a-loss.

Conclusion

As a frisson of social damnation the beggar in public space imparts to the passer-by dissociative motion that is not only physical but also a self-motion upwards into enviability-at-a-loss, walking on air after stepping on the beggar's face. Passer-by selves are plucked from anonymity by an enviability they can only increase whether they give to the beggar or stride past. The beggar too collects a tithe of enviability in the recognition of their shamelessness, security of social place (you cannot go a lot lower), and closeness to reality (real economic straits). The emotion of enviability, catalysed by beggars, excites interactants to become distanced identities. And the excitations of non-beggar selves passing beggars by prompt giving or refusing to give, in either case adding to a diffuse urban enthusiasm whose lack is said to herald cellular paranoia (Sennett, 1995). On account of their exhibition of economic impotence, a beggar thus works on the body politic like a dose of Viagra.

Second cartography: begging as the dramatic restraint of a pornographic by a softcore frame

Tableaux of beggary displace and deny its reality. Just as softcore eroticism is a frame superposing a pornographic frame (MacCannell, 1989), so beggars' despairing petitions are a grim muzak that muffles truly desperate appeals[3]. MacCannell's frame analysis (following Goffman, 1974) of sexual representations, if applied to beggary, exposes how beggars' apparently subversive displays of poverty *affirm* an affluent symbolic order. But what is MacCannell's difference between pornographic and softcore frames?

Introducing MacCannell's cartographic frame

In the pornographic frame, faces authentically demonstrate the confrontation between sexual desire and language-led exogamous sexual intercourse (MacCannell, 1989). This is MacCannell's principal argument, that having sex beyond one's own family/tribe/culture/community depends on the evolution of new language that the sexual act, as it were, can strangle at its inception. MacCannell writes of pornography's representations: "[T]he sexual trauma that accompanied the invention of language" (1989, p 158) is expressed in "faces [that] reflect a grammatical conjugation between individuals for whom language is the only common ground. Under these conditions, the [pornographic] denial of language [by faces *in extremis*] is an affirmation of a new kind of intimacy" (p 164). Pornographic sexual ardour therefore 'speaks' erotic reality as an exogamous "gesture of utter defiance of the linguistic moral order" (p 166). Such defiance authenticates the power of interpersonal attraction driven – even more than by sexual desire – by "opposition to normative structures" (p 167).

Conversely, the frame of softcore commercial eroticism is reticent about its pornographic subtext while disguising that reticence. Typically, it features a disengaged young female, smooth as Narcissus' mirror, into which the viewer can only pour their self-love. The softcore frame, where "sexual doings might occur but don't", suspends and denies sexual desire (MacCannell, 1989, p 170). Hinting at origins in pornographic expressions, it opposes those, so as to repress the exogamous intersubjectivity that language made possible. Softcore eroticism is restrained yet posed as how sex should be seen. This is because "the everyday response [to exogamous speech] is a multiple repression of the intersubjective powers of speech, sexually based solidarity, *and* the pornographic frame" (MacCannell, 1989, p 173).

Cartography of softcore suppression of a hardcore frame in begging interactions

- *Foreclosure of intersubjectivity by the beggar's softcore summons.* The speech of beggars to passers-by seldom consists in agonised cries, screams, and wails but is characteristically a chant or recitative prayer ("Got any spare change, please"). Never too loud and usually intoned as though the beggar articulates a generalised condition, the summons does not voice personal desperation yet is despairing. Beggars appear to flaunt their want but actually envelop it in restraint. If beggars did nakedly express desperation (in the fractured speech of a pornographic proposal of quasi-kinship between strangers potentially joined in language), they would invite their arrest. Most neatly, the beggar's acutely-distressing experience of hunger and homelessness may be represented and masked by the simple written sign, 'Hungry and Homeless'. This sign stands in relation to the need it proclaims as might a sign reading 'I have been run over' held up by a road accident victim who is bleeding to death. And every aspect of the beggar's demeanour is in line with the 'Hungry and Homeless' sign. Foreclosed though traded upon by the beggar's adoption of nearly liturgical speech forms, intersubjectivity expires in dramatic restraint. Within tight propriety limits, the spectacle of beggary substitutes for the pornography of suffering a 'softcore destitution'.

- *Beggars affirm an affluent symbolic order.* By formulating their beggary as an instantly-recognisable and therefore conventionalised spectacle of itself, the beggar supports a request for spare change that when responded to is a mockery of what is needed. As though subscribing to the same social policies that shaped their prospects of becoming their casualty, a beggar – deadpan, almost asocial – conveys that they can be self-helped only by piecemeal charity from the 'private sector'.

  Softcore eroticism blends with and infuses commodity advertisement culture by outlawing from plain sight the reality of fucking, yet at the same time it injects sanitised sex into public life wherever it can. Similarly the frame of 'softcore destitution' (superposing 'pornographic destitution') is like a homeopathic dose of penury in streets full of shoppers who are marching to the rhythms of "suicide and consumption" (Warde, 1994, p 884). Softcore destitution, like softcore eroticism, solicits the passer-by's decision to give or not give money on behalf of beliefs that are unreal. While in the case of softcore eroticism the belief is in the possibility of fulfilment through unbridled consumption (Durkheim's 'egoism'), in the case of softcore destitution the unreal belief is that the victim has *sole* responsibility for responding as they do to social conditions urging their victimage. Where the models of softcore eroticism are paid to present themselves as self-displayed 'for fun', beggars – no less hypocritically – present themselves as privatised tax collectors who, enterprisingly, cut out the middleman (the interventionist state).

- *Reverse-narcissism inspired by beggars.* MacCannell says that the softcore erotic model is like Narcissus' mirror in which the viewer can gaze upon an idealised reflection wiped clean of real sex. By *identifying with* the model and not just *identifying* the model *as* a softcore model, one can fleetingly become the model, frozen, slightly bored, *being-for-oneself*, and serenely desirable (I elucidate the disjunction between *identification with* and *identification as* in Travers, 1995). Similarly, but towards a contrary end of the viewer's disidentification, beggars model poverty as softcore destitution without venting its pornographic emotions (rage and shame). They inveigle viewers' repulsion (reverse-narcissism) that is on the order of, 'Ugh! That's not me!' or, more generously, 'There but for the grace of God go I, but not today (thank God)'. Instead of *identifying with* the beggar, the viewer, *disidentifying from* (see again, Travers, 1995) the beggar, completes the disidentification by giving small change or by jumping into the identity of one who does not give to beggars, either way *identifying with* 'I am not a beggar'.

Thus, with great delicacy, beggars offer passers-by a titivating glimpse of what happens to someone who falls through the bottom of affluence. Beggars, the very last people from whom non-sociologists might expect such self-denying decency, draw themselves as a veil over their experience of endless social descent. Passers-by duly see the beggar as a unit of self-controlled poverty that frees them from its involving implications.

• *Aggressive begging.* The spectacle of beggary may be rent by explicit (pornographic) appeals from the heart. When passers-by are accosted, shouted out, abused, and threatened by beggars, then the 'spectacle' (softcore destitution) gives way to reality (hardcore destitution). The call for legislation to control the pornographic aggression of beggary is, naturally, instantaneous[4], and often rests on the allegation that beggars *always* menace passers-by (and so neither deserve nor need charity). Two examples suggest how difficult it is to think that aggressive begging is on a par with, say, mugging. At Brixton tube station a woman dodges back and forth at the exits of the barriers screaming, 'Spare change!'. Her manner is that of a rugby defender preparing to tackle the player with the ball, and her face is both vicious and pleading. Outside a Bristol arts complex, a girl who looks about 14 (seen by me on several occasions leaning against a pillar and holding out her hand for coins while sweetly whispering, 'Any spare change?') is tearfully yelling 'I'm a human being!' and darting furiously into a crowd that is trying to calm her down. In neither case does the beggar touch anyone, but in both cases the beggar is treated like a beast that has slipped its leash.

Conclusion

The beggar votes for affluent normal appearances but masquerades assent as abstention. It is to the dramatic restraint from urgent appeal that the reward of their recognition as a bona fide beggar – through either donation or non-donation – is given (this is clarified later). Yet the beggar is a self like any other self, stuck with self and using it at the dramaturgical limits of situational propriety to eke out a miserable existence within an affluent symbolic order. At a standstill on the margins of the pursuit of replete consumerhood, the beggar is a token victim, a sort of human trampoline not so much trampled as compressed into self-denial ('I am *only* a beggar'), the better to catapult passers-by into identities that may also be denying any other need than the need to consume.

Insofar as the spectacle of beggary incites the feeling of relative wealth, the beggar works for capital (Gans, 1972). One might even feel that the beggar is a capitalist par excellence, because he or she poses the proposition that money is everything. From each beggar flows the implication that a self is worth only what the identity it constructs can sell itself for. As a beggar, the self capitalises itself in a dimension of disgrace, however. This may be because 'wealth creation' by beggary betrays governmental disinvestment in poverty through the promotion of consumerism.

Third cartography: begging as a scene

Begging interactions have four features in common with a *scene* (an encounter that stops short of a row). They focus interactants on the here and now; they produce, in their closure, identities hitherto only tentative; they produce those identities as if from prior inclinations towards them; and they flirt with violent closure.

Introducing Frank's cartographic frame

A scene is an interaction that does little else but define interactants' selves as antipathetic identities in a gradual eruption whose non-violent closure is crescive and ambiguous (Frank, 1976, 1982). By achieving public recognition, Frank says, identities that had been tentative but convinced that they should make themselves felt are "*defined through the interaction* [the scene]" (1976, p 411) to appear to have been real prior to the scene *and all along to have been asking to be reckoned with*. It is the scene's use of an 'improper closing' that marks the scene as such. A scene closes when interactants snub each other from identities produced by the scene.

Frank claims that the improper closing of a scene cannot be fully understood as the conduct of speakers deemed unworthy of study beyond their origins in sequences of talk (but see Schegloff, 1988; and also see the deconstruction of Schegloff's argument in Goffman, 1981, pp 5-77, 1983b). A scene's closure, breaking a cycle of repudiation and counter-repudiation, is not only faulty 'repair' left dangling, but also cooperative and motivated rule-violation that 'keys' (Goffman, 1974) the 'frame' that is being closed (Frank, 1982, p 369). By means of an improper closing, interactants balance the unkeyed frame of propriety against the keyed frame of impropriety. The consequent ambiguity terminates interaction in mutually-prejudicial, close-call vindications of identities who fight shy of violence. Only Goffman's (1974) frame analysis of closings, says Frank (1982, p 369), "makes clear what conversation analysts can allow us to forget ... [that] [m]embers' purposes fill in the sense of any closing", and that one of their purposes in scenes is to make their "purposes not ... too intransigent".

A scene, then, is like the negotiation of a bitter truce after a war that, declared by the truce, never broke out.

Cartography of a begging interaction as a scene

- *The begging scene as its own topic.* By asking for money and so exacting more of other people than their civil inattention, the beggar is an obstacle to passers-by, upsetting their sense of having "no reason to fear ... others, be hostile to them, or wish to avoid them" (Goffman, 1963, p 84). The beggar, of course, already offers a clear identity, that of beggar, but this identity, if not confirmed by donations, will become a millstone instead of a lifejacket. The beggar as well as the passer-by is caught in their own identity suspense.

  Because the only exit for the passer-by from a begging interaction is by way of an identity that expresses internally and externally what he or she thinks of the beggar, the passer-by is split into two potential identities, donor and non-donor, the latter further fraying into a number of performative attitudes towards beggary, each dragging behind it 'the kind of identity' who would behave like *that*. So, merely by begging, the beggar both opens him or herself to repudiation and opens up the passer-by into several possible counter-identities (that, whatever their inner certainty, still have to be expressed, for the first time, *here*). The beggar, just because money, not civil inattention, is his or her 'total identity' request, thus initiates a tiny scene, a rapid mime of a full-blown confrontation. Developing at exactly the pace of the passer-by, a scene is inevitable, since it has to be dealt with immediately at the expense of other topics.

- *Tentative identities are publicly recognised in the begging scene's closure.* A proprietous closing of the begging interaction is the handing over of money. Tinkling coins confirm the beggar as a beggar and at the same time grant the donor an identity of one who has not slighted the beggar and who therefore honours other people's interactional identities regardless of their status. But, because the propriety of giving money is within the beggar's improprietous frame, the donor becomes a 'faulty person' (Goffman, 1953, pp 258-72), a knock-on advertisement for beggary. The propriety of giving, exacerbating the impropriety of begging, boosts the beggar and momentarily lights up the donor as a donor more than anything else. In this way the donor cannot help but repudiate the beggar, as the beggar will have hoped they will, by clarifying the donor identity that perfectly reverses the beggar identity.

  The more frequent exit from a begging interaction of not giving money necessitates behaviour towards the beggar that expresses an identity through its deliberated repudiation of the beggar. Non-donating repudiations come in several types. 'Not seeing' is the main one. Other types are ridicule, abuse, and assault. Not seeing is accomplished by physical manoeuvres such as 'eyes straight ahead', 'acceleration of pace', 'giving a wide berth', and 'increasing self-involvement' or, when passers-by are dyads or groups, 'self-and-other(s)-involvement'. A frequent method of ridiculing a beggar is to walk past the beggar while jingling change in one's pocket (this is done by males). Abuse is either verbal ('Get a job!' 'Fuck yourself!' 'Don't look at me!') or gestural (a casual V-sign or a finger – two examples – plainly indicate 'I hate you but not enough to concern me'). However they behave, the non-donor simultaneously affirms the beggar and pronounces a precise counter-identity to that of the beggar, instantly inferable and available for retrospective expansion in the lineaments of repudiation.

- *Terminal identities seem to pre-exist the begging scene.* In public places, where the solo interactant is very often a stranger among other strangers, bad or good behaviour – unless the interactant wears the uniform of an institution – carries only a small risk of repercussion to other realms, provided the interactant can forget the scene later[5]. Becker's (1970, pp 261-73) idea of commitment within interaction, built up by the interactant's 'side-bets' (concurrent commitments to identities generated in other social realms) is relevant here[6]. Clearly the pressure of side-bets is reduced in public places. Even members of dyads or groups, who may be pressured by co-members' expectations of them, belong to entities as exempt from side-bets as the solo interactant. Only superficially constrained by faceless civil inattention, a person who is somewhat released from commitments may feel, if and when a scene presents itself, that they are discovering what they are 'really' like. The public scene can become a test case in which the rapid advent of a situational identity will make it seem that the situational identity derives from a latency that awaited just such an opportunity to assert itself. And, because this situational identity is so precisely defined, it will not feel situational (situations are not usually scenes, and so permit only vague definitions of identity). Paradoxically, therefore, a self in a scene can feel – with its side-bets off – that it is discovering an identity that in embryo pre-existed the scene and was hitherto *obscured by* commitments and side-bets.

Whichever way it goes, of course, the scene more deeply commits the beggar to that identity which started it.

- *The ambiguous closure of the begging scene is a close-call vindication.* After the begging interaction is closed, both parties will have received a slight overdose of identity but one that depends on awareness of the other as having administered it. Thus begging unbalances everyone beyond the closure of its interaction, but, being tiny scenes between strangers in public places, begging scenes do not have portentous consequences for the next meeting of the interactants (escalate the scene, deny that the scene was a scene, apologise for the scene, cut dead the other, make a new scene out of the other's response[s] to the old scene). Instead, begging scenes vindicate people who through them assume identities that can behave as though they were not close-called and did not need vindicating.

- *When the scene does not come off as a scene.* In my interactions with beggars, I found that, by sitting beside them and striking up a conversation, I dissolved the scene before it could become one. On no occasion when I sat down with beggars did a beggar ask me to go away, and on every occasion the talk that ensued was relaxed and friendly. Through talking to beggars on their own level, I learned that it is the structure of the begging interaction *as a scene* that gives the passer-by the feeling that the gap between beggar and non-beggar is difficult to cross. And that very gap stimulates some people to widen it by looking mean and/or ludicrously myopic and others to unwittingly widen it, on the beggars' terms, by handing over money.

Conclusion

In scenes, selves are other than the ricochetting identities they might *identify with* (Travers, 1995) after the event. The selves under discussion here are interactional selves that unite to conspire their separation. As it were, the beggar identity is a transformative interaction turnstile that is not opened *by giving or not giving money* but which, *in the process of reciprocal self-work*, dispenses either money or its unequivocal denial. Such money as the beggar receives, then, is actually only a *byproduct of the begging scene's self-work*. This is to say, *the passer-by does not give (or refuse to give) to the beggar as one monad spatially and temporally in apartheid from another monad. The passer-by and the beggar, interactive at first sight, work up a scene so as to become two self-extricated identities in two distinct realms.* The pay-off is both a demeaningly-confirmed identity for the beggar and an uneasily detached identity for the passer-by. Money, given or withheld, merely lubricates this 'self-process' of identity manufacture.

Summary: the face that begs

Reading backwards from the above into any face-to-face interaction, one might say that face-to-face interaction requires for its continuing interactivity that interactants, perhaps taking turns, create others' enviability-at-a-loss (superiority excited by a facilitative but not necessarily contemptible abasement). Interactivity may need selves that beg to be trodden flat even while they maintain a demeanour as hard as paving stone. Selves, though almost invisible in Goffman's and Garfinkel's 'normal appearances', apologetically protrude – in the form of identities – just enough, we may say, to be routinely crushed in the interests of interactional order, both actual and analytical (Travers, 1994a).

One might further say that raw experiences of real emotions are interactionally taboo while their sanitised simulations are treated as real. A self, after MacCannell, wishing to express naked truths of human life will be strongly deterred from greeting others with strangled pleas for recognition in a language that fosters only rude intersubjectivity. Face-to-face communication, to be acceptable, will thus have to be a collusion against truth, arrogating to itself an emptied, glossed-over semblance of the truth. It follows that in face-to-face interactions, selves, to earn identities, will be 'converted' to society's ethos of distance-equals-membership in the politest possible way (Travers, 1992a).

Finally one might say that whatever the officially ratified nature of any interaction, it is only not a scene because none of the interactants deliberately makes a scene. This is to suggest that whatever the unacknowledged identities that a potential scene could deliver, processual selves beg off from them with behaviours that attempt to conceal their begging off. However an interaction develops, then, it must be between selves politely begging (in the modes of asking, requesting, demanding) to be taken seriously. But selves to avoid scenes should not take themselves more seriously than as selves that are taken seriously primarily because they are selves busy with hidden identity work. And this identity work is the work of selves burying identities in the interests of peace or – when the interaction becomes a scene – the work of defining, defending, and asserting identities despite the risks of conflict.

Goffman implies that a self presenting identity has an inner agency that is only intersubjective in the mood of alienation. The idea of self developed in this chapter (drawing from Travers, 1992a, 1992b, 1994a, 1994b, 1995) carries with it a contra-Goffman assumption that full intersubjectivity is a given of face-to-face interaction. Interactants in this way of thinking only *resort to* behaving apropos identities when for whatever reason they become self-conscious. A self never can be more than a promise of some impossible-to-finally-describe identity which consists in further promises. The promises are necessary to vary 'normal appearances', since interactivity would be insufficiently involving to hold interactants in mutual moral accountability if interactants only churned out more of the same hegemonic appearances. But, when selves are eager to dissociate, their promises of self-hood turn into entreaties ('Please leave me alone') which, through the respect they (the entreaties) receive, construct antipathetic identities. Entreaties are begging behaviours but under a tautening veneer of politeness.

Since interaction – if we see it through Goffman's eyes – is a climate of potential insult at all times, selves may spend their whole lives taking care not to give good cause for their having to apologise. So now it can be said that taking such care is every variety of begging behaviour by selves of selves with respect to potentially offensive identity ascriptions. If it is, *self is the face that begs*. So the self's begging behaviour is its very nature, hitherto, by Goffman and everyone else, masked by the polite ruse of calling politeness a mask, as if the mask of politeness could be ripped off without tearing an interactant's face to shreds.

This chapter has argued that actual beggars in the street maliciously demean themselves by performing identities that are beneath contempt so as to create enviability-at-a-loss. It has also argued that beggars, by *politely* foreclosing bare-wire intersubjectivity, affirm the ontological affluence of passers-by. They can do all that – according to the third cartography – by making tiny scenes which create after-the-fact identities presumed to pre-exist the scenes. Beggars, of course, wear masks of spectacular beggary (to which their faces are welded by the gaze of strangers). But they know how to do this, the paper suggests, because every face knows already that if it wants to be a self for others it begs to be seen as a self, by masking its wants with inseparable identities. As a rule, or law, then:

> **If an interactant (X) expects to be taken seriously by another interactant (Y), then, to the degree that seriousness regarding identity is conveyed, interactant X *begs* to be treated as at least a self that could righteously take exception to not being taken that seriously. And the same goes for Y in the same time.**

For even the interactant who passes by a beggar in the street begs the beggar to see him or her as other than a beggar, in a social copula that, by being severed from within, saves both the faces from the intimacy that the language of this chapter postulates outside society on behalf of social interaction.

Acknowledgements

The Nuffield Foundation supported my begging research. Thanks are due to Greg Martin for supplying media materials; to the Julian Trust for letting me stay in the night shelter; to my informants for sharing their ideas with me; and to Greg Smith for helpful comments on an earlier version of this paper.

Notes

[1] Of 32 interviews and more than 200 observations mostly in Bristol and London late in 1994.

[2] Goffman's thoughts on 'face' (1955) and the extensive literature they

have spawned would also open up begging interactions, but are not referred to here for lack of space.

³ Some appeals might be cynical, but then to be this cynical is to be desperate.

⁴ Teir (1993) reviews American constitutional difficulties when freedom to beg conflicts with the demand for freedom from beggars. See also Chapter Thirteen in this volume.

⁵ Gardner (1989) makes the case that self-work in public settings, especially if painful, can damage gender identities that have to be lived with elsewhere.

⁶ Thanks to Barry Barnes for directing me to Becker on commitment.

References

Bamisaiye, A. (1974) 'Begging in Ibadan, Southern Nigeria', *Human Organization*, vol 33, no 2, pp 197-202.

Becker, H. (1970) 'Notes on the concept of commitment', in H. Becker, *Sociological work*, Chicago, IL: Aldine.

Bergson, H. (1956) *Comedy*, New York, NY: Anchor Books.

Blum, A. (1994) 'The ethical face of commonplace malice: convolutions of the divided subject', *Studies in Symbolic Interaction*, vol 16, pp 215-49.

Cahill, S.E. and Eggleston, R. (1994) 'Managing emotions in public: the case of wheelchair users', *Social Psychology Quarterly*, vol 57, no 4, pp 300-12.

Cioffi, F. (1971) *The proper study*, London: Macmillan.

Cooley, C.H. (1902) *Human nature and the social order*, 1983 edn, New Brunswick, NJ: Transaction Books.

Debord, G. (1983) *Society of the spectacle*, Detroit, MI: Black and Red.

Edmondson, R. (1984) *Rhetoric in sociology*, London: Macmillan.

Fabrega, H. (1971) 'Begging in a Southwestern Mexican City', *Human Organization*, vol 30, no 3, pp 277-87.

Frank, A.W. (1976) 'Making scenes in public: symbolic violence and social order', *Theory and Society*, vol 3, pp 395-416.

Frank, A.W. (1982) 'Improper closings: the art of conversational repudiation', *Human Studies*, vol 5, pp 357-70.

Gans, H. (1972) 'The positive functions of poverty', *American Journal of Sociology*, vol 78, no 2, pp 275-89.

Gardner, C.B. (1989) 'Analyzing gender in public places', *The American Sociologist*, vol 20, no 1, 42-56.

Gardner, C.B. (1995) *Passing by: Gender and public harassment*, Berkeley, CA: University of California Press.

Gilmore, H.W. (1940) *The beggar*, Chapel Hill, NC: University of North Carolina Press.

Gmelch, G. and Gmelch, S.B. (1978) 'Begging in Dublin: the strategies of a marginal urban occupation', *Urban Life*, vol 6, no 4, 439-54.

Goffman, E. (1953) 'Communication conduct in an island community', PhD Thesis, University of Chicago.

Goffman, E. (1955) 'On face-work', in E. Goffman, *Interaction ritual*, 1972 edn, Harmondsworth: Penguin.

Goffman, E. (1963) *Behavior in public places: Notes on the social organization of gatherings*, New York, NY: Free Press.

Goffman, E. (1972) *Relations in public*, Harmondsworth: Penguin.

Goffman, E. (1974) *Frame analysis*, Cambridge, MA: Harvard University Press.

Goffman, E. (1981) *Forms of talk*, Oxford: Basil Blackwell.

Goffman, E. (1983a) 'The interaction order', *American Sociological Review*, vol 48, no 1, pp 1-53.

Goffman, E. (1983b) 'Felicity's condition', *American Journal of Sociology*, vol 89, no 1, pp 1-53.

Gore, M.S. (1958) 'Society and the beggar', *Sociological Bulletin* (India), vol 7, no 1, pp 23-48.

Heirling, J. (1990) 'A sociology of panhandling', Unpublished Master's Thesis, Department of Sociology, University of Arizona.

James, W. (1890) *The principles of psychology*, Volume 1, London: Macmillan and Co.

Lévi-Strauss, C. (1962) 'Crowds', *New Left Review*, vol 15, pp 3-6.

Lofland, J. (1980) 'Early Goffman: style, structure, substance, soul', in J. Ditton (ed) *The view from Goffman*, London: Macmillan.

Lofland, L. (1989) 'Social life in the public realm', *Journal of Contemporary Ethnography*, vol 17, pp 453-82.

MacCannell, D. (1989) 'Faking it: face-work in pornography', *American Journal of Semiotics*, vol 6, no 4, pp 153-74.

Manning, P.K. (1980) 'Goffman's framing order: style as structure', in J. Ditton (ed) *The view from Goffman*, London: Macmillan.

Meir-Dviri, M. and Raz, A.E. (1995) 'Rituals of exchange in the social world of Israeli beggars: an exploratory study', *Symbolic Interaction*, vol 18, no 2, pp 99-119.

Misra, P.K. (1971) 'Nomads in a city setting', *Man in India*, vol 51, no 4, pp 317-33.

Ratnapala, N. (1979) *The beggar in Sri Lanka*, Sri Lanka: World Vision International.

Rawls, A.W. (1987) 'The interaction order *Sui Generis*: Goffman's contribution to social theory', *Sociological Theory*, vol 5, no 2, pp 136-49.

Santos, M.D., Leve, C. and Pratkanis, A.R. (1994) 'Hey buddy, can you spare 17 cents: mindful persuasion and the pique technique', *Journal of Applied Social Psychology*, vol 24, no 9, pp 755-64.

Schak, D.C. (1989) *A Chinese beggars' den*, Pittsburgh, PA: University of Pittsburgh Press.

Schegloff, E. (1988) 'Goffman and the analysis of conversation', in P. Drew and A. Wootton (eds) *Erving Goffman: Exploring the interaction order*, Cambridge: Polity Press.

Sennett, R. (1995) 'Bodily experience in public space', in S. Edgell, S. Walklate, and G. Williams (eds) *Debating the public sphere*, Aldershot: Avebury.

Shichor, D. and Ellis, R. (1981) 'Begging in Israel: an exploratory study', *Deviant Behavior: An Interdisciplinary Journal*, vol 2, pp 109-25.

Simmel, G. (1955) *Conflict*, Glencoe, IL: Glencoe Free Press.

Smith, G. (1994) 'Snapshots "Sub Specie Aeternitatis": Simmel, Goffman and formal sociology', in D. Frisby (ed) *Georg Simmel: Critical assessments*, Volume 3, New York, NY: Routledge.

Smith, G. (ed) (1999) *Goffman and social organization*, London: Routledge.

Teir, R. (1993) 'Maintaining safety and civility in public spaces: a constitutional approach to aggressive begging', *Louisiana Law Review*, vol 54, no 2, pp 285-338.

Travers, A. (1992a) 'The conversion of self in everyday life', *Human Studies*, vol 15, pp 169-238.

Travers, A. (1992b) 'Strangers to themselves: how interactants are other than they are', *British Journal of Sociology*, vol 43, no 4, pp 601-37.

Travers, A. (1994a) 'Destigmatizing the stigma of self in Garfinkel's and Goffman's accounts of normal appearances', *Philosophy of the Social Sciences*, vol 24, no 1, pp 5-40.

Travers. A. (1994b) 'The unrequited self', *History of the Human Sciences*, vol 7, no 2, pp 121-40.

Travers, A. (1995) 'The identification of self', *Journal for the Theory of Social Behaviour*, vol 25, no 3, pp 303-40.

Warde, A. (1994) 'Consumption, identity-formation and uncertainty', *Sociology*, vol 28, no 4, pp 877-98.

Watson, R. (1989) 'Le travail de l'incongruité', in I. Joseph (ed) *Le parler frais d'Erving Goffman*, Paris: Les Editions de Minuit.

Weber, M. (1947) *The theory of social and economic organization*, New York, NY: Oxford University Press.

White, H. (1978) *Tropics of discourse*, Baltimore, MD: Johns Hopkins University Press.

NINE

Word from the street: the perils and pains of researching begging

Margaret Melrose

In a world where people have problems,
In a world where decisions are a way of life....
Other people's problems, they overwhelm my mind.
Compassion is a virtue, but I don't have the time.
(David Byrne, *'No compassion'*, from *Talking Heads '77*,
Index Music, Inc/Bleu Disque Music Inc (ASCAP) 1977)

In recent years attention has increasingly focused on the "actual 'doing' of research" (Song and Parker, 1995, p 241); on investigating the research process itself and analysing the researcher's 'location of self' (Hertz, 1996), that is, on issues of 'reflexivity' (Hertz, 1996; Arendell, 1997) and on the 'politics and ethics' of the research that we do (see Oakley, 1981; Finch, 1984; Punch, 1986; Homan, 1991; Sieber, 1993; Song and Parker, 1995; Dean, 1996). Given these developments, it is remarkable that the role of emotions in shaping research processes and products has remained relatively neglected (Kleinman and Copp, 1993), and that analyses of the gender dynamics in the research process have been mainly limited to women doing research on other women (for example, Oakley, 1981; Finch, 1984; Riessman, 1991; Cannon et al, 1991; Reinharz, 1992; Edwards, 1993; but see Scott, 1984; Bolak, 1996; Arendell, 1997 for exceptions).

By reflecting with honesty on the "pains and perils" (Punch, 1986) of research upon which I have recently been engaged I hope to contribute to our understanding of the emotional impact that research may have on the researcher and to explore the role of gender dynamics in facilitating or inhibiting the research process.

The research and the researcher

The project upon which I am now reflecting is that reported in Chapter Six of this volume. It involved face-to-face semi-structured interviews with people currently engaged in begging. Begging is an activity which is illegal in England and by choosing to investigate it we had entered into "difficult fields of morality, illegality and deviant behaviour" which render both researcher and participants vulnerable (Eardley, 1996, p 72). The interviews were conducted during July and November 1997, all in urban settings. Each interview typically lasted 30 to 40 minutes, although a few were longer. From a total of 25 people (23 men and 2 women) who I approached, a sample of 19 men was achieved. While heterogeneity was achieved to some extent in terms of the ethnic mix of the sample, it certainly was not achieved in relation to the sexual mix of participants (see Cannon et al, 1991). This is a point to which I shall return. Regardless, however, of the constitution of the sample achieved, we are unable to say whether, or to what extent, it might reflect the actual population of those engaged in begging because we were faced with the difficulty of sampling an unknown population (see Lee, 1993).

Participants were given assurances of confidentiality and were allowed to remain anonymous if they wished. In the event, such assurances seemed irrelevant to many participants (see Finch, 1984; Arendell, 1997). This may have been because, although what they do may be illegal, it is also very public and visible. Altogether eight interviews were conducted at the begging sites; six were conducted inside cafés or bars and five were conducted outside at pavement cafés or bars. Gathering the data was therefore a very exposed and public activity as opposed to the (private) intimacy which is often associated with interview situations (see Oakley, 1981). Begging was narrowly defined so that only those engaged in unlawfully soliciting 'a voluntary unilateral gift in a public place' were considered for interviewing. In practice this meant consciously ignoring those overtly engaged in other informal economic activities such as busking or selling *The Big Issue*.

The project had originally been conceived and its form had been initially developed as a research degree project at the University of Luton where I am currently employed (on fixed-term contracts) as a researcher. In the event, the postgraduate student who began the project could not complete it. At the time the renewal of my contract of employment at the university was under negotiation and I was invited to undertake some interviewing and to help generate some findings on the basis of the work which had already been undertaken. As a consequence of my precarious position as an employee at the university, on the one hand, and of my personal biography and identity – that is, the 'baggage' (Arendell, 1997, p 343) which I, as a white, working-class woman bring to my work, on the other, I was keen to 'salvage' something from a worthwhile project, and I agreed to attempt some interviewing.

Along with the student who had begun the project and my colleague who was supervising it I thought that the contemporary phenomenon of begging warranted research attention because it is an activity which has been often condemned but little understood (see Dean and Barrett, 1996; *The Guardian*, 28 May 1994, *Times*, 6 September 1995). I shared in the general hypothesis that the apparent increase in begging during the last decade might result from an increasingly grudging benefits system combined with the hypercasualisation of the labour market and diminishing opportunities for unskilled manual workers (see Chapters Four and Five in this volume). Additionally, I was conscious that the increased availability and use of heroin (particularly among unemployed young people) throughout the 1980s (Dorn and South, 1987, p 2) might play a part. The possibility that, for subordinate groups, begging might constitute one of many strategies of resistance was also worthy of investigation (see Jordan, 1996, pp 75-6). However, I was interested, primarily, in 'learning from' (Reinharz, 1992) those engaged in begging the meanings they attached to the activity, and to let them explain, in their own words, their reasons for employing this particular informal economic activity. I also wanted a new contract! My motivations in agreeing to work on the project stemmed therefore from intellectual curiosity, personal commitment *and* self-interest!

I approached the research, first, with an "emotional and intellectual commitment" (Finch, 1984, p 86) to make the research serve the interests of "dominated, exploited and oppressed groups" (Kirby and McKenna, 1989, cited in Robson, 1995, p 293; see also Becker, 1967; Gouldner, 1968; Oakley, 1981; Stanley and Wise, 1993; Finch, 1984; Beresford, 1996), an approach to research which has a long and increasingly respectable history; and second, with a commitment to reducing the distance between "researcher and researched" (Oakley, 1981). My approach was therefore broadly feminist and interpretive (see Arendell, 1997).

Mann (1996, p 64) has asked "What is it that motivates people to spend their time with the poor, criminals, prostitutes, welfare 'scroungers' and other 'unrespectable' groups?" While he is right to question the motivations of people engaged in this kind of work and correct to insist that we be clear about our own reasons for doing it, in posing the question thus, Mann reasserts the power relations obscured by such distinctions between 'self' (researcher) and 'other' (researched) (see Sarup, 1994). He contributes to an objectifying dynamic which strictly demarcates the lives of those to be studied from those doing the studying, which keeps the latter "hidden from analytical scrutiny" (Stanley and Wise, 1993, p 3). This serves to confirm the traditional hierarchy of the researched/researcher relationship (see Oakley, 1981; Finch, 1984; Stanley and Wise, 1993) which, as I have explained, I felt personally committed to breaking down.

Perils of the field: gaining access

Gaining access to people engaged in begging was never going to be an easy task: as with most 'sensitive' topics this project taxed our 'methodological ingenuity' (Lee, 1993, p 2). The idea of accessing people through statutory or voluntary agencies involved in providing food and shelter for homeless people had been considered but rejected on the grounds that this would 'skew' the sample in favour of those who were *homeless* and begging *and* making use of such services. We were concerned that such an approach to constructing the sample would lead to the issues of begging and homelessness being conflated as they are in much of the existing literature. In the event, just under half (nine) of those interviewed were actually 'homeless' to the extent of being literally 'roofless'.

We agreed instead to employ a system of 'outcropping'. This involves the researcher locating a site where members of the group under investigation are likely to be and 'studying' them there (Lee, 1993). For this pilot project, this meant walking around, or 'hanging around' at likely begging sites (for example, railway and tube stations and busy shopping/tourist areas) and, when people were seen to be begging, approaching them to ask for an interview. We decided that it was preferable for me to work alone because it was felt this would be less intimidating than approaching potential participants in pairs and would, therefore, make it more likely that they would agree to be interviewed. We also felt it to be ethically questionable for the researcher to work with a covert 'back-up', but not reveal to participants that she was doing so.

Through the chosen method of sample construction I was exposed to both 'presentational' and 'anonymous' dangers (Lee, 1993, p 10). On the one hand, my *presence* might provoke hostility or aggression and the danger that I would meet with a belligerent, or even hostile response was ever present (and always anticipated) (Mann, 1996). As Bourgois (1996, p 14) has pointed out, "extreme settings full of human tragedy are psychologically overwhelming and can be physically dangerous". On the other hand, by walking the streets, 'hanging around' in railway stations, and conducting interviews on the pavement at begging pitches (for example, sharing blankets in Tottenham Court Road and Princes Street with the interviewees), I was also exposed to *anonymous* or "otherwise avoidable dangers" (Lee, 1993, p 10). By sitting with the participants at their 'pitch' I was drawing attention to myself and the participants. This might have resulted (but fortunately did not) in the arrest of the participant or myself; however, I felt that this risk was unavoidable if that was where the participant wanted to be interviewed and if I was to maintain their confidence (see Eardley, 1996). Further, it was not possible to let colleagues know where I might be at any particular moment: the best that could be achieved would be to say that I would be in such and such an area during the morning and such and such an area in the afternoon. In terms of personal safety this was obviously not ideal but our chosen method of sample construction required compromise at the level of personal safety if we were not to compromise our ethics or the data obtained. I initially insisted that I was quite happy and confident about this compromise.

The dangers researchers face, and the compromises they will require, are of course more or less salient depending on the sex of the researcher. This research required that I (a female researcher) approach people (predominately men) in the street to ask them to be interviewed and/or to invite them for a cup of tea or drink while the interview was conducted. The "common worry for women about being alone with strange men" (Scott, 1984, p 173) was compounded by necessity of having to approach 'strange men' in the street. This worry therefore became "part of the job" (Scott, 1984, p 173). It was reduced the more public and visible the interview situation, which is perhaps paradoxical because, as I have indicated, visibility carried with it other risks.

Approaching these men was potentially threatening to both the researcher and researched because in some ways such actions transgress gender norms without necessarily challenging the conventional gender hierarchy (see Arendell, 1997). Given that hierarchy, it would be quite possible for such actions to be misconstrued by participants. Indeed, after completing one interview (which I conducted in a waiting room on a railway station), and after I had turned off the tape recorder, the participant said he had "better get back to the office" (meaning his begging pitch which was just outside the railway station). When I wished him good luck for the rest of the day he asked me if it wouldn't "just be easier" if he came home with me! Given that we were virtual strangers and that he knew nothing about my living arrangements or personal life, I was momentarily shocked by his suggestion and unsure how to respond. Because he had just 'given' me an interview, rather than challenge his comment I dismissed it in a 'good natured' way (see Arendell, 1997, p 358). Unfortunately, as Gurney has pointed out, "there are no ready prescriptions for female researchers' coping with such situations" (Gurney, 1985, cited in Arendell, 1997, p 362) but such incidents do raise questions about what we should tolerate and where we should draw the line in our quest for data.

The panoptic effect of surveillance sytems often made me terribly self-conscious when I was 'hanging around' in main railway stations, and especially those which are notorious for prostitution and drug-dealing. In these situations my gender became uncomfortably the most salient aspect of my subjectivity. Not only did I often feel physically vulnerable but I realised that, if I were 'caught on camera' just hanging around (pretending to wait for a train), I might well be taken to be 'soliciting' or 'loitering' by security personnel. On the other hand, if they were to see me approaching someone begging they might think I was an acquaintance and would be liable to evict me from the station. In the event, none of the interviewees were encountered in stations, probably because these are sanitised and 'socially secured' spaces from which 'marginal street people' can be excluded (Wardhaugh, 1996, p 703).

The chosen method of sample construction, as well as presenting dangers, was extremely time-consuming and very often frustrating. As I trudged the streets of various cities, often unsuccessful in my search for potential interviewees, I was continually engaged in an internal dialogue which questioned my own motivations (especially when it was cold and raining), the sagacity of the method of sample construction, and the inhumanity of a social system which renders some people destitute while bestowing such riches on others (see, for example, Dean with Melrose, 1999). My frustrations (at not finding participants) often gave rise to inappropriate anger – sometimes with myself for having agreed to do the research; sometimes with the economic forces and government policies which appeared to make begging necessary for some (and with my own powerlessness in the face of such complexity); sometimes with *The Big Issue* sellers who were found in abundance in all three cities but whom we had agreed I should not interview. I began to feel that if it were not for the intervention of *The Big Issue*, or if we had defined 'begging' less narrowly, then my job of finding potential participants would have been much easier. Sometimes I felt angry with beggars themselves (simply for being there and necessitating the research) and, when I did not find interviewees, with beggars for *not* being in the places I expected they would be. This latter feeling gave rise to a complete contradiction between my professional and political interests: in terms of my professional interests as a researcher I wanted to find people to interview but in terms of my personal/political values I would not want to find people begging on the streets. When I did not find participants, however, I felt that I was not doing my job well enough, that I had chosen the 'wrong' places or that I was 'failing' in some way, which engendered yet more frustration.

On one particularly hot day in July I walked around Central London from 9.30 am until 5.30 pm taking in the Strand (about three times), Hungerford Bridge, the Royal Festival Hall, Charing Cross and Embankment stations, Shaftesbury Avenue, and other places, but saw no one begging, although there were buskers and people selling *The Big Issue*. On the other hand, when I did achieve interviews, as a result of the harrowing accounts they often elicited, I sometimes wished I was not a researcher. I was quickly disabused of the idea that 'fieldwork is fun' (Kleinman and Copp, 1993). This mixture of feelings provided a potent recipe within which ambivalence towards both the project and the participants could develop.

Pains of the field: establishing rapport

The ambivalence generated by the chosen method of sample construction was deepened by the accounts participants gave me during the interviews. I had started the project with the expectation (born of past experience) that in the field I would be able to establish rapport with participants and that I would be able to empathise with them; that I would be able to see the world from their point of view (see Mead, 1934; Oakley, 1981). In this instance, however, I was not prepared for just how traumatic some of the participants' narratives might be. Reinharz (1992, p 36) has suggested that the shock of discovering 'more pain' in interviewees' lives than the researcher had expected eventually forces her "to confront her own vulnerability" and is at the root of stressful reactions to interviews. After the first two interviews in London (which were conducted in one day) and in which I was 'pulled into' the interviewees' problems (Edwards, 1993), I began seriously to question, not only my capacity to empathise, but also my desire to do so. The sheer complexity and multidimensional nature of the 'problems' participants experienced (homelessness, addiction, unemployment, poverty) seemed to me overwhelming and made me despair. I realised that I did not want to see the world from where these participants saw it; it was just too awful. My notes from my first day of fieldwork in Edinburgh (where I achieved the 15th and 16th interviews) read, 'Both the interviewees today were traumatised – and I don't have the skills to cope!!! I am traumatised!!' My emotional discomfort confronted me with my own vulnerability as a person and as a professional researcher.

My identification and emotional involvement with participants did indeed 'spill over' (Kleinman and Copp, 1993, p 8) into the rest of my life. On returning home after the first two interviews I felt physically sick and rather depressed and did not know what to 'do' with the feelings or quite how to manage them. Although I was not living with those I was studying it certainly felt for a time as though they were "living inside my head" (Kleinman and Copp, 1993, p 8). I also felt that I did not want them to be there, but neither could I 'get rid' of them. Their narratives haunted me (cf Thompson, 1990, cited in Reinharz, 1992, p 35). I began to feel (inappropriately) angry with participants for having such distressing tales to tell and that I didn't want to know how messed up and awful they felt or how bad their lives were. I began to tell myself I didn't care and (humming the David Byrne song which provides the epigraph to this chapter to myself as I walked around) I began to worry that my compassion might actually have evaporated.

Acknowledging these feelings forced me to face one of my biggest fears – that I was not so much empathetically 'incompetent' (Kleinman and Copp, 1993, p 28) as empathetically bankrupt and thus incompetent as a researcher. I was forced to do a lot of 'emotion work' (Kleinman and Copp, 1993, p 28) in an attempt to transform my negative feelings towards participants, the project and myself and to accept that rather than generating positive feelings, "the day to day work of research in any setting involves feelings of like and dislike, boredom and annoyance, fear and shame" (Warren, 1988, p 46).

My emotional response to the first two interviews in particular made me feel that, for the sake of my own sanity and emotional health, I needed to distance myself from the participants; that my expectations of 'rapport' and 'identification' were placing (perhaps impossible) demands on me and producing negative feelings (Kleinman and Copp, 1993, p 34). I realised that if I continued to feel as I did I would be unable to carry on with the work. My emotional discomfort made me confront the possibility that, despite its desirability, identification is not always possible, and indeed, in circumstances such as these, it might not even be desirable. I had to confront the possibility that despite theoretical objections (particularly from feminist researchers) to the notion of 'detachment' (for example, Oakley, 1981; Finch, 1984; Reinharz, 1992), it might actually be necessary to foster a certain level of detachment in order to cope emotionally in situations such as these.

This too led to feelings of discomfort. It went against the grain of my personal and political commitment and seemed unsuited to the epistemological aims with which I had begun the project. It seemed, however, the only means by which I could continue with the work and I therefore attempted to cultivate a distance between myself and the participants. I could engage, but not identify, with them: I attempted (probably unsuccessfully) to remain ethically committed but emotionally uninvolved; to 'sympathise' rather than 'empathise' (Mead, 1934) with their problems. In short, I became quite 'numb'. This may have protected me from experiencing feelings of despair, hopelessness and powerlessness, among others, but as Kleinman and Copp (1993, p 33) point out, "numbness itself is an *overpowering* feeling state" and "numbness and self-estrangement spill over into other realms of our lives".

I felt tremendously guilty about my reluctance to identify with participants, about my own "comparative riches" (Kleinman and Copp, 1993, p 29) and about the fact that I was listening to what for me were distressing narratives and then just walking away, unable to offer anything in return which might be of practical help. The fact that I had a home, employment, family became the 'unavoidably salient aspects' of my subjectivity in the context of the interview situation (Kleinman and Copp, 1993, p 10). I was forced to confront the enormous gulf between my own life and the lives of the participants and to recognise that in relation to them, my location in a world from which they had been virtually excluded was relatively powerful. I began to wonder if there was something almost parasitic about what I was doing. As a result, about half way through the project we decided to pay participants £5 for an interview and although this went some way towards alleviating my guilt it did not entirely relieve me of it.

Researchers have been troubled by the idea of paying people to participate in research (Homan, 1991). It has been argued that financial inducement might represent a form of 'coercion' (especially among some of the most vulnerable people in society) or that it may in fact distort the data. However, given the context of this particular research I think it was necessary to 'give something back' (Sieber, 1993); to alleviate my guilt by allowing me to feel that I was giving some practical assistance, to demonstrate my appreciation for their participation and to compensate them in a small way for giving me their time because, whether I sat at the site with them or took them away from the site for a cup of tea, I would inevitably affect their 'earnings'. In this instance, therefore, payment did not constitute an "improper influence" (Homan, 1991, p 71). It was usually only after I had asked people if they would be willing to be interviewed, and they had agreed, that I told them I would pay them. Their motivation for participating did not, in most instances, appear to be economic; the participants seemed to be primarily concerned with furthering our understandings of their situations and circumstances in the hope that 'some good' might come of it (Melrose, 1996); that their personal circumstances might be improved or that other young people might be forewarned. One participant (who was not paid) told me, "I mean listening to this, listening to what I've been going through and what some others have gone through, it'll put youngsters off really, sort of running away and sort of going on the streets". Indeed there is little, if any, discernible difference between the data produced in those interviews in which interviewees were paid and those in which they were not.

Gender dynamics in the field

My observations suggest that begging itself is a highly gendered activity. Bourgois (1996, p 3) has argued that "male income generating activities in the underground economy are more publicly visible" than those employed by women, and the absence of women begging would certainly seem to confirm this. As I have indicated, out of the 25 people observed, just two were women. This may be because women turn to other income-generating strategies, such as prostitution, or because their destitution is 'hidden', but given that as a group young women (under 25 years of age) are more vulnerable to homelessness than young men, and especially if they become pregnant are often reduced to destitution by "aggressive housing and social security rules" (Douglas and Gilroy, 1994, p 149), the relative absence of women engaged in this activity warrants some further investigation.

To all intents and purposes I, a woman, was entering a 'male' terrain (the public space of the street) and attempting to gain access to what appeared to be predominantly a 'male' world (constituted by those who beg). Accessing participants was much more difficult than entering the terrain, although the latter was not without its dangers. Access was difficult not because people were not willing to be interviewed but because sometimes it was just so difficult to find anyone to ask. Suspecting that the people I sought might be mistrustful of those appearing to be in 'authority' (Reinharz, 1992), I would make sure to wear jeans and casual wear, so as not to look too formal, but, paradoxically, when hanging around in such places as railway stations, I felt the 'dressed-down' look might make me look suspicious to station personnel.

Gaining access presented me with combining the challenges faced by many female researchers, that of being non-threatening, "with that of being a credible competent professional" (Gurney, 1985, cited in Arendell, 1997, p 351). I wanted participants to feel they could trust me but, paradoxically, because of their mannerisms and/or appearance, I was often initially unsure about trusting them. A few of the participants were very animated during our conversations and displayed signs of aggression, anger or agitation. However, this was not directed specifically at me; more at some anonymous "generalized other" (Mead, 1934). A few of the participants had numerous facial piercings and/or tattoos (some on their faces). One participant had his head shaved and a pattern of noughts and crosses shaved into it as well as numerous tattoos, facial scars and piercings. Many wore army fatigues. Often they did not look like the most accessible people and I often felt aware of my own physical vulnerability as I approached them. However, in order to gain access and establish rapport I had to overcome any misgivings I might have had. As Punch (1986, p 10) has pointed out (and in this instance understated!) in work of this kind "the researcher has to learn to sustain relationships with people with whom one normally might not easily mix". I rationalised my anxieties as the 'effects' of negative stereotypes through which images of those who beg are mediated in the wider culture and was able to overcome them in this way. Usually, the process of the interview confirmed that my anxieties were unfounded.

Although their appearance signalled aggression this often, in fact, appeared to be just a surface impression; a kind of exterior they displayed to the world, almost like a coat they wore to cope with the harshness of their lives. Very often in the course of the interviews participants exposed themselves as chronically vulnerable (emotionally and physically). For example, one person admitted to being scared and another to being lonely. I think they felt able to do so *because* they were talking to a woman (see Arendell, 1997). I was, as Arendell describes, "the token nurturing, caretaking woman" listening attentively and "doing the 'work women do' in conversations with men" (Arendell, 1997, p 356). Perhaps the men related to me "as a position in an imagined relation – as a feminized Other" (Pierce, 1995, cited in Arendell, 1997, p 348).

Female researchers may be confronted with the choice of "accepting sexism on the one hand and the acquisition of knowledge in the interests of furthering careers on the other" (Warren, 1988, p 36). It is a distasteful choice over which we have little control. Indeed, some of the men interviewed were quite patronising or chauvinistic. I have already recounted how one of the participants suggested he might come home with me. On another occasion the interviewee wanted me to let him pay for the coffees we had had, and on another, as I was walking with a participant to a café, he counselled that I should "be careful who you walk off with" because "some of these homeless guys are rapists and that". His comment immediately made me worry (needlessly) that he might be making a self-reference. Another man I approached (about 8.30 in the evening) said he would give me an interview and 'take' me 'for a drink' if I would come back to meet him in half an hour. I asked him if we could meet during daylight hours the next day and he patronisingly told me that there were "no serious beggars in Edinburgh during the day time". (I had actually interviewed two people earlier that day.) My instinct and common sense told me it would be foolish to meet him at the time he suggested and for the sake of my personal safety the interview was forsaken. I felt that this man was viewing me as a 'potential date' (Arendell, 1997, p 357) rather than as a professional with a job to do.

I also 'put up with' racist and homophobic comments without challenging them. One respondent (paradoxically an African-Caribbean) blamed his lack of opportunity to work on "too many immigrants" and said that he was considering joining the National Front; another assured me that he was "not like that" (meaning not gay) when he said that he occasionally slept with friends (meaning at their houses): he told me that he would not like me to "get the wrong idea". Accepting such views without challenging them must make us question the extent to which we collude with participants in reproducing negative stereotypes of other groups for the sake of gathering data (see Arendell, 1997) with which, paradoxically, we might hope to undermine negative stereotypes of the group we are studying. The views that were expressed and the sexist or patronising comments that I endured suggest that, when it is women interviewing men, the participants are not necessarily disempowered in relation to the researcher and that defining the situation as 'an interview' does not necessarily invert the established gender hierarchy (Arendell, 1997). In relation to the wider society, these were some of the most vulnerable and marginalised men, but some of them still felt themselves empowered (and asserted their power/superiority) in relation to the gender, racial and sexual hierarchy.

All participants agree to take part in research "for their own reasons" (Arendell, 1997, p 344) and often they want something from the researcher (such as understanding, attention or help) as much as she wants something from them (Lee and Renzetti, 1993). For the men perhaps participating in an interview was "status enhancing" (Bolak, 1996) and/or, possibly, they enjoyed the attention. The men perhaps accepted me as an 'incompetent' (Lofland, 1972 cited in Brewer, 1993, p 133; see also Scott, 1984). Although I might have represented a threatening 'official' world which they are disinclined to trust, I was non-threatening by virtue of the fact that I am a woman (see Warren, 1988; Reinharz, 1992). On other occasions I seemed to be treated as an 'honorary male' (Warren, 1988; see also Bolak, 1996; Arendell, 1997). I was allowed access to the inner world of their thoughts and feelings and "invited to share the scope of their anger and frustration *as men*" (Arendell, 1997, p 356). For example, some expressed anger about their status, their inability to get work or housing; and they told me of their frustrations at not being able to fulfil a traditional role as provider and breadwinner. In relation to men I was therefore able to access situations which male researchers might have found more difficult.

After I had interviewed 19 men we decided that I should try to correct the gender imbalance by looking only for women and ignoring any further men that were observed. On the first day of looking (in London), between 10 am and 4 pm I saw no women begging at all. On the second day I decided to vary the time at which I was looking and went out in the mid-afternoon, intending to take in the rush hour. I saw two women, both of whom, when approached for an interview, refused in a rather aggressive and hostile manner. To them I seemed to represent an 'official interrogator' (Finch, 1984) rather than a 'confidante' who shared "a structurally subordinate position" (Finch, 1984, p 76; see also Oakley, 1981). I was both hurt and shocked by the hostility the women expressed towards me: because of my personal biography and identity I did not recognise myself as a representative of the world they obviously saw me representing. It was clear that men and women positioned me very differently (see Song and Parker, 1995). This raises a question about why the women appeared to place me in one way and the men in another. It seems to suggest that, in this instance, it was our 'gender congruity'

(Riessman, 1991) which evoked such hostility. It was *because* I failed to recognise the *differences* of status and power which these women perceived that I was unable to establish rapport with them (see Lourde, 1984).

Many feminists argue that 'gender congruity' (Riessman, 1991) facilitates the establishment of rapport in the research situation (Oakley, 1981; Finch, 1984; Reinharz, 1992). This was not my experience in the begging research. With the women I approached, "woman to woman affinity was not something easily established on the basis of our shared sex alone" (Edwards, 1993, p 188). In this particular situation gender was 'not enough' (Riessman, 1991). While my gender appeared to facilitate access to men who were begging it seemed, on the contrary, to provide an obstacle in terms of gaining trust and establishing rapport with women. The ease with which access and rapport can be established rather seems to depend on the play of class, race, gender, age and sexual dynamics in the interaction (see Lourde, 1984; Riessman, 1991; Edwards, 1993; Song and Parker, 1995; Arendell, 1997). It depends on how participants 'place' the researcher in relation to these categories. When attempting to interview women who are (economically and/or socially) disempowered in relation to the researcher, and in relation to the society more generally, it seems highly unlikely that the interviewee would recognise that she and the interviewer share a "structurally subordinate position" (see Oakley, 1981; Finch, 1984).

It seems to me that the idea that gender alone can facilitate the establishment of good rapport with research participants is overly simplistic. Such arguments are based on a notion of '*fixed* identities' and do not allow for "the partial and simultaneous commonality and difference between the researcher and the interviewee" (Song and Parker, 1995, p 249; see also Arendell, 1997, p 356). As Song and Parker (1995, p 253) argue, much more attention needs to be paid to "how researchers themselves may be actively constructed and perceived by interviewees".

Conclusions

This chapter has raised a number of questions for which there are no ready or easy answers and, at the same time, provides some salutary warnings about future work involving people engaged in begging or other street-level activity.

I have pointed to the importance of the 'placing' of the researcher by interviewees and have suggested that this is crucial to shaping interactional dynamics in the research process. In particular I have suggested that class, gender, ethnicity, sexuality are factors which will determine such placings and that perceived 'congruity' (Riessman, 1991) or 'difference' (Lourde, 1984) work in complex ways in each interview situation to facilitate or inhibit interaction. I have also explored the ways in which these interactional dynamics may take their toll emotionally on the researcher, depending on the extent to which they might correspond or diverge from the interviewer's self-image.

There are a number of practical implications for future research of this nature. First, the importance of 'placing' – of the interviewee by the interviewer and the interviewer by interviewee – suggests that, in terms of sampling procedures, it is probably preferable for introductions to potential participants to be effected by a gatekeeper. This may mean liaising, for example, with voluntary agencies which have contact with people who beg or whose services are used by them. This would mean accepting the consequent limitations of the sample this might produce, although it ought to be possible to extend that sample using 'snowballing' techniques to make contact with other people who beg using the members of the original sample as gatekeepers. Through these methods both participants and researcher would have some reassurance about whom they were being introduced to/approached by. A strong case can also be made for ensuring that more than one interviewer should be available to a project of this nature in order that interviewers of different sexes and different class and ethnic backgrounds can have the opportunity to access different participants and different aspects of the data.

Second, the chapter demonstrates the importance of ensuring that researchers engaging in this sort of field work are well supported by colleagues; and that they are always afforded adequate opportunities for debriefing to ensure that they maintain a distinction between their own lives and those of their participants. I have shown that prescriptions regarding empathy between fieldworkers and interviewees may place an enormous strain on fieldworkers. This leads to the third of the practical conclusions which I would draw, namely that researchers working in fields such as this must be prepared to accept certain principled methodological compromises.

If in practice it is not possible to achieve the degree of empathy which researchers may seek with those who participate in their research (or if the emotional cost of achieving such empathy is intolerable), it may be necessary on occasions to accept the objectifying dynamic of the self/ other (Sarup, 1994) or researcher/researched relationship (Oakley, 1981; Finch, 1984). This need not, I submit, negate or undermine the researcher's ethical commitment to the group being studied or compromise the epistemological aims of the research. Similarly, I have raised questions about what we, as researchers, are willing to tolerate for the sake of gathering data: we need, for example, to be aware of when we might be colluding with racism, sexism and homophobia for the sake of maintaining or establishing rapport. Such collusion may lead the researcher to be angry with herself at a later stage and it is important when thinking through the compromises which fieldwork can inevitably entail that commitment to the needs or interests of the group being studied should not necessarily be allowed to outweigh other ethical commitments. It is an issue of particular significance when one is interviewing participants whose means of expression can be as extreme as their lives are extraordinary. When you are on the street, it is easy to be overwhelmed by the horrors in the lives of those who live there. The effect is to engulf the researcher in a kind of empathic paralysis which can numb the capacity for compassion. The word is – be warned!

References

Arendell, T. (1997) 'Reflections on the researcher–researched relationship: a woman interviewing men', *Qualitative Sociology*, vol 20, no 3, pp 341-68.

Becker, H. (1967) 'Whose side are we on?', *Social Problems*, vol 14, pp 239-47.

Beresford, P. (1996) 'Challenging the "them and us" of social policy research', in H. Dean (ed) *Ethics and social policy research*, Luton: University of Luton Press/Social Policy Association.

Bolak, H. (1996) 'Gender and self-other dynamics in studying one's own in the Middle East', *Qualitative Sociology*, vol 19, no 1, pp 107-30.

Bourgois, P. (1996) *In search of respect: Selling crack in El Barrio*, New York, NY: Cambridge University Press.

Brewer, J. (1993) 'Sensitivity as a problem of field research: a study of routine policing in Northern Ireland', in C. Renzetti and R. Lee (eds) *Researching sensitive topics*, London: Pluto Press.

Cannon, L., Higginbotham, E. and Leung, M. (1991) 'Race and class bias in qualitative research on women', in J. Lorber and S.A. Farrell (eds) *The social construction of gender*, Thousand Oaks, CA: Sage Publications.

Dean, H. (ed) (1996) *Ethics and social policy research*, Luton: University of Luton Press/Social Policy Association.

Dean, H. and Barrett, D. (1996) 'Unrespectable research and researching the unrespectable', in H. Dean (ed) *Ethics and social policy research*, Luton: University of Luton Press/Social Policy Association.

Dean, H. with Melrose, M. (1999) *Poverty, riches and social citizenship*, Basingstoke: Macmillan.

Dorn, N. and South, N. (1987) *A land fit for heroin? Drug policies, prevention and practice*, Basingstoke: Macmillan.

Douglas, A. and Gilroy, R. (1994) 'Young women and homelessness', in R. Gilroy and R. Woods (eds) *Housing women*, London: Routledge.

Eardley, T. (1996) 'On legality and morality', in H. Dean (ed) *Ethics and social policy research*, Luton: University of Luton Press/Social Policy Association.

Edwards, E. (1993) 'An education in interviewing', in C. Renzetti and R. Lee (eds) *Researching sensitive topics*, Thousand Oaks, CA: Sage Publications.

Finch, J. (1984) '"It's great to have someone to talk to": the ethics and politics of interviewing women', in C. Bell and H. Roberts (eds) *Social researching: Politics, problems, practice*, London: Routledge and Kegan Paul.

Gouldner, A. (1968) 'The sociologist as partisan', *American Sociologist*, vol 3, pp 103-16.

Hertz, R. (1996) 'Ethics, reflexivity and voice', in R. Hertz (ed) *Qualitative Sociology*, vol 19, no 1, 'Methods special issue', pp 3-10.

Homan, R. (1991) *The ethics of social research*, Harlow: Longman.

Jordan, B. (1996) *A theory of poverty and social exclusion*, Cambridge: Polity Press.

Kirby, S. and McKenna, K. (1989) *Experience, research and social change: Methods from the margins*, Toronto, Canada: Garamond.

Kleinman, S. and Copp, M. (1993) *Emotions and fieldwork*, Thousand Oaks, CA: Sage Publications.

Lee, R. (1993) *Doing research on sensitive topics*, London: Sage Publications.

Lee, R. and Renzetti, C. (1993) 'The problems of researching sensitive topics: an introduction and overview', in C. Renzetti and R. Lee (eds) *Researching sensitive topics*, London: Pluto Press.

Lourde, A. (1984) 'Age, race, class, sex: women redefining difference', in A. Lourde, *Sisters outsiders*, New York, NY: Crossing Press.

Mann, K. (1996) '"Who are you looking at?" Voyeurs, narks and do-gooders', in H. Dean (ed) *Ethics and social policy research*, Luton: University of Luton Press/Social Policy Association.

Mead, G.H. (1934) *Mind, self and society*, Chicago, IL: University of Chicago Press.

Melrose, M. (1996) 'Enticing subjects and disembodied objects' in H. Dean (ed) *Ethics and social policy research*, Luton: University of Luton Press/Social Policy Association.

Oakley, A. (1981) 'Interviewing women: a contradiction in terms', in H. Roberts (ed) *Doing feminist research*, London: Routledge and Kegan Paul.

Punch, M. (1986) *The ethics and politics of fieldwork*, Thousand Oaks, CA: Sage Publications.

Reinharz, S. (1992) *Feminist methods in social research*, New York, NY: Oxford University Press.

Reissman, C.K. (1991) 'When gender is not enough: women interviewing women', in J. Lorber and S.A. Farrell (eds) *The social construction of gender*, Thousand Oaks, CA: Sage Publications.

Robson, C. (1995) *Real world research*, Oxford: Blackwell.

Sarup, M. (1994) 'Home and identity', in G. Robertson, M. Marsh, L. Tickner, J. Bird, B. Curtis and T. Putnam (eds) *Travellers' tales: Narratives of home and displacement*, London: Routledge.

Scott, S. (1984) 'The personable and the powerful: gender and status in sociological research', in C. Bell and H. Roberts (eds) *Social researching: Politics, problems, practice*, London: Routledge and Kegan Paul.

Sieber, J. (1993) 'The ethics and politics of sensitive research', in C. Renzetti and R. Lee (eds) *Researching sensitive topics*, Thousand Oaks, CA: Sage Publications.

Song, M. and Parker, D. (1995) 'Commonality, difference and the dynamics of disclosure in in-depth interviewing', *Sociology*, vol 29, no 2, pp 241-56.

Stanley, L. and Wise, S. (1993) *Breaking out again*, London: Routledge and Kegan Paul.

Wardhaugh, J. (1996) '"Homeless in Chinatown": deviance and social control in cardboard city', *Sociology*, vol 30, no 4, pp 701-16.

Warren, C.A.B. (1988) *Gender issues in field research*, Thousand Oaks, CA: Sage Publications.

TEN

Public attitudes to begging: theory in search of data

Michael Adler

This chapter is based on the thinking which informed a proposal to study the public's experience of and public attitudes to begging. Since a stand-alone survey would have been very expensive, it seemed more appropriate to seek funding which would make it possible to include a set of questions on begging as part of an ongoing survey and, because of its primary focus on public attitudes, the most obvious candidate was the annual British Social Attitudes (BSA) Survey. This survey comprises a common core, which is repeated every year, and a set of modules dealing with specific topics, either on a one-off or an intermittent basis (for a full account see Bryson et al, 1998). For a much smaller cost than a stand-alone survey, funding a module containing questions about begging would enable the data that are generated to be analysed in terms of the attitudinal, demographic and socioeconomic data that are collected for other purposes. An application to the Economic and Social Research Council was successful and, as a result, a set of questions on begging will be included in the 1999 British Social Attitudes Survey. However, since, at the time of writing, the survey has not yet been administered and the questions on begging have not even been formulated, this chapter is necessarily speculative. As such, it can identify some possible topics for investigation but cannot report on any findings.

Previous research on beggars and begging

Despite its prevalence, and its increasing salience as a public issue, there has, until very recently, been little systematic research on begging (defined as the soliciting of a unilateral gift, normally of money, in a public place) in the UK. Although there have been a number of academic studies which have examined begging historically and comparatively (see, for instance, Beier, 1985; Huggins, 1985; Ratnapala, 1985; Ribton-Turner,

1987), published studies of begging in post-war Britain (for example, O'Connor, 1963; Sandford, 1971) are largely journalistic or anecdotal. Modern sociologists do not seem to share the fascination of the 'Chicago School' with 'hobos' (Anderson, 1923) or other 'down and outs' (Wallace, 1965) or of symbolic interactionists with different forms of deviance (see Becker, 1963; Cohen, 1974; but see Chapter Eight in this volume). Consequently, the frequently-expressed concerns of politicians and journalists have contributed to a sense of 'moral panic' and have not been informed by an understanding of the phenomenon derived from empirical research on begging itself or on public attitudes to it.

One possible starting point would have involved carrying out a census of those engaged in begging. However, not least because there is no appropriate sampling frame, the methodological problems entailed by a census would have been formidable. As is evident from the chapters in Part II in this volume, ethnographic studies and in-depth interviews with beggars can be a very fertile source of ideas. However, other methodological approaches can also provide valuable insights.

As Dean (1998) has recently demonstrated, discursive interviews with a structured sample of the public can be used to explore prevailing beliefs and popular discourses in relation to a range of issues, such as poverty, citizenship and the welfare state, all of which are germane to the phenomenon of begging, and thus provide a different set of insights into it. However, although the knowledge derived from such studies can certainly contribute to our understanding, it does not necessarily provide a sufficient basis for generalising to the population as a whole. Nor does it permit a statistically reliable exploration of the social correlates of the beliefs and attitudes in question. On the other hand, a large-scale survey of public attitudes may not only complement such insights into the ways in which people respond to and think about begging and related issues, but also provides a means of analysing these responses and attitudes in terms of a range of antecedent factors.

Theoretical concerns

There is no single, over-arching body of theory which informs our proposal; rather there is a set of interrelated theoretical concerns which are relevant to it. These are set out below.

Begging and its relationship to other forms of economic activity

Those who think that begging is different in kind from other forms of economic activity usually point to the fact that begging involves 'getting something for nothing', while other forms of economic activity all involve getting something in return. On the other hand, those who think the difference is merely one of degree point to the fact that some other forms of street-level economic activity (for example, busking and selling *The Big Issue*) are not really that different from begging. Nevertheless, 'getting something for nothing' is, arguably, what makes begging so problematic. We live in a market economy and market values, which include the principle of exchange (normally of goods and services for money), are all pervasive: so much so that we feel uncomfortable with transactions, like begging, that do not reflect this principle. However, George Orwell famously challenged the distinction between begging and other remunerated activities, arguing that:

> ... [t]here is no essential difference between a beggar's livelihood and that of numberless respectable people. Beggars do not work, it is said; but then what is work? A navvy works by swinging a pick. An accountant works by adding up figures. A beggar works by standing out of doors in all weathers and getting varicose veins, bronchitis etc. It is a trade like any other; quite useless of course – but then many reputable trades are quite useless. (Orwell, 1932, p 154)

By examining how the public responds to begging and other remunerated occupations, the survey will provide an opportunity to assess the significance of market values by ascertaining whether begging is regarded as different in kind, as merely different in degree or as being no different at all from other types of economic activity. In the first case, we would expect their reactions to begging to be different to their reactions to all other remunerated occupations including busking and selling *The Big Issue;* in the second case, that their reactions to begging would be similar to their reactions to busking and selling *The Big Issue* but different from their reactions to other remunerated occupations; in the third case, that they would be much the same as their reactions to other remunerated occupations.

Norms of reciprocity and beneficence

In a seminal article, Gouldner identified a universal *norm of reciprocity*. According to this norm, "people should help those who have helped them and, therefore, those whom you have helped have an obligation to help you"(1960, p 143). However, in a subsequent paper, Gouldner made the important observation that, if people were guided solely by the norm of reciprocity, many who need help might never receive it, and he identified a complementary *norm of beneficence* (or charity). This norm requires people "to give to others much help as they need ... without thought of what they have done or we can do for them and solely in terms of a need imputed to the recipient" (1973, p 266). In short, it calls on people 'to give something for nothing'.

Giving alms and helping the poor are encouraged by many religions that regard charity as one of the highest virtues. However, the norm of beneficence is almost certainly a weaker norm than the norm of reciprocity and plays second fiddle to it. This is because, as explained above, it conflicts with the ideology of the market, which is hostile to the view that people should get something for nothing. Indeed, some people have argued that market values are themselves a special case of the norm of reciprocity. According to this view, people try to keep their transactions with others on an even keel. A does something for B, B does something for A – not necessarily exactly the same thing but something roughly equivalent in value. This kind of transactional equivalence prevents one party from being too dominant and the other from being too dependent.

Perhaps begging is problematic because dominance and dependency make people feel uncomfortable (see Chapters Eight and Eleven in this volume). Nevertheless, if the norm of beneficence did not exist, no one would give to beggars and, if that were the case, beggars would almost certainly stop begging. According to Gouldner, the duty of beneficence is particularly incumbent on the 'high and mighty' (that is, the rich and powerful, who not only have more to give and can give at less personal cost to themselves but can also hope to gain some public *kudos* for their generosity).

It is, of course, important to note that post-modern critics have cast doubt on the continued existence of universal concepts such as social norms, arguing that a multiplicity of particular differences, such as those associated with class, gender, race, age, employment have effectively undermined them (for example, Hillyard and Watson, 1996). However, these claims have not been empirically tested and one very important function of the survey will be to test the extent of popular support for each of the two norms in question and thus the validity of the post-modern critique.

If giving to beggars itself reflects the norm of reciprocity, then one might expect that those who are relatively poor would give more often and more generously, on the grounds that they are more likely than others either to have been, at some point in the past, or to find themselves, at some point in the future, in the beggar's position. If, on the other hand, it reflects the norm of beneficence, then one might expect those who are better off to give more generously, for the reasons set out above. However, it is perhaps worth noting that, although gaining *kudos* may well apply to other forms of charitable giving (for example, to supporting 'good causes' in ways that attract favourable publicity among those whose opinions are thought to matter), it is less clear that this applies to giving to beggars.

The aims and achievements of the welfare state

Should the welfare state make begging redundant? If a welfare state is defined as a state which takes responsibility for the welfare of its citizens, the question must be answered in the affirmative and the recent growth of begging in this country is an indictment of successive governments (see Chapters One and Two in this volume). If, on the other hand, a welfare state is defined as a state which encourages citizens to take responsibility for their own welfare, the question may be answered in the negative and the recent growth of begging in this country is not so much an indictment of successive governments as of the beggars themselves. Thus, responses to begging may reflect attitudes to the welfare state.

A recent British Social Attitudes Survey indicates that there are considerable differences of opinion among the public (see Table 10.1).

Table 10.1: Attitudes towards the welfare system (%)

	Agree	Neither agree nor disagree	Disagree
The welfare state makes people nowadays less willing to look after themselves	44	24	30
If the welfare state were not so generous, people would learn to stand on their own two feet	33	24	42

Source: Bryson (1997, p 78)

There is clearly some support for the general view that the welfare state has made people 'less willing to look after themselves'. More than four people in 10 (44%) take this view, while three in 10 disagree. But, when it comes to the more specific view that benefits actually prevent people from 'standing on their own two feet', only a third agree with slightly more than four in 10 (42%) disagreeing. Attitudes have fluctuated somewhat over the previous decade and Bryson concludes that public opinion has become somewhat less favourable to welfare measures in recent years.

However, successive BSA surveys indicate that a majority of the public does not want either to abandon the existing welfare state as it is or to recast it into 'new welfare' (Taylor Gooby, 1995). Every year since 1983, respondents have been asked about their willingness to pay for extra provision on health, education and social benefits (for example, pensions and benefits for the unemployed). As Table 10.2 shows, when taxation and expenditure are explicitly linked in this way, the majority of respondents consistently opts for higher taxes and higher expenditure. Indeed, the majority has shifted over the years from support for the status quo to a desire for higher spending and a willingness to pay for it.

When asked about specific services, public willingness to finance increased expenditure varies markedly. Support for spending on universal services – like health, education and pensions – is strong, while support, for example, for spending on benefits for unemployed people is weak (Taylor Gooby, 1995).

The survey will provide an opportunity for determining whether public attitudes to begging are related to attitudes to the welfare state and to the willingness to pay more in taxes for better services, in particular, higher levels of benefit for the unemployed. Through the survey, it will also be possible to investigate whether public attitudes to begging are related to public perceptions of whether recipients of social security are 'victims' of social injustice or 'villains' who are themselves responsible for their plight.

Table 10.2: Trends in attitudes to taxes and public expenditure (%)

% supporting:	1983	1987	1991	1995
Increased taxes and more spending on health, education and social benefits	32	50	65	61
Keeping taxes and spending on these services the same as now	54	42	29	31
Reduced taxes and less spending on these services	9	3	3	3

Source: Brook et al (1996, p 187)

Table 10.3: Causes of need (%)

% who think that there are people in need because:	1986	1989	1994
they have been unlucky	11	11	16
of laziness or lack of willpower	19	19	15
of injustice in society	25	29	29
it is an inevitable part of modern life	37	34	32

Source: Taylor Gooby (1995, p 9)

In the 1994 BSA Survey, respondents were asked which of four possible reasons came closest to their view of why some people are in need. As Table 10.3 shows, the distribution of responses has changed relatively little since the mid-1980s.

Comparative data indicate that the British are less likely than other Europeans to attribute poverty to 'injustice in society' and somewhat more likely to attribute it to 'laziness or lack of willpower' (Golding, 1995). That notwithstanding, the survey will make it possible to investigate whether attitudes to begging are related to responses to this question.

The role of charities

Previous surveys have sought to ascertain whether resources for certain areas of expenditure (for example, housing for homeless people and food aid for poor countries) should come from government or from charities (Barnett and Saxon-Harrold, 1992). Respondents were presented with six areas of expenditure and invited to say whether the money needed should be raised from government, from charities or from both. As Table 10.4 indicates, those areas in which support for government funding is greatest concern the alleviation of human suffering or, indeed, saving lives in Britain. Other worthy activities in the UK (for example, protecting rare animals and providing holidays for disabled people), or similar activities elsewhere (for example, food aid for poor countries), are seen as being more appropriate for charities. From this, it can be inferred that most people would regard support for indigent and impoverished people as the responsibility of the government.

The effect of begging on established charities is, to date, unknown. For example, it is not known whether beggars who are (or claim to be) homeless have had a negative effect on contributions to Shelter, and, likewise, whether young and vulnerable beggars have a negative effect on

Table 10.4: The roles of government and charities (%)

Funding should be:	entirely/mainly from government	shared equally	entirely/mainly from charities
Kidney machines	93	5	1
Housing for the homeless	86	9	2
Lifeboats	65	21	12
Protecting rare animals	29	36	27
Holidays for disabled people	31	34	30
Food aid for poor countries	29	34	30

Source: Barnett and Saxon-Harrold (1992, p 199)

contributions to organisations like Dr Barnado's or the NSPCC/RSSPCC? If there is a fixed pool of resources for charitable purposes, that would be a problem, but this may well not be the case. Once again, the survey will make it possible to explore such issues.

Begging and social justice

According to Miller (1976), there are three conflicting principles of social justice which can be used to determine what is due to an individual:

* to each according to his/her *needs*;
* to each according to his/her *deserts*; and
* to each according to his/her *rights*.

Unfortunately the three principles conflict with each other. People who are seen to be in need may not be regarded as deserving, while those who are regarded as deserving may not be deemed to have any right to the item in question. In such circumstances, one can either *choose* between the competing principles or try to *combine* them in some way. Miller (1976) and Walzer (1983) favour the first approach, the former by arguing that one principle should be chosen 'across the board', the latter by suggesting that different principles are appropriate in different 'spheres'. Rawls (1972) is the most famous recent example of someone who advocates a procedure for combining different principles and, in so doing, adopts the second approach.

Deserts necessarily conflict with needs because the former are based on behaviour while the latter are based on circumstances. Those who beg on the streets are frequently thought of as 'undeserving', either because it is thought that they should be working (in some recognised form of employment) or claiming benefit, or that they are claiming benefit and not declaring their takings, or that they are dependent on alcohol or drugs. Their life-style may be seen as a challenge to conventional social norms and, for reasons such as these, they may be thought not to deserve support. On the other hand, their needs are frequently all too apparent and their willingness to demean themselves by begging is evidence for the veracity and urgency of their needs.

The principle of rights is more complex. Rights may be (negative) rights to forbearance, which impose little cost on the community, or (positive) rights to resources, whose realisation necessarily conflicts with other rights (for example, property rights – see Plant and Barry, 1990). It is clearly the latter that are relevant here. However, to the extent that beggars have rights to be supported by the community, these are based on the fact that they are in need or that they deserve support. Thus, in this instance, the principle of rights is actually redundant.

Whether or not people give to beggars may depend on which of the other two principles (deserts or needs) they give priority to, both in general and, in particular, in the sphere of financial support (Walzer, 1983; Miller, 1992). This is another issue which it should be possible to address through the survey.

Returning to the general issue of social justice, Titmuss (1971) made an important distinction between proportional (or equitable) justice and creative (or individualised) justice, arguing that the income maintenance system needed both and that the problem was to find the right balance between them. While the former should be based on socially recognised needs which, in order to guarantee equity, should be as precise and inflexible as possible, a degree of flexibility is also needed to guarantee individualised justice (that is, to ensure that decisions take account of the peculiar circumstances of the individual case). The discretionary powers retained in parts of the social security system were intended to secure this objective but they have been substantially reduced and there is little evidence that they actually achieve this aim (Adler, 1996, 1997).

Ignatieff points out that the welfare state has distanced those who give from those who receive. As he puts it,

My encounters with [the poor] are a parable of moral relations between strangers in the welfare state. They have needs and, because they live in a welfare state, these needs confer entitlements – rights – to the resources of people like me. Their needs establish

> a silent relationship between us.... They are dependent on the
> state not upon me, and we are both glad of it. We are responsible
> for each other but we are not responsible to each other. (Ignatieff,
> 1984, pp 9-10)

A vast phalanx of professionals is employed within social services to make difficult moral decisions on behalf of the public, both by ensuring that the requirements of proportional justice are met, and by exercising an appropriate measure of creative justice. Although their emphasis is more on creative justice than on proportional justice, a similar situation exists in large charitable organisations like Oxfam or Shelter. What is peculiar about begging, and arguably makes it so problematic, is that the public are confronted with the task of making such decisions themselves. Do those who give avoid the problem by giving indiscriminately (for example, by giving to everyone), or by adopting a rule of thumb (for example, by giving to the first so many beggars they encounter), or do they attempt to discriminate between those they give to and those they ignore? And are those who do not give 'risk averse', perhaps because they are afraid of being conned?

The survey will provide an opportunity of ascertaining whether Ignatieff is right in claiming that the public dislikes having to assess the claims of individuals and prefer such decisions to be taken on their behalf by the state (which they are required to support through taxation) and/ or by charitable organisations (which they are free to support by their contributions).

Begging and citizenship

In a recent article, Plant (1998) contrasted two different conceptions of citizenship. The first sees citizenship as a status that is not fundamentally altered by an individual's virtue (or lack of it). According to this view, all citizens should be able to claim their rights, which include positive rights to benefits and services (that is, to resources) as well as negative rights to non-interference (that is, to forbearance), even if their way of life is disapproved of and even if they are not discharging what others may regard as their proper contribution to society. The second conception of citizenship places much less emphasis on rights and focuses instead on responsibilities – on obligation, virtue and contribution. On this view, citizenship is not a kind of pre-existing status but, rather, something that is achieved by contributing to the well-being of society. Whereas the first conception played the dominant role until recently, Plant argues that one of the main aims of the current ('New' Labour) government's proposals for welfare reform is to promote the second conception of citizenship.

A change such as this would represent the substitution of a conception of citizenship imposed from above for one which, arguably, grew from below (Turner, 1990) and would have enormous implications for those who do not work (and thus, in the government's view, do not contribute to society) and for those whose way of life is not regarded as virtuous. Orwell's views notwithstanding, it is likely that beggars are widely regarded as members of both these categories.

As is pointed out in Chapter Two in this volume, beggars may be thought of as people who exclude themselves from citizenship or as people who are excluded from it, as people who have rejected the obligations of citizenship or as people who are responding to the fact that their expectations of citizenship have been betrayed, and it is hoped that the survey will be used to determine just how they are regarded by the public. The results should also throw some light on the extent of public support for the contrasting rights-based and obligation-based conceptions of citizenship outlined above.

Poverty and social exclusion

Until recently, poverty researchers focused on the disposable income (or expenditure) of an individual or household. Although Townsend, the most distinguished of these poverty researchers, defined poverty in terms of "resources that are so seriously below those commanded by the average individual that they are, in effect, excluded from ordinary living patterns, customs and activities" (Townsend, 1979, p 1), the term 'social exclusion' did not catch on until the 1990s when, in response to the hostility of some governments to the term 'poverty' (notably the British and the German governments), it was taken up and championed by the European Commission.

There are several differences between poverty and social exclusion (see, for example, Room, 1995; Walker and Walker, 1997). Whereas poverty refers to a lack of resources and is effectively a unidimensional concept, social exclusion refers to a wider set of deficiencies, which can include powerlessness, social isolation, chronic insecurity and anomie. Although poverty can lead to social exclusion and is clearly of enormous importance in determining an individual's life-chances, other factors (for example, poor health, educational disadvantage, poor employment opportunities, inadequate housing and racial discrimination) may also give rise to disadvantage. In addition, whereas poverty focuses on distributional issues, in particular the lack of resources at the disposal of individuals or households, social exclusion focuses primarily on relational issues, in other words inadequate social participation and detachment from the moral order. Thus, according to Room (1995), social exclusion can be analysed in terms of the extent to which an individual is bound into membership of the moral and political community.

As far as poverty is concerned, previous BSA surveys have sought to measure how poverty is understood by the public. In 1994, around one third of the respondents thought of poverty in relative terms, another one third adopted an absolute conception of poverty and another one third adopted an extremely restrictive conception.

Notwithstanding the large proportions holding absolute and restrictive conceptions of poverty, nearly seven in 10 (69%) believed that there was quite a lot of real poverty in Britain at the time and that the extent of poverty had increased over the last 10 years (68%). Moreover, more than half the respondents thought that poverty would increase over the next 10 years (Taylor Gooby, 1995).

As reported above, BSA surveys have also sought to measure public attitudes to recipients of social security and the extent to which the public blames 'the victim' or 'the system' for their situation (Bryson, 1997). Data such as these are clearly relevant to a study of public attitudes to begging

Table 10.5: Popular conceptions of poverty

Respondent would say someone in Britain was in poverty if ...	% of total	% in that category but not previous one	conception of poverty
they had enough to buy the things they needed but not enough to buy the things that most people take for granted	28	28	relative
they had enough to eat and live, but not enough to buy other things they really needed	60	32	absolute
they had not got enough to eat and live without getting into debt	90	30	restrictive

Source: Taylor Gooby (1995, p 8)

and one might surmise that, other things being equal, those who adopt a relative conception of poverty, who think poverty is widespread and increasing, and who attribute poverty to injustice in society would be more inclined to give to beggars than, for example, those who adopt an absolute conception of poverty, who think poverty is residual and decreasing, and who attribute poverty to misfortune, laziness or lack of willpower. Through the survey, it should be possible to explore such relationships in detail.

As far as social exclusion is concerned, Perri 6 (1996) has made an important distinction between two sets of social bonds: those that link people to others in the same position as themselves, for example, family members, people living in the same community or immediate colleagues at work; and those that link people to others in very different positions – in particular, those who are in contact with opportunities in the wider society which can be brought to their attention and which they can, potentially at least, take advantage of. Perri 6 proceeds to argue that our social policies typically concentrate disadvantaged people together with others like themselves instead of helping them to make the second type of link with people who can provide ladders for them to escape their disadvantages. This may be true but it is not clear that it applies to beggars. It is well-established that people are most prepared to give to their nearest and dearest: to their parents, brothers and sisters and children (that is, to their immediate family). The evidence for this comes from financial support, caring and, in extreme cases, from organ transplants. The propensity to give diminishes as the social distance from the donor to the recipient increases and, thus, an important matter is the point at which a willingness to give stops. Since one can assume that people are more prepared to give to others whom they regard as members of their 'community', where the boundaries of the community are drawn and whether beggars are seen to fall within or outwith those boundaries (that is, whether they are regarded as members of the same community as the potential donor) become very important questions.

In *The gift relationship*, his study of blood donation, Titmuss (1970, 1997) asked the question "Who is my stranger?" (that is, who is the person to whom I am giving?). The answer is everyone who can benefit from the gift of blood, that is the whole society, including the donor, his family and friends. To give blood is to create the possibility for others (and indeed for oneself) to receive blood. Titmuss argued that the act of giving (which he called altruism) is grounded in the norm of reciprocity and promotes a degree of social integration in society. However, begging would appear to be different since, except for poor people who might give to beggars today in the anticipation that they may change places with them tomorrow, most of those who give to beggars will themselves never be beneficiaries. Recent research (Dean, 1998) indicates that fear of poverty is widespread and it may be that those who fear poverty most are more inclined to give for that reason. It should be possible to explore this possibility through the survey but the most salient issue is undoubtedly whether or not giving money to beggars, although it is not supported by the norm of reciprocity in the same way as giving blood, likewise promotes social integration. If, as Levitas (1996) argues, social integration is now equated, within a new hegemonic discourse, with integration into the labour market and the only route to social integration is through paid employment, this goal may be unattainable.

The survey of public attitudes

The survey should provide a very effective means of collecting data relevant to each of the themes outlined above, that is, to the relationship between begging and other forms of economic activity, the norms of reciprocity and beneficence, the aims and achievements of the welfare state, the role of charities, social justice, citizenship and social exclusion. The application identifies a number of key areas for investigation, all of which will first be explored in discussions with focus groups. Given that the survey will be exploring uncharted territory, this is particularly important. At the most basic level, we will need to make sure that what our understanding of 'begging' matches that of the general public.

Encounters with begging

The survey will make it possible to estimate the prevalence of encounters between the public and beggars. In addition to estimating the proportion of the population that has encountered begging on the streets, the survey will enable us to measure how frequent these encounters are, where they take place (in cities, large towns, small towns, suburbs or rural areas), and whether there are any significant regional variations. Such data, though no substitute for a 'headcount' survey of beggars, is, in sociological terms, just as significant.

Responses to begging

The survey will also examine responses of the public to beggars and be used to estimate what proportion of the population gives to the beggars they encounter. Such data should make it possible to examine whether there is a relationship between the propensity of people to give to beggars and the frequency with they encounter them, that is, to ascertain whether those who encounter beggars on a regular basis are more or less likely to give than those who encounter them less frequently. It should also be possible to estimate how much people give, to find out whether they give selectively and, if so, the characteristics and circumstances of those they give to. For example, it should be possible to find out whether people are more or less likely to give to the young and vulnerable or to the old and derelict, or to women rather than men, and if they respond differently to pavement musicians, 'squeegee merchants' and sellers of *The Big Issue*, all of whom provide something tangible in return, and to beggars who do not. Finally, it should be possible to investigate whether giving to beggars on the street is related to other forms of charitable giving, for example, in street collections, door-to-door collections or in response to a TV or radio appeal, supporting charitable organisations or attending a charitable event (previously examined by Barnett and Saxon-Harrold, 1992) and, if so, whether or not giving to street beggars has any effect on their other charitable donations. Those who give to beggars may be the kinds of people who give in other ways, but giving to beggars may reduce their willingness to do so. It will also be possible to analyse the respondents' answers to survey questions in terms not only of their demographic and socioeconomic characteristics, such as age, sex, household income, economic position, religion, educational qualifications, marital status, receipt of benefits, but also in terms of three attitude scales (a left–right scale, a libertarian–authoritarian scale, and a welfarism scale) which have been developed from responses to the BSA Survey (see Bryson et al, 1998) and thereby to build up a profile of public responses to begging.

Attitudes to beggars and begging

In addition to examining people's responses to begging, the survey will examine a broader set of attitudes related to this phenomenon. How are public attitudes to begging related to attitudes to other forms of street-level economic activity? Many buskers regard what they do as charging for a 'performance', and sellers of *The Big Issue* are certainly encouraged to see themselves as newspaper vendors, but it is not clear whether the public see these activities as any different from begging (but see Chapter Eleven in this volume). Thus the research will examine whether, and to what extent, the public differentiates between begging and other forms of street-level economic activity.

Although different people react to beggars in different ways (see above), why do people generally not give to beggars? Does it stem largely from embarrassment or guilt? Is it because people wish to avoid making a difficult decision about whether the beggar's needs are genuine or not? Is it based on a negative assessment of the efficacy of an individual donation? Or does it reflect a perceived lack of reciprocity in the transaction?

Beggars frequently claim to be 'hungry and homeless' – do they tap the same altruistic motives tapped by organisations like Oxfam and Shelter which promote the claims of hungry and homeless people (albeit in an impersonal way)? Are they seen as 'deserving', perhaps as unfortunate people who have fallen on hard times? Or are they seen as 'undeserving', 'fakes', 'chancers' or 'scroungers' simply out to get something for nothing? Some may view all beggars in the same light, while others may discriminate between beggars with different characteristics. And do the personal characteristics, appearance or demeanour of the beggar make a difference?

It will also be important to examine the feelings that begging provokes among the public and, in this respect, the survey will a bring a different kind of lens to bear on some of the questions raised, for example, in Chapters Eight and Eleven in this volume. Is begging perceived as a problem? Do people feel 'harassed' by beggars, as has been asserted by some prominent politicians? Or are other feelings more readily evoked, such as guilt, indifference or sympathy? Of course, once again, these responses may depend upon the personal characteristics, appearance or demeanour of the beggar.

Policy responses to begging

To the extent that people regard begging as a problem, the survey will attempt to identify whose problem they think it is, who they think should deal with it, and the degree of public support that exists for various policy options. Such options will include those which emphasise a 'carrot' (for example, the provision of incentives such as employment, training, accommodation and other facilities) and those that emphasise a 'stick' (for example, an outright ban on begging in public places and its criminalisation). The survey will also attempt to assess the degree of public support for alternative methods of channelling support to destitute people, such as 'diverted giving' schemes which attempt to tap the same charitable impulses as street begging but seek to avoid some of the most problematic aspects of encounters between beggars and the public (see Chapter Twelve in this volume). In this connection, it should also be possible to examine public preferences for different mechanisms of targeting resources on the destitute. For instance, do people prefer to give money 'anonymously' (through taxation or through a recognised charity) or to give directly to those they encounter face-to-face?

Postscript

It is our hope that the survey be used not only to examine the ways in which people respond to and think about begging and related issues and to analyse their responses and attitudes in terms of a range of antecedent factors, but also to inform a discussion of possible responses to begging. This debate will need to take account of the broader policy agenda in which responses will be formulated and will inevitably reflect the government's policy agenda. Three emerging themes seem to merit special attention. First, the range of 'Welfare to Work' measures which comprise the 'New Deal' and are based on the premises that work should pay and that everyone who can work should do so. Second, the new emphasis on communitarianism which, in the version promoted by New Labour, is a response both to the neo-liberalism espoused by the Conservatives and the social democracy associated with Old Labour (Driver and Martell, 1997) and, as such, is associated with the 'Third Way'. And, third, the declared commitment to combat social exclusion. These three themes provide the context for any discussion of responses to begging but, since begging is, in many ways, a test case for each strand in the policy agenda, it is our hope that it will also be possible to use the data on public attitudes to begging obtained from the survey to assess their viability.

Acknowledgements

I would like to thank Alison Park of SCPR, with whom I will be working on the project and with whom I have discussed many of the ideas in this chapter.

References

6, Perri (1996) *Escaping poverty*, London: Demos.

Adler, M. (1996) 'Rights and discretion in social security – did Titmuss get the balance right?', *Richard Titmuss Memorial Lecture*, Paul Baerwald School of Social Work, Hebrew University of Jerusalem.

Adler, M. (1997) 'Decision making and appeals in social security: in need of reform?', *Political Quarterly*, vol 68, no 4, pp 388-405.

Anderson, N. (1923) *The hobo: Sociology of the homeless man*, Chicago, IL: University of Chicago Press.

Barnett, S. and Saxon-Harrold, S. (1992) 'Interim report: charitable giving', in R. Jowell, S. Witherspoon and L. Brook (eds) *British social attitudes: The 9th report*, Aldershot: Dartmouth.

Becker, H. (1963) *Outsiders: Studies in the sociology of deviance*, New York, NY: The Free Press.

Beier, A.L. (1985) *Masterless men: The vagrancy problem in England, 1560-1640*, London: Methuen.

Brook, L., Hall, J. and Preston, I. (1996) 'Public spending and taxation' in R. Jowell, J. Curtice, A. Park, L. Brook and K. Thompson (eds) *British Social Attitudes: The 13th report*, Aldershot: Dartmouth.

Bryson, C. (1997) 'Benefit claimants: villains or victims' in R. Jowell, J. Curtice, A. Park, L. Brook and K. Thompson (eds) *British Social Attitudes: The 14th report*, Aldershot: Dartmouth.

Bryson, C., Brook, L. and Park, A. (1998) *British Social Attitudes 1997: Technical Report*, London: Social and Community Planning Research.

Cohen, S. (ed) (1974) *Images of deviance*, Harmondsworth: Penguin.

Dean, H. (1998) 'Popular paradigms and welfare values', *Critical Social Policy*, vol 18, no 2, pp 131-56.

Driver, S. and Martell, L. (1997) 'New Labour's communitarianisms', *Critical Social Policy*, vol 17, no 1, pp 27-46.

Golding, P. (1995) 'Public attitudes to social exclusion', in G. Room (ed) *Beyond the threshold: The measurement and analysis of social exclusion*, Bristol: The Policy Press.

Gouldner, A. (1960) 'The norm of reciprocity', *American Sociological Review*, vol 25 pp 161-78, reprinted in A. Gouldner (1973) *For sociology*, London: Allan Lane.

Gouldner, A. (1973) 'The importance of something for nothing', in A. Gouldner, *For sociology*, London: Allan Lane.

Hillyard, P. and Watson, S. (1996) 'Postmodern social policy: a contradiction in terms?', *Journal of Social Policy*, vol 25, no 3, pp 321-46.

Huggins, M.K. (1985) *From slavery to vagrancy in Brazil*, New Brunswick, NJ: Rutgers University Press.

Ignatieff, M. (1984) *The needs of strangers*, London: Chatto & Windus.

Levitas, R. (1996) 'The concept of social exclusion and the new Durkheimian hegemony', *Critical Social Policy*, vol 16, no 1, pp 5-20.

Miller, D. (1976) *Social justice*, Oxford: Clarendon Press.

Miller, D. (1992) 'Distributive justice: what the people think', *Ethics*, vol 102 (April), pp 555-93.

O'Connor, P. (1963) *Vagrancy*, Harmondsworth: Penguin.

Orwell, G. (1932) *Down and out in Paris and London*, London: Victor Gollancz.

Plant, (Lord) R. (1998) 'So you want to be a citizen?', *New Statesman*, 6 February, pp 30-1.

Plant, R. and Barry, N. (1990) *Citizenship and rights in Thatcher's Britain: Two views*, London: IEA Health and Welfare Unit.

Ratnapala, N. (1985) *The beggar in Sri Lanka*, Sri Lanka: Palihawadana.

Rawls, J. (1972) *A theory of justice*, Oxford: Oxford University Press.

Ribton-Turner, C.J. (1987) *The history of vagrants and vagrancy and beggars and begging*, London: Chapman and Hall.

Room, G. (1995) 'Poverty and social exclusion: the new European agenda for policy and research', in G. Room (ed) *Beyond the threshold: The measurement and analysis of social exclusion*, Bristol: The Policy Press.

Sandford, J. (1971) *Down and out in Britain*, London: Peter Owen.

Taylor-Gooby, P. (1995) 'Comfortable, marginal and excluded: who should pay for a better welfare state?' in R. Jowell, J. Curtice, A. Park, L. Brook and D. Ahrendt (eds) *British Social Attitudes: The 12th report*, Aldershot: Dartmouth.

Titmuss, R. (1970, 1997) *The gift relationship: From human blood to social policy*, London: Allen and Unwin (1st edn) and LSE Books (2nd edn).

Titmuss, R. (1971) 'Welfare "rights", law and discretion', *Political Quarterly*, vol 42, no 1, pp 113-32.

Townsend, P. (1979) *Poverty in the United Kingdom*, Harmondsworth: Penguin.

Turner, B. (1990) 'Outline of a theory of citizenship', *Sociology*, vol 24, no 2, pp 189-217.

Walker, A. and Walker, C. (eds) (1997) *Britain divided: The growth of social exclusion in the 1990s*, London: Child Poverty Action Group.

Wallace, S.E. (1965) *Skid row as a way of life*, Totowa, NJ: The Bedminster Press.

Walzer, M. (1983) *Spheres of justice: A defence of pluralism and equality*, Oxford: Basil Blackwell.

ELEVEN

"I feel rotten. I do, I feel rotten": exploring the begging encounter[1]

Ian McIntosh and Angus Erskine

This chapter is based upon research which aimed to gain an understanding of people's reaction to, experiences of and attitudes towards being approached in the street for money by people begging. The research was motivated by what we saw as something of a lacuna in much of the academic literature on begging, which puts the focus mainly upon the activities, strategies and experiences of those who beg (Gmelch and Gmelch, 1974; Heilman, 1975; Shichor and Ellis, 1981; Meir-Dviri and Raz, 1995; Williams, 1995; Wardhaugh, 1996). Much of this literature provides rich ethnographic material and illuminating insights into the world of begging, but it rarely dealt with a number of questions and issues that we were keen to explore. We wanted to understand begging from the other side of the begging interaction – those who are approached for money in the street – rather than the experiences and strategies of those who beg. Given that the focus within much social scientific research is upon the powerless rather than those with more power within particular social interactions and contexts, this approach seemed to us to offer a different and novel perspective on the begging encounter.

We were interested in specific questions: how do people recognise and understand begging activity? how is begging distinguished from other forms of street-level activity? why is the begging encounter often a problematic and uncomfortable one given the generally very small amounts of money involved? what explanations do people construct for the existence of begging? We were also interested in practical considerations that are addressed during a begging encounter: when do people decide either to give or not to give money? on what basis is a decision reached as to how much money should be given? how frequently do people give? what is perceived of as 'aggressive begging? In essence we want to shed some further light on the often problematic encounters across an "open palm" (Heilman, 1975; see also Chapter Eight in this volume).

"Edinburgh has got a bit of an attitude about it on the whole"

To explore these questions we decided to interview individuals who, on a regular and consistent basis, were likely to encounter, confront, or pass by people begging. Edinburgh was deemed to be the best location for our research in Central Scotland as it is a place that has witnessed recurring debates about the 'begging problem' and the issue of 'aggressive begging' is still very much a live one (*The Scotsman*, 10 September 1997 and 11 September 1997, *The Daily Record* 21 May 1998). Thus it seemed likely that the subject of begging and beggars would be one that those we interviewed would have recently given some attention to.

Permission was given by the management to interview staff at two large department stores on Edinburgh's Princes Street, Edinburgh's most famous and busiest street and a well-known location for begging and other forms of street-level economic activity. We piloted our interview schedule in one store where we had a low response rate among staff and then conducted the bulk of our interviews in the second, where due to the commitment of senior management in the store, we were able to interview as many people as we wanted, in privacy, and in the store's time. The staff we interviewed came from a range of occupations (sales people, designers, managers, warehousing, security etc) with differing lengths of service and a variety of positions within the stores and working different shifts. Of the 55 people we interviewed, the majority (38) were women. All had encountered people on the street asking for money and this, they reported, was a common, almost routine, part of arriving at, and departing from, work.

"I believe that you have got your genuine ones..."

A common theme that emerged across almost all interviews was a concern with whether or not people who were begging were 'genuine':

> "I would give to someone that you could look at and say that person is genuinely homeless." [man, 20s]

> "I seriously believe that there are the ones that aren't genuine, right, that are running two cars and living in a flat and things like that." [woman, 20s][2]

The notion of the 'genuine beggar' was central to participants' accounts, explanations and experiences of begging and was employed to decide how much to give and when to give. Whether a beggar was seen to be genuine or not impacted upon how they experienced the interaction and understood the activity. However, there was little consistency in the way the notion of 'genuine' was understood and applied. Who the 'genuine beggar' is seems to depend less upon the person begging and more upon the feelings of the passer-by.

> **"I just normally judge on the face.... I am more likely to give if it is a nice innocent face."** [man, 20s]

> **"... you can usually tell the genuine ones when you are coming along the road in the morning that really haven't had a wash for days and they look sort of pale."** [man, 20s]

> **"Well you've only got to look at them and see. I think if you look into their eyes you can tell."** [woman, 50s]

> **"Just if I feel sorry for them, if they're sitting out when it's raining and really cold and I think, well they must be genuine beggars if they're sitting out in this weather."** [woman, 30s]

Of course for people such as those we interviewed who encounter people begging regularly, these quickly made assessments can form the basis of 'typifications' (Schutz, 1972) of beggars which can be drawn upon consistently. It became clear to us that these constructions of 'typical' or 'real' 'beggars' became quite strongly held, even to the extent that it would be confused with actual 'begging activity' – a point discussed more fully below.

People believe that a large number of those begging are in some way not 'real' – a fake. A common view was that people beg as a, potentially, lucrative way of supplementing an existing income rather than begging being the sole source of their income, as with a 'genuine beggar'. As one respondent told us:

> **"[There are] two reasons [why people beg]; one, well they've just no' got the money and they can't get a job and then the other reason, as I said to you, is that they are just at it. You know they are no' really needing to beg but they've got it down to a**

fine-art.... I believe that you have got your genuine ones and the ones that are just complete con-men." [woman, 40s]

This division between the 'genuine' and the fraudulent caused concern:

> "They are probably on the social and what not and still claiming and still going out on the street.... That's where the people that are genuine always lose out and that's why people aren't giving so much." [woman, 30s]

The authenticity of the beggar is a key determining factor in people's understanding of their encounter with them. It is, of course, based upon a very partial knowledge, which was acknowledged by those we interviewed. As we were told, judging whether someone is a genuine beggar was a difficult task:

> "It's hard to work out whether people are genuine or whether they are just faking it." [man, 20s]

> "... to be honest you're not sure if they're genuine ones.... I don't mind giving to the genuine ones but I suppose there is no way of telling. It's very difficult, it's very difficult I must admit but I suppose it just depends on whether you feel sorry for them when you're looking at them." [woman, 30s]

> "At that initial point I think this person is maybe not more deserving but ... I don't know how you would describe which ones I would give money to and which ones I wouldn't. I mean you don't know their situation so you can't really say which one's more deserving than another." [woman, 20s]

"They just sit there"

Respondents reported that the body posture of those begging was used to assess whether they were genuine and deserved money. But while the body was important, there were inconsistent interpretations of position and demeanour. Looking too destitute or passive might result in people being less likely to give:

"Well why should I give my money to someone who is just sitting there not getting off his butt and doing something about being homeless or in hard times.... I work hard for my money and I don't have that much to give away." [woman, 20s]

"A lot of the time they are asleep and they've got the hat out or something like that so they are not even asking you for it. I just get the impression that a lot of them don't need it." [man, 40s]

This passivity could be interpreted as a deliberate strategy:

"... I was thinking why they sit down and maybe it is because if they come to you, you might think they're a threat so maybe they sit down to make you feel superior to them." [woman, 40s]

Others thought that beggars were becoming increasingly passive and therefore less deserving of money:

"... I think a wee while ago beggars used to actually do stuff like busk and stuff and get their money but now they just sit there, and obviously they look miserable, but they just sit there." [woman, 40s]

Yet, others came to a completely different conclusion, such as one woman, who said:

"I think the true people wouldn't speak and that they'd just sit there with their head down. I think genuine people wouldn't talk, they would just sit and not say anything with their head down." [woman, 40s]

An individual's posture could be used as a clue to how genuine they were and their general trustworthiness:

"... it's like even with people's posture, someone that sits upright or walks really upright rather than someone who slouches you tend to trust the one that's upright.... I would tend to go for the person who is more upright." [woman, 20s]

Yet Harman (Viles and Furnivall, 1869, p 31) warns against the 'upright man', one of the categories of beggars he found in Elizabethan London. Whether viewed positively or negatively, bodily expression is used today to judge the worthiness and genuineness of people begging.

Homelessness and begging

It was clear from the interviews that there was a strong connection made between being homeless and begging. Interviewees assumed that all the people they encountered on the street begging must be homeless; this, in fact, was a clue to whether they were 'genuine' or not – it seems a beggar with a home is not treated as a 'proper' beggar. As one interviewee said:

> "... there is a lot of people begging around this vicinity who, in a lot of people's views are not really homeless." [man, 20s]

When asked if selling *The Big Issue* was the same thing as begging, one woman made the conflation between begging and homelessness clear:

> "I suppose what makes it the same is that we know that a lot of people who sell *The Big Issue* are homeless so that's what makes it the same." [woman, 40s]

Another refused to believe that those he often saw begging were real beggars because they did not look homeless:

> "I would have thought that if you were homeless you would have been sleeping rough, you are going to look really rough, you are going to be dirty and your clothes are going to need a wash. The people begging around here don't look like that to me." [man, 30s]

Again this was employed as a way of deciding whether those begging were genuine and whether to give money or not, as one woman put it:

> "Well I mean if I genuinely knew they were homeless and had nothing I mean I would give, but if its just unemployed people I wouldn't give to them." [woman, 30s]

Being poor, it seems, is not enough for many people to convince them of the authenticity of those who beg, as it seems that being homeless as well as poor is central to their understandings of the genuine beggar – this is an assumption not supported by research. Anderson et al (1993) found that only 20% of those currently sleeping rough reported begging as a source of income.

It was notable from the interviews that there was a constant conflation, among those we talked to, of large-scale homogenous categories of socially excluded groups – the 'homeless', the 'poor', 'beggars' the 'unemployed' and so on. Such categories seemed to form a central part of our respondents' understandings and explanations of those they encountered on the streets.

Our interviews reflected such a strong conception of what a beggar was, and was not, that we can usefully make a distinction between a 'beggar' and 'begging activity'. It became clear that people would dismiss certain forms of activity as being something other than begging because those involved did not 'look' like beggars to them or they did not, in various ways, meet their criteria of authenticity. Often, however, it was the case that those we interviewed observed what they described as beggars, but when probed acknowledged that often no requests were being made for money.

It seems that people can 'see' beggars but no actual begging – and vice versa – thus making the categories of 'beggar' and 'begging' much more ambiguous and hard to define than might be first thought. Sometimes groups of younger people hanging around, often with dogs (two of those we interviewed told us how people get an 'extra allowance from the social' for owning a dog), would be described as beggars even if no actual begging activity was taking place. This seemed to be borne out by our own observations in and around Princes Street. Often we were told that beggars filled many shop doorways – as one woman put it, "begging is quite rife along Princes Street" – and that begging would be encountered every 50 yards or so, but what we saw was individuals who may have fitted people's conception of beggars but much less often did we actually encounter 'begging activity'. In 10 or so hours we spent in Edinburgh walking to and from the stores, we rarely saw someone asking anyone for money.

"It is more of a life-style these days"

It seems that young people can never be 'proper' beggars and will always have an ambiguous begging identity. 'Real beggars' are older homeless men – the 'down-and-out' tramp that emerged from interviews, at times in a romanticised manner. As one man said when asked what a genuine beggar was:

> "Probably the older gentleman, if you can call them that, the one that's probably weather beaten and you can see that he's a real tramp. If anything I would probably give to him." [man, 40s]

Another said:

> "I think there's more young people now than there used to be and we tended to think that it would be the older ones that were genuine." [woman, 30s]

Another interviewee told us about:

> "… an old chap, everyone knows who he is, and I've gave money to him … but I wouldn't say that I gave to the younger ones 'cos you feel as if they are not doing anything." [woman, 30s]

Younger people on the streets begging, it seems, are seen to be choosing a particular life-style. To amend the old adage it seems from our field work that 'choosers' cannot be 'beggars'. This notion of begging as a life-style choice among younger people was a recurrent notion. Another respondent stated that:

> "I don't think you realise why they are begging. I mean the older men used to beg because they just didn't have anywhere to go you know, I think the younger people who are begging are quite wealthy some of them you know." [woman, 50s]

Generally it was thought that to 'choose' to beg meant that they were not genuine because they could do something about their situation. As one man told us:

> "I just get the impression that it is more of a life-style these days than it used to be … I really don't believe that a lot of people begging are real cases, yeah they may be out of a job but it might be their choice to beg 'cos they can make more money

doing that ... I don't believe they are all genuinely homeless or have fallen on hard times ... I equate real begging with being desperate, having no choice but to do it." [man, 30s]

This theme of begging and choice emerged frequently during our interviews.

"Sometimes I can pass people begging and I don't feel anything"

The begging encounter is perplexing and contains within it the possibility for ambivalence and confusion. Contradictory views of beggars and begging was a feature of all the interviews we conducted. People we talked to found it difficult to be certain about what they thought about being asked for money in the street, acknowledging that their opinions on the subject were rarely formed definitively and were subject to change. A typical response would be the following:

"It comes down to how you feel. Sometimes I can pass people begging and I don't feel anything and sometimes a person makes you feel, oh, frustrated, its a mixture isn't it of emotions." [woman, 40s]

As another person put it:

"Sometimes it is a guilt thing, depending on the individual asking for money sometimes you feel obviously that they are there for a reason but other times you feel, you know, why can't they do something about it?" [woman, 30s]

During the course of the interview, respondents vacillated between taking a hard line in relation to the presence of beggars and giving money to a position that was much more sympathetic. This can be epitomised by the person who initially stated that they "can categorically say I have never given money", then went on to say:

"It's possibly a beautiful sunny day.... And they're sitting there all huddled up with their blankets you know looking quite pathetic and they're forcing a reaction.... Yeah you feel guilty that you're not giving to them that, you know, your life's fine and you know, you know, you just feel guilty. I suppose that I am feeling that I am being selfish.... And not giving to them ... 'cos I mean everybody should have a Christian attitude shouldn't they and help?" [woman, 30s]

Another interviewee's response is indicative of the ambivalent attitude people have towards those who beg:

"I don't think there is such a thing as a free lunch ... these people could do a great deal to help themselves ... but I am not really adverse to the idea of people begging ... I suppose it is a thing that could happen to anyone." [man, 30s]

"I often cross the street"

It seems then that the 'beggar' is a figure that people often find difficult to deal with. Certainly we found much evidence that they appear to constitute a troubling presence on the street, one that rarely fails to evoke a reaction and a response even from those that encounter them frequently. So much so that a potential interaction with a beggar leads to strategies of avoidance. As one person said:

"I often cross the street to avoid someone begging, to stop me feeling bad when I walk past. It's about yourself though, you feel bad and you can imagine how they feel." [woman, 20s]

Avoidance of eye contact is common:

"I do tend to feel genuinely sorry for most of them, being in a position where they have to do that, so I don't have a problem with people asking for it.... I feel sympathetic towards them.... I have occasionally ignored them.... If you're in a busy street and you do feel a bit conscious of people around you and yeah to be honest I have ignored them on occasion ... your eyes go down ... I feel guilty." [woman, 30s]

We found other reactions such as guilt and embarrassment to be very common among those we spoke to:

"I feel embarrassed, you know, to think that somebody's having to come up to you and say 'can you give me some money please'." [man, 40s]

"I think its embarrassment but also at the same time guilt ... 'cos I mean I would hate if that was me so you just feel guilty and you feel like its your fault that person was there." [woman, 20s]

"I don't feel guilty but you know, some of the ones that are sitting on the street when you are going home at night ... you think God, that's him for the night and yeah it does make you wonder what it's all about." [woman, 30s]

"I feel quite mean a lot of the time. I think there are some people that don't deserve money, like the people who use dogs and things but I'd give the money more because of the dog than the people, I don't think they deserve money." [woman, 30s]

"I think because they make you feel so awkward. If you don't give you feel so guilty and I think its because you've got this guilt feeling that you don't give to them when they ask you." [woman, 30s]

"All these sorry faces and trying to get money for nothing"

It is worth reminding ourselves of the normally tiny sums of money that are involved in giving to beggars. Explanations as to the troublesome nature of the begging encounter cannot be found on purely financial or economic grounds – how much upset would be caused to most of us when discovering that we had lost 10 pence? Within the begging relation, as evidenced by the comments of our interviewees, moral decisions are brought into the foreground over more strictly economic ones. The begging relation is a graphic example of how many apparent economic or monetary transactions operate within a powerful moral framework, a point brilliantly made long ago by those such as Adam Smith (Smith, 1966) and Emile Durkheim (Durkheim, 1984). It seems to us that this foregrounding of moral issues which have to be made within the, otherwise familiar, context of a monetary transaction which one feels 'forced' into, is a key source of the often fraught nature of the begging relation.

The troubling nature of the begging encounter in terms of a lack of equivalence is often utilised as a line of demarcation between begging and other forms of street-level economic activity:

> "Buskers are just making an extra bit of money ... it's about giving and receiving, by giving entertainment you pay them for watching them for a few minutes." [woman, 20s]

In relation to giving money to *Big Issue* sellers, one person commented:

> "... the main difference is that you are getting something for it ... people would be more open to give money if they are getting something for it." [man, 20s]

As one interviewee put it:

> "Well with buskers you're getting a song aren't you.... Selling *The Big Issue*? You're getting something aren't you, so its not like proper begging." [man, 20s]

Not everyone who buys *The Big Issue* reads it, and some people told us they often buy more than one copy of the same issue. The clear existence of some form of an 'equivalence' makes the interaction a much less problematic one and more akin to the reciprocated exchanges that one is accustomed to, even when receiving essentially useless items.

When asked if busking could be compared to begging, the following responses were typical:

> "Well I suppose they are entertaining you aren't they? And they are earning money, they're doing something rather than just asking you know, they are actually doing something ... it's almost like working and that's why there is a bit of a difference." [woman, 30s]

> "They are doing something rather than just sitting there ... all these sorry faces and trying to get money for nothing ... buskers say, 'well I can play an instrument, I need money', so in a way it's like a job isn't it?" [woman, 20s]

Only rarely did those we interviewed equate the selling of *The Big Issue* with begging, the presence of a tangible object of exchange apparently satisfying a rudimentary 'principle of reciprocity' and immediately elevating the activity above that of begging. One typical response came from one man who, when asked if selling *The Big Issue* was a form of begging, replied:

> **"No, it's selling ... they're accountable for the stock and whatever they sell they get a profit from, so its definitely not begging."**
> **[man, 40s]**

The mere presence of an object of exchange brings the activity much more into the more familiar and comfortable world of market and monetary exchanges and one that even mirrored the practices and routines of 'proper jobs'.

The aggressive beggar?

During the course of the interviews we only spoke to three people who had encountered what they described as 'aggressive begging'. All of these encounters involved the same person, a man in a wheelchair who begs in Princes Street. He had sworn at them for not giving money. More commonly, people had heard stories about aggressive begging even if they had not directly experienced it themselves. This is interesting given the recent debates that have taken place in Edinburgh in relation to the 'problem' of aggressive begging. People may find collecting for charities through tins in the street much more intrusive than either begging, selling *The Big Issue* or busking. As one woman explained:

> **"It's hard to get away from them if you don't want to give money, you see them on the street shaking a tin and you think 'oh God not again'." [woman, 20s]**

One man gave a typical response:

> **"They annoy me more than anybody, oh yeah, they just stick the tin in your face and expect money from you." [man, 20s]**

Another interviewee took great exception to those who collected money by rattling open buckets:

> "I don't like this bucket in your face ... that puts you right off ... if you want to give you don't need it stuck under your nose you know." [woman, 40s]

This was echoed by a man who said:

> "I hate them ... it doesn't matter what way you are going you get caught once then you walk down another couple of blocks and you get caught by another load of them ... they just seem to be there, always sticking it in your face.... It's no' the same as begging because it is going to something that is worthwhile but it's just a pain." [man, 20s]

We were given many examples like this. So, it seems that, on the main streets of Edinburgh at least, individuals who collect money through charity tins can be much more difficult to deal with than those begging for money for themselves. However, the two activities were rarely seen to be the same mainly because as we were often told, you at least "knew where the money was going".

"You know where your money is going"

One of the common rationales that we encountered during the research for not giving money to people begging, or at least being reluctant to do so, was that it was unclear what was going to be done with the money or that the money would be used for the 'wrong' reasons. One man told us that he would give more:

> "If they are putting that money to use for buying like clothes or buying food or something that is going to be of benefit to them. I mean I am not saying that they are not entitled to a drink or a cigarette but that is like maybe sort of second to, you would sort of think that they would need to do something more important first of all." [man, 20s]

Another interviewee told us that she never gave to people begging:

> "No, not to beggars. I don't mind, like, charities like the Salvation Army or whatever and people that are actually gonna use the money for what they say they're gonna use it for." [woman, 30s]

Having some vague notion of where the money was going made the giving of money less problematic, as one woman told us:

> "I think probably because with it being a charity you know that money is going to be used because it is an official charity and you know your money is going to a good cause it is going to be used in the right way. Whereas if I am giving money to somebody who's begging how do I know If that money is not going for drugs, if it's going for drink, to feed a habit or if it's generally going to go for food for them." [woman, 20s]

Others had a different perspective, reckoning that with begging they could 'see' where the money was going – to the person asking for it:

> "My reason for not giving to charity ... is 'cos the money doesn't go to the people who need help.... I give to them [beggars] they need help so they are using it." [woman, 50s]

However, one interviewee expressed succinctly a concern in relation to giving, when she said that:

> "Well if you give your money to someone in the street it is going straight to them but, are they using it in a constructive way?" [woman, 20s]

"I think it is a bit of both"

Asked to explain the existence of begging, people we spoke to, apart from agreeing that it was on the increase, vacillated between seeing it as the fault of the individual and viewing it as a social problem that required a response from 'the government'. In this way the prescience and continued relevance of C. Wright Mills' distinction between 'private troubles' and 'public issues' is clearly illustrated (Wright Mills, 1970). As one person said:

> "I think it is a bit of both ... I think it is more that they should help themselves rather than depend on the government and all that to help them, but I think that the government should take a look and see all the people who are begging and try and do something to help them out. Because maybe if they gave them help they would help themselves and then in the end it would be all right. I think it is definitely a bit of both." [woman, 20s]

Those individuals who came down clearly on one side or the other were the exception. People's responses were much more ambivalent and uncertain; of course, this could have been because it was the first time they had been asked to formulate their thoughts on the subject:

> "I think that society has got a lot to do with it but on the other hand, I mean, although its only hearsay you hear about these people who won't even try and get a job, I mean because the pay's low they don't think it's worth it but I really think it's society because the cost of living is so high and people can't afford to have their kids living with them so they send them out and they become homeless and you know I'd say society's got a lot to do with it." [woman, 30s]

Explaining the presence of beggars is, it seems difficult:

> "Em, because I think they have a very low opinion of themselves, they don't have any self-esteem to go and get a job whatever and they are just absolutely desperate. Or they could be just very lazy, I don't know and I do think that it has got a lot to do with habits as well like you know maybe drugs or maybe drink or I dunno." [woman, 20s]

> "Well I think years ago people didn't have money and they made do.... They didn't ask for all the benefits that people are getting now ... it's a lack of pride I think." [woman, 30s]

The notion that begging was inevitable and unavoidable came across clearly from the interviews:

> "Some people just don't have luck, because there can be terrible sets of circumstances in people's lives and if there was nothing they could have done to change that then ultimately society, the government or whatever should be there to protect the individual in the end. I don't think in this day and age that we should have things like that." [woman, 40s]

As another person said:

> "... if we lived in an ideal world they wouldn't be there but it's not an ideal world so they will always be there." [woman, 20s]

Fatalistic attitudes such as these served both to explain the existence of begging on the street and to distance individuals from it. Begging is something that will always happen but probably to someone else:

> "I hope that there is not much chance of that happening to me. I don't think I would ever be reduced to begging." [woman, 20s]

Conclusion

The motivations and reasons for giving money to a stranger on the street are often unclear for the giver. Why *should* they hand over their money to someone for nothing obvious in return is a question which our interviewees posed themselves in one way or another. It is a deeply ambivalent experience.

Bauman (1991, p 1) usefully defines ambivalence. It involves, "the possibility of assigning an object or event to more than one category". He goes on to say that such ambivalence manifests itself in "the acute discomfort we feel when we are unable to read the situation properly and choose between alternative actions". Such a depiction of ambivalence resonates with interviewees' responses. The begging interaction involves a confusion of moral issues and monetary exchanges and an, albeit brief, emotional involvement of varying intensities with someone who is often a complete stranger. Added to this is the problematic nature of what often appears to be a one-sided and non-reciprocated exchange.

Reciprocal exchanges have long been recognised as a central component of social and economic life. As Georg Simmel put it:

> **Most relationships among [people] can be considered under the**
> **category of exchange. Exchange is the purest and most**
> **concentrated form of all human interactions in which serious**
> **interests are at stake. (quoted in Levine, 1971, p 43)**

Further, as Simmel states, "... all contacts among men rest on the schema of giving and returning an equivalence" (in Gouldner, 1960, p 162). The begging encounter involves, of course, a potential exchange where the equivalence involved is not clear to either party, particularly those being asked for the money. Within societies such as ours, where reciprocated exchanges are a normal and routine part of social life, the begging encounter/relation can be a perplexing one. The non-reciprocated nature of the exchange is all the more stark because the object of the request within the begging encounter is that of money. And money is the token that is most symbolic (Giddens, 1990; Neary and Taylor, 1998) of reciprocated market exchanges. Again, to quote Simmel: "The functioning of exchange, as a direct interaction between individuals, becomes crystallised in the form of money..." (quoted in Craib, 1997, p 151).

The begging relation involves a monetary exchange that is unlike the vast bulk of exchanges between strangers and in part that is why it is problematic. It is a monetary relation that lies on the periphery, if not completely outside, our normal routine understandings of such exchanges and has the potential to undermine and usurp a central social relation around which gravitates much of our understanding of social and economic life and the smooth running of our daily routines (Goffman, 1971).

One person put it to us very succinctly "I feel rotten. I do, I feel rotten." (man, 20s).

Notes

[1] The authors would like to acknowledge the support from the Nuffield Small Grants Scheme, who provided us with the resources to tape and transcribe our interviews, and we would particularly like to thank the people we interviewed and the management of the two stores that we worked in. Their cooperation was essential, extensive and gratefully appreciated.

[2] To preserve the anonymity of respondents, we have not given their precise ages or their occupations.

References

Anderson, I., Kemp, P. and Quilgars, D. (1993) *Single homeless people*, London: HMSO.

Bauman, Z. (1991) *Modernity and ambivalence*, Cambridge: Polity Press.

Craib, I. (1997) *Classical social theory*, Oxford: Oxford University Press.

Durkheim, E. (1984) *The division of labour within society*, London: Macmillan.

Giddens, A. (1990) *The consequences of modernity*, Cambridge: Polity Press.

Gmelch, G. and Gmelch, S.B. (1974) 'Begging in Dublin: the strategies of a marginal occupation', *Urban Life*, vol 6, no 4, pp 439-54.

Goffman, E. (1971) *Relations in public*, Harmondsworth: Penguin.

Gouldner, A. (1960) 'The norm of reciprocity: a preliminary statement', *American Sociological Review*, vol 25, no 2, pp 161-78.

Heilman, S.C. (1975) 'The gift of alms: face-to-face giving among Orthodox Jews', *Urban Life and Culture*, vol 3, no 4, pp 371-95.

Levine, D. (ed) (1971) *Georg Simmel: On individuality and social forms*, Chicago, IL: Chicago University Press.

Meir-Dviri, M. and Raz, A.E. (1995) 'Rituals of exchange in the social world of Israeli beggars: an exploratory study', *Symbolic Interaction*, vol 18, no 2, pp 99-119.

Mills, C. Wright (1970) *The sociological imagination*, Harmondsworth: Penguin.

Neary, M. and Taylor, G. (1998) 'Marx and the magic of money: towards an alchemy of capital', *Historical Materialism*, no 2, pp 99-118.

Schutz, A. (1972) *The phenomenology of the social world*, London: Heinemann.

Shichor, D. and Ellis, R. (1981) 'Begging in Israel: an exploratory study', *Deviant Behaviour*, vol 2, pp 109-25.

Smith, A. (1966) *The theory of moral sentiments*, London: Frank Cass.

Viles, E. and Furnivall, F.J. (1869) *Awdeley's fraternity of vagabonds, Harman's caveat, Haben's sermon &c*, Oxford: Early English Text Society/Oxford University Press.

Wardhaugh, J. (1996) '"Homeless in Chinatown": deviance and control in cardboard city', *Sociology*, vol 30, no 4, pp 710-16.

Williams, B.F. (1995) 'The public I/eye: conducting fieldwork to do homework on homelessness and begging in two US cities', *Current Anthropology*, vol 36, no 1, pp 25-51.

TWELVE

Policing compassion: 'Diverted Giving' on the Winchester High Street

Joe Hermer

In contemporary Britain, begging in public places is governed by a complex of official and informal techniques that are linked within a framework of vagrancy, charity, welfare and local 'good government' legislation. These techniques are implemented by agents who work both 'within the scene' and from a distance, and are located not just in traditional offices of social control such as the police, but also in related regimes of public space administration, such as tourism and economic development, town centre and estates management, and environmental health and highway engineering.

Within this field of begging governance, some charitable appeals for pedestrian pocket change are configured as illegitimate and criminal, such as the case with visibly indigent begging, while other begging behaviour, such as charity collections, busking and *Big Issue* selling are tolerated, legitimised and even encouraged. By including this spectrum of behaviour under the rubric of 'begging', I acknowledge how the criminal character of vagrancy has historically encompassed a wide array of indigent, itinerant and peripatetic street characters – such as pedlars, hawkers, vendors, roundsmen, image sellers and various types of street entertainers, including ballad singers.

In my examination of the interregulated character of begging encounters, I am particularly interested in how begging is governed by discourses of urban order that evoke the tropes of 'civic renewal' and 'urban regeneration'. The writing of Michel Foucault, especially his later work on 'governmentality' (1991), provides a rich theoretical stance from which to understand such programmes. The Foucauldian notion of governance recognises that political power is exercised "through a multitude of agencies and techniques, some of which *are only loosely associated* with the executives and bureaucracies of the formal organs of state" (Miller and Rose, 1990, p 1; my emphasis). To speak of 'government' in this wider sense is to describe an array of mentalities and practices that work to direct social actors and configure individual subjectivity, often in highly peculiar ways, that are centred in moralising programmes of self-regulation.

This conceptualisation of government liberates us from a narrow, instrumentalist view of law which posits a compliant 'subject' that can be commanded, repressed, restricted and prohibited. Instead, we can consider how social actors are 'made up' through a set of discursive trajectories that normalise particular social relations and spaces. Governmental forms of power are primarily positive and constitutive in character: individuals are governed through both the enforcement of particular social roles and identities, such as 'welfare recipient' or 'hospital patient', as well as more loosely constituted modes or trends of conduct which are congruent with ideas of taste, style and fashion.

Central to this mode of power are the deployment of specific representational technologies that are capable of 'acting at a distance' on spaces, events and people. As Bruno Latour has so vividly illustrated, such inscriptions (such as statistical correlations) make 'absent people present' and allow regulatory agents to "speak in the absence of speakers" (1986). The 'No Loitering' sign provides an exemplar of this sort of governance technology in public space: individuals are targeted and 'moved on' by the police under the authority of the sign, while more subtly, such 'official graffiti' acts to inscribe social space in a way which marginalises and excludes particular individuals and groups who are *seen* as 'loitering', such as visible minorities, young people, or the visibly indigent[1].

In this chapter, I want to focus on an exceptional example of begging governance which unfolded in the Cathedral City of Winchester. The Winchester scheme is significant, but not because it represents a regulatory effort that is 'new' or successful. Rather, Operation 'Diverted Giving' is worthy of our attention in how officials actively attempted to intervene in the giving conduct of the pedestrian public through a specific visualisation of compassion and tolerance.

Operation 'Diverted Giving'

'Diverted Giving'

This governance effort surfaced in the Summer of 1995, when local officials and traders became alarmed at the number of 'winos', 'drunks' and 'aggressive beggars' who are 'littering up' the city centre in this affluent community. As the Deputy Mayor of Winchester City Council commented:

> "... even three of four young people laying around the streets begging and drinking was an offence to some people ... so they said what is the city council going to do about it." (interview, 19 June 1997)

This concern coincided with the opening of a new Tesco superstore on the outskirts of town, an event which was, according to the Chair of the Winchester Chamber of Commerce "of great concern" to the traders (interview, 23 June 1997). In response to this perception of a declining city centre, a 'City Centre Forum Group' was formed to look at ways in which the pedestrianised core could be made more attractive. This committee immediately focused on the presence of beggars on the downtown streets, especially 'aggressive beggars', a relatively new persona on the crime and disorder control landscape.

This governance scenario can be briefly stated as this: *'Community' comes together to rejuvenate declining downtown in the face of suburban supermall competition*: a routine scenario in urban regulation. But in Winchester, things take an unexpected twist when, instead of mounting a campaign to simply sweep the streets of 'undesirables', city officials – the police, traders, city councillors – turn their attention to what they referred to as 'the problem' of public compassion and tolerance, to the giving habits of pedestrians. As one member of the committee, the Head of Tourism (Winchester City Council) stressed:

> "We actually have a situation where half the people say 'we don't want these people here' and the other half of the residents giving them money ... encouraging it by the nature of what they were doing." (interview, 20 June 1997)

The idea of diverting public donations away from the hands of beggars to local charities through officially designated charity boxes was advanced by the committee as a way to deal with 'the problem' of public compassion, alleviating the apparent guilt and embarrassment that the passer-by felt when presented with an out-stretched hand. A programme utilising charity boxes in private stores would, according to the Head of Tourism:

> "... deal with the issue of people in the city who felt that they
> wanted to be charitable ... consequently they could be assured
> that their money was going where it needed to go ... and therefore
> that took out the thing of 'should I give someone money or
> shouldn't I give someone money?'." (interview, 20 June 1997)

Officials suggested that the programme would resolve the 'begging
problem' by having two effects. First, what they called the 'deserving'
and 'worthy' beggars, those who beg because of lack of food or
accommodation, would no longer need to solicit pocket change on the
street as they could avail themselves of the social services which would
be supported by the begging box income. The 'unworthy' and undeserving
beggars, those who were considered to be 'professional' and 'aggressive
beggars', the so-called 'drunks and winos' who 'drank their money', would
simply move on and find another city that was a 'soft touch' as the
donations dried up. A key tenet of this logic was that beggars who stayed
on the streets could more easily be judged as unworthy and moved on by
the police, who had promised what one Hampshire Constabulary Police
Inspector called "an increased level of support" to traders in the downtown
area (interview, 26 November 1996). Thus, the begging box programme
was described by the Winchester City Council Estates Officer as an
"experiment" and "economic tool" (to reduce begging), one that would
"target the undesirables" (interview, 16 June 1997).

One of the most remarkable features of this programme was the
seriousness with which city officials believed it could relieve the guilt of
the pedestrian who was racked with the dilemma of 'to give or not to
give'. Posters were designed to be displayed in strategic locations though
the pedestrianised city centre to meet incoming tourists so that, when
someone saw 'a beggar' they knew they could discharge their conscience.

"You are asked not to give money to beggars."

The poster states,

> **"If you have sympathy with these people please make your
> donation go where you can be SURE that it will help. Collection
> boxes are located around the city for the Night Shelter and Trinity
> Centre.... The nearest collection box is in...." (Launch poster,
> entitled 'City Centre Begging')**

While traders and the city council were enthusiastic about the programme, they were reluctant to spend very much money on start up costs for something considered to be 'an experiment'. Five wooden boxes were 'cobbled together' by a local carpenter at a cost of £20 each, paid for by the City Council as part of what its Estates Officer described as a "town centre management" initiative (interview, 16 June 1997). The programme was launched with a photo opportunity at the high street Marks and Spencer store on 2 December 1995.

The programme was immediately heralded as a great financial success: stories abounded that people were leaving "notes rather then coins" (Estates Officer, interview, 16 June 1997) and that boxes were overflowing with money. The abovementioned police inspector noted that someone had deposited a £35 cheque, and commented that someone "wouldn't have given that to a beggar" (interview, 26 November 1996). The local newspaper, the *Hampshire Chronicle*, ran a story one week after the programme, entitled 'shoppers' seasonal generosity' and reported that WHSmith had raised £100 in the first two days.

Encouraged by what appeared to be an unqualified success, and flattered by modest national media attention, the city believed that the operation could be significantly expanded. The Estates Officer recruited a specialised 'diverted giving' committee to redesign the programme and plan a relaunch for the summer of 1996. The committee was composed of the Trinity Day Shelter manager (one of the two shelters to participate in the scheme), a city tourism officer, a regional security manager from Marks and Spencer, a city centre inspector, and an official from the city planning department.

The committee believed that the scheme could be expanded to include as many as 15 boxes within shops, with an additional 24 external boxes located on the street, and that as much as £10,000 could be raised per year, an outrageously optimistic goal based on inaccurate donation estimates ('Diverted giving' scheme project [Relaunch Committee] meeting minutes, May 1996, 22 May 1996 and 23 June 1996).

I want briefly to focus on two specific aspects of the redesign of this programme, which illustrate how precisely the committee acted to construct an aesthetic of public compassion.

First, the committee felt that the posters were unattractive and awkwardly written and did not effectively emphasise a notion of 'social responsibility'. Committee members were aware of how fragile public opinion was about the programme, that they had to be "very careful about how things were written" (interview with Tourism Services Manager, June 1997). In considering options for refining the poster message, the idea of using some form of graphic to depict a notion of 'giving' was agreed upon. The task of redesigning the poster was given to the police inspector, who utilised a police artist from General Headquarters to follow up on committee ideas.

Over a series of three meetings, the committee attempted to come up with a suitable illustration which visualised the 'giving' idea. The police artist created several images that the police felt would be appropriate: the first one was an image of a visibly indigent character crouching on the street, a "scruffy looking drunk with a dog and a couple of bottles" as the Trinity Day Centre Team Head saw it (July 1997). A second depiction introduced a notion of charity, with a similar 'Ralph Mctell' character on the pavement wrapped up with a blanket with someone "in a suit throwing money at him" (interview with Trinity Day Centre Team Head, July 1997). The Tourism Services Manager and the Trinity Day Centre Team Head balked at the stereotype of homelessness, although they did agree with the other committee members who approved of the depictions, that it was nonetheless important to illustrate the notion of 'giving'. The dilemma, according to the Tourism Services Manager, was to illustrate giving in such a way that it did not look like someone 'distributing largesse' (June 1997).

After some discussion on how 'giving' could be more specifically represented, the police artist responded with the image of two hands, one of which was moving towards another in a 'reaching', 'helping' action. At first glance, the committee liked the look of this caring dramatisation, but after reflecting on the image further, they worried that the helping hand really looked like a hand reaching out to arrest and apprehend someone (Tourism Services Manager, June 1997; Trinity Day Centre Team Head, July 1997).

In order to address the ambiguity of this image – a depiction that seemed to represent both arrest and assistance, control and help – the committee decided to introduce the image of money clearly dropping from one hand into another, and it was this depiction that was refined for the new operation graphic. The effort to construct a representation of 'diverted giving' produced an image of direct exchange between two human hands, precisely the conduct that the programme was attempting to banish (see Figure 12.1).

To accompany the new illustration of giving, the poster text was edited to present a softer, less pedantic message: reference to those 'who take sympathy with these people' was edited out, as was references to 'pseudo-buskers'. The shift in the visual depiction from the character of the beggar

Figure 12.1: The 'Make It Count' poster

to the notion of 'giving' was complemented by the replacement of the poster title 'City Centre Begging' with the phrase of 'Make It Count', a suggestion of the Trinity Day Centre Team Head (interview, July 1997).

The second main task of the committee was the development and procurement of new charity boxes. The original wooden ones were seen as 'quaint' and 'amateurish' looking, and were considered neither big nor secure enough.

The job of finding new boxes was taken up by the Marks and Spencer manager who turned to a security contractor called Tuskguard. Tuskguard produced a series of technical drawings which the security manger brought to the meetings for consideration and comment, and eventually a charity box design was agreed upon, one that, according to a committee member, could be "mounted on a variety of surfaces and positions" and be "highly mobile and adaptable to specific environments". The committee ordered 15 of the customised cylindrical steel boxes at a cost – according to the final invoice – of £1,970.95. This cost, along with those associated with the poster production, was paid for with donations of £2,000 from the Hampshire Constabulary, and £500 from Marks and Spencer (interview with Estates Officer, 19 August 1997).

When the relaunch day of 2 July arrived, Tuskguard had installed boxes in Marks and Spencer, Boots the Chemist, McDonalds, WHSmith, Sainsbury's and the tourist information centre. Despite their ambitious plans, the committee could find only one new box location, leaving nine of the paid-for boxes to be stored in the council basement (interview with Estates Officer, 19 August 1997).

Operation aftermath

The effects of the programme are by no means obvious or visible, most notably because of the way the programme attempted to reconfigure the *idea* of public charity. Officials constantly evoked a view of society that relied on a crude form of structural-functionalism: that the pedestrian conscience could be triggered or activated on the 'sight' of a 'beggar'. Certainly, there is something authoritarian about a notion of human agency that is so mechanical and function-oriented.

How much money did the programme raise? Did money given to the programme go to those 'in greatest need', as city officials claimed?

In examining the financial character of the scheme, one is immediately drawn to the manner in which the programme was administered. Despite the fact that the 'Diverted Giving' programme was presented as a 'public' scheme, the council made no effort actually to monitor how the boxes were administered or how the charities spent the money. This is especially significant considering the extent to which the council made authoritative statements about the financial success of the programme, both to the media and to other councils which it advised on the 'success' of the scheme. Even 18 months into the programme, the city council had not collected any information on the amount each location was depositing, and only after I made repeated requests to the city for information, did the estates officer circulate a form asking for amounts deposited from individual store managers[2].

When we consider the actual role of the city in administering the boxes, operation 'diverted giving' was operated as a *private* charity: each store location had the responsibility of emptying their box, counting the money, recording the amount in a paying-in book, and depositing the money into an account shared by the treasurers of each charity[3]. While the programme was ostensibly presented as a 'public' scheme, the programme operated as a loosely coordinated series of private charity boxes under the control of each of the retailers. And because the boxes were inside the private space of retail shops, they were exempt from public charity law. No system of accountability was put in place to monitor the administration of the donated funds[4].

Despite this lack of accountability, I was able to reconstruct the deposit amounts for the five major locations over the first two-year period of the programme from three major sources[5]. The highly irregular deposit patterns of each of the five locations make it impossible to construct detailed patterns of giving. However, by averaging these deposits out per month, we can tell that officials consistently overestimated the actual amounts being raised by the boxes, both in public statements, and in private communications with other cities interested in the scheme. For example, officials repeatedly reported that the scheme raised £500 per month, when in fact the scheme averaged £258 per month in the first six months, an amount which would drop to £110 per month in the last six months of 1997. It seems most likely, that, making no effort to find accurate figures, officials were more then happy to carry on with the 'success' story of the first few weeks.

So, while officials provided an inaccurate picture of the financial state of the programme, did the money nevertheless provide assistance to those 'in greatest need' as the city claimed? Certainly, when one reviews the operations of each of the two 'diverted giving' charities, the amount contributed is negligible. For the operating year of 1996/97, the 'diverted giving' money accounted for 1.34% of the operating budget of the night shelter, and 1.77% of the Trinity Day Centre – an amount which was a "drop in the ocean" according to the Night Shelter Manager (Trinity Centre Annual Report, 1996-97; Winchester Churches Nightshelter Annual Report, 1996-97; interview with Winchester Churches Nightshelter Manager, July 1997). Not only did the programme generate very little meaningful revenue, there is considerable evidence, especially in the case of the Trinity Day Shelter, that the programme exacerbated an already underfunded, financially stressed work environment. Both shelter managers reported that, shortly after the programme started, individuals showed up at their centres asking for free or reduced services. The Night Shelter Manager reported that users routinely asked if the nightly fee could be waived as the centre had received money from the scheme: the manager of Winchester Churches Nightshelter characterised these requests as "crap" (interview, July 1997) and refused to change an already rigid fee scheme.

The Trinity Centre manager faced a far more serious problem in dealing with users. The manager keeps a very small welfare fund of about £20 a week that is doled out in emergency cases – he is constantly having to say 'not this time' to users who come to him for pocket-change. With the introduction of the boxes, the manger had a much more difficult time justifying his decision to say 'no' to people:

> **"Now when they come and ask for something and I'm saying no we haven't got enough, [they say] 'just read in the *Chronicle* that you got £2,000 from the begging boxes, what you have done with the money?'." (interview, July 1997)**

These demands heightened an already tense environment to the point that the staff felt they had to justify the fact they charged 50p a meal. The Trinity Day Centre management decided to lower the price of lunch meals to 25p, so that the staff could "have something to tell them". Certainly, several of the centre users who had been subjected to the harsher policing regime came into the centre and made their displeasure known to the staff. It is little wonder that the Trinity Day Shelter manager insisted that the name of his charity be removed from the begging boxes for the relaunch.

A more serious occurrence at the Trinity Day Centre that was widely seen to be related to the begging box programme was when the centre shut down for a period of two weeks after two users of the centre became violent with staff. Certainly, the closure of the centre was seized on by the proponents of the programme as a sign that the scheme was having some effect. As one trader commented, the shut down was inevitable as the centre users "[understandably] saw their income disappearing. They [the centre staff] got quite a lot of grief. People that were giving them money weren't" (interview with Head of Tourism, 20 June 1997).

Was the programme successful in removing the 'professional' and 'aggressive' beggars from Winchester High Street? The overwhelming sentiment among city officials and traders was that the programme was successful; several prominent officials cited a survey that was carried out by the tourism department which apparently demonstrated how the 'Diverted Giving' programme had worked. However, when examined closely, the survey in question gauged people's opinion about their perception of safety, rather then addressing the actual presence or absence of people begging in the pedestrianised area[6].

There is no evidence to suggest that the begging boxes decreased (or increased) the number of people begging through the 'drying up' donations. And while it is beyond this study to trace the street behaviour of police towards those begging, there is strong evidence to suggest that the police did, in various phases, initiate a crackdown in the pedestrianised area as part of a 'package of measures' which included the begging boxes. The response of the police is complex, but there is little doubt that, in conjunction with a number of management initiatives, they followed through with a programme of more robust 'moving on' of begging types in the downtown area, as an expression of the 'increased level of support' which the police had agreed to provide to the retailers (interview with Police Inspector, 20 November 1996). The programme implicitly gave the police a greater moral authority to 'swoop down hard' on those who were begging. In moving beggars on, as the deputy mayor commented, the police would have "something positive for them to say" (interview, 19 June 1997). The police would:

"... have some place to direct people to ... they didn't need to beg around here.... If you're short of food or a bed, we've got a place for you to go." (Deputy Mayor)

The effect was to displace those begging from the city centre area to a park south of the city centre, an area known as Andover Park. And despite the insistence of officials that the programme would simply 'dry up' street donations and drive the 'professionals' out of town, this police-generated displacement was in fact anticipated by members of the 'Diverted Giving' committee as a desirable outcome. As the Tourism Services Manager recalled:

> "... we determined that early on as part of that group that what was going to happen is that was going to shift our problem to somewhere else ... that we couldn't solve social problems and that this might have to be a measurable success." (interview, 20 June 1997)

Certainly, the police seemed as unwilling as anyone else to deal with the hard core of drinkers that the programme appeared to target. As one inspector stated, these individuals were "low quality prisoners"; they smelled and were dirty, and provided little status for young officers keen to deal with more serious crime.

Operation 'Diverted Giving' can be understood as a private form of policing, where retailers donate money collected from their customers under the guise of public charity, and transfer it to two charities which were seen to deal with the 'homeless problem' in Winchester. In exchange, retailers benefited from a moralised environment where anyone begging in the downtown area could be labelled as unworthy and subjected to being moved on.

Conclusion: a 'free gift'?

In examining the character of urban programme of regulation, one should always be cautious in offering a 'conspiracy' explanation of regulation, where unseen forces act to dominate and oppress individuals. Too often, in explaining the 'law in action', socio-legal researchers assign agency to social actors in ways that present questionable notions of causality. Social life is rarely coherent or transparent enough to be simply 'read' like a book, and researchers must tread carefully in reconstructing regulatory efforts whose material traces are often buried well below the surface of observable phenomena.

Yet, in the Winchester case, there is little doubt that the official goals of the programme were not sincerely and thoughtfully held by the majority of the participants, and that individuals who are in the position to understand the workings of the programme were willing to participate in the guise of public interest. And despite the contradictory and unanticipated elements of the programme, the operation nevertheless generated a coherent and concrete set of circumstances which was aligned with the interests of city officials, retailers, and the police: to 'target the undesirables' and configure public compassion in a way that made the 'moving on' of beggars acceptable to the pedestrian conscience.

In conclusion, I return to the notion of 'diverted giving' as illustrated by the operation graphic of the giving hands (Figure 12.1). In order to suggest the idea of 'social responsibility' in a way that did not moralise the character of the giver or recipient, the committee evoked the social form of money dropping from one hand to another, an image that powerfully evokes the moral authority of 'the gift'. In his work on the 'gift relationship', Mauss explores the nature of reciprocity that exists in societies that do not yet rely on personal contract in a market where money circulates (Mauss, 1990, p 46). "What power resides in the object given" asks Mauss, "that causes its recipient to pay it back?" (Mauss, 1990, p 3). Even in the money economy of the 20th century, Mauss suggests that our lives are still "permeated with the same atmosphere of the gift" (Mauss, 1990, p 65). This permeation is perhaps most vividly illustrated by Titmuss in his study of the gift relationships of blood donation, which generates a profound complex of trust and altruism that fuses the politics of welfare with "the morality of individual wills" (Titmuss, 1970, p 12).

There is no such thing as a 'free gift', as Mary Douglas (1966) suggests in her reading of Mauss (Mauss, 1990, p vii). And, as we have seen, the 'free gift' of 'diverted giving' is no free gift at all: the programme created a moralised climate that constructed a notion of compassion which was congruent with the 'moving on' of those begging. 'Diverted giving' provided city officials and retailers with a form of 'moral capital' (Valverde, 1994) that could be used to moralise the activity of begging through the construction of an official form of charity.

'Diverted Giving' was not a 'free gift' in a way that is absolutely central to the governance of begging on contemporary streetscapes. The very qualities of money which allowed the 'diverted giving' team to evoke notions of a charitable gift – the morally neutral character of money – are the same qualities which, for city officials, make money so dangerous in the hands of those begging, as exemplified by the constant worry of officials that beggars would simply go off and 'drink' their money. As Simmel writes,

> To the extent that money, with its colourlessness and its indifferent quality, can become a common denominator of all values it

> becomes the frightful leveller-it hollows out the core of things,
> their peculiarities, their specific values and their uniqueness and
> incomparability in a way which is beyond repair. They all float
> with the same specific gravity in the constantly moving stream
> of money. (Simmel, 1971, pp 330, 1978)

Certainly, it is not difficult to detect the hypocrisy of high street retailers who defend notions of consumer 'choice' and 'freedom' for their own customers, while depriving these very same democratic qualities of money to those who do not appear to be profitable consumers. By participating in the 'diverted giving' scheme, retailers are reacting to money as a 'frightful leveller' which makes no judgement between the street beggar and the most respectable of high street shoppers. I suggest then, that an account of begging encounters in public space must not only take into account the policing of visible indigence and legitimate charity, but also how such begging governance attempts to 'colour' the morally neutral character of money and delineate notions of worthiness within the social relations that constitute public space.

Notes

[1] For an analysis of the relationship between visualisation and regulation in urban governance see Hermer (1997).

[2] Certainly, the Estates Officer seemed irritated at my requests for the donation amounts, and somewhat embarrassed at having to admit that the city had no real information about the performance of the boxes. This irritation was compounded by the fact that the bank would not release statements to him on the 'charity box' account as he was not a holder of the account: he was forced to circulate a form asking each of the participants to volunteer information they had recorded in their paying-in books.

[3] The account was held at the local branch of a high street bank.

[4] Of all the contributors, the deposit amounts of one stood out as peculiar in this regard. Made at highly irregular intervals, the deposits were always rounded off to the nearest £50. Since it seems improbable that these rounded-off amounts occurred randomly from box donations, there must have been some form of rounding-off (either up or down) done by the

store. With no outside system of accountability, we have no way of knowing if individual locations 'top up' deposit amounts, or shave some off (NatWest account statement for 'Winchester City Centre Collection' account for 10 February 1997 to 9 January 1998; completed 'Winchester Make It Count' forms for several retailers as returned to the Estates Officer; various reports from paying-in books from project participants).

[5] Namely, selected bank account statements, returns by the retailers to the Estates Officer and additional information provided by the project participants (see Note 4 above).

[6] This survey (Winchester Visitor Survey 1996, Southern Tourist Board) appears to be part of a growing industry which provides local authorities with 'scientific' evidence to support city centre management initiatives.

References

Douglas, M. (1966) *Purity and danger: An analysis of concepts of pollution and taboo*, London: Routledge and Kegan Paul.

Foucault, M. (1991) 'Governmentality', in G. Burchell, C. Gordon, and P. Miller (eds) *The Foucault effect: Studies in governmentality*, Hemel Hempstead: Harvester-Wheatsheaf.

Hermer, J. (1997) 'Keeping Oshawa beautiful: policing the loiterer in public nuisance by-law 72-94', *Canadian Journal of Law and Society*, vol 12, no 1, pp 171-91.

Latour, B. (1986) 'Visualization and cognition: thinking with eyes and hands', in H. Kuklick and E. Long (eds) *Knowledge and society: Studies in the sociology of culture past and present*, Greenwood, CT: JAI Press.

Mauss, M. (1990) *The gift: The form and reason for exchange in archaic societies* (translated by W.D. Halls), London: Routledge.

Miller, P. and Rose, N. (1990) 'Governing economic life', *Economy and Society* vol 19, no 1, pp 1-31.

Simmel, G. (1971) 'The metropolis and mental life', in D. Levine (ed) *Georg Simmel on individuality and social forms*, Chicago, IL: University of Chicago Press.

Simmel, G. (1978) *The philosophy of money*, London: Routledge and Kegan Paul.

Titmuss, R. (1970) *The gift relationship: From human blood to social policy*, London: George Allen & Unwin.

Valverde, M. (1994) 'Moral capital', *Canadian Journal of Law and Society*, vol 9, no 1, pp 213-32.

THIRTEEN

Tolerance or intolerance? The policing of begging in the urban context

Roger Hopkins Burke

This chapter is about the policing and regulation of begging in the contemporary urban context. In Britain, as has been explained in previous chapters, begging remains a criminal offence in England and Wales – although not in Scotland – and those involved can be dealt with by the criminal justice process in that jurisdiction in accordance with the 1824 Vagrancy Act. In reality, many people found begging are not prosecuted. While respected sociologists of policing observe that the primary function of the public sector police service has always been to target and control the socially excluded elements of society, among which those found on the streets begging feature prominently (Reiner, 1997; Crowther, 1998), there is, nonetheless, evidence to suggest that many individual police officers have a – often officially sanctioned – tolerant attitude towards those encountered begging on our streets. Intervention and prosecution invariably requires the person to have compounded their actions with aggressive behaviour (Hopkins Burke, 1998a). The recent introduction of zero-tolerance policing strategies suggests a change in emphasis towards the targeting of all beggars, both passive and aggressive. The reality – as we shall see below – is somewhat different.

The evidence of history suggests that more coercive measures have usually been taken against those found begging when the numbers involved visibly escalate and, not surprisingly, this is – notwithstanding the difficulties there are in quantifying the phenomenon – inclined to occur at times of persistent economic recession and social upheaval (for a comprehensive review see Postan, 1972; Slack, 1974; Beier, 1985; Rose, 1988; Rogers, 1991; Coldham, 1992; Hopkins Burke, 1998a). At such times, the authorities have tended to favour some form of repressive intervention with the intention of maintaining social order and the protection of the status quo (Hopkins Burke, 1998a).

In the years following the Second World War – with economic boom conditions, full employment and the new social security system – there were relatively few people to be found begging on the streets (Rose 1988). Their substantially reduced ranks predominantly consisted of men with alcohol-related problems living in derelict buildings and sleeping rough (Conroy, 1975; Archard, 1979; Healey, 1988). The return to begging on a large scale occurred following the collapse of the long post-war economic boom and the subsequent retreat from the welfare state that has epitomised the subsequent government response (Jessop, 1990). From 1973 onwards the growing world recession reintroduced mass unemployment to the UK and the increasingly tougher rules limiting welfare benefit to certain groups can be seen as a major reason why there are now a greater numbers of beggars on the streets of London (Murdoch, 1994) and other major cities in the UK (Rose, 1988; Hopkins Burke, 1998a); a situation replicated in the USA, in general (Kelling and Coles, 1996) and New York City, in particular (Bratton, 1997; Currie, 1997; Taylor, 1997). According to the Fiscal Policy Institute, New York has the most extreme income distribution in the US between the upper and lower classes. Families at the top fifth of the income spectrum earned more than US$132,000 per annum, while families at the bottom fifth earned less than US$7,000 (approximately £4,375) (NY1 Television News Channel Internet Service, 4 November 1997). At the same time, recent years have seen a substantial reduction in welfare entitlement in the city (Currie, 1997).

It can be legitimately argued that the recently much publicised 'zero-tolerance' policing initiatives – particularly those introduced both in New York City and London – are merely a return to a long established tradition of targeting the poor and socially excluded at times of economic and social upheaval (Currie, 1997; Taylor, 1997; Crowther, 1998). Those contemporary libertarians who favour a substantially more tolerant response, nonetheless, need to consider the following not inconsiderable moral conundrum.

Evidence from a study conducted in Leicester (see Hopkins Burke, 1998a), discussed below, acknowledges that, while on the one hand, the vast majority of those found begging on our streets can be considered an economically excluded group worthy of a humanitarian intervention, on the other hand, these very same people can provide an intimidatory presence to be negotiated by ordinary people going about their legitimate activities. Furthermore, the more politically radical reader who considers the economic plight of beggars sufficient to warrant a policy of non-intervention in their activities should consider three closely related issues. First, many members of the general public intimidated by the activities of beggars are themselves relatively poor – albeit that they might be in employment – and, in some way, vulnerable members of society. Second, people begging on the streets are at significant risk of violence from other members of society; indeed this scenario is as likely – if not more so – than the reverse situation (see Murdoch, 1994; Hopkins Burke, 1998a; and see Chapter Six in this volume). Third, there is the issue of intimidation and aggression used to self-regulate the internal world of the beggar. The excellent autobiography of reformed alcoholic/vagrant turned chess grand master, John Healey (1988), portrays the terrifying world of the vagrant beggar – the 'grass arena' – where the law is enforced with the broken bottle, the boot and the knife. In short, the world of the beggar is a violent and frightening environment where those rules of politically correct behaviour that have increasingly come to dominate middle-class lives – especially those of public sector professionals and academics – have completely failed to penetrate. A libertarian policy of radical non-intervention in the activities of those found begging on our streets is considered by this author to be morally irresponsible. Some form of policing and regulation is essential for the benefit of all – beggars and the general public – alike.

This chapter has the following structure. First, there is a brief examination of the issue of begging in contemporary North America. This discussion both illustrates the universality of the problem for post-industrial (or post-modern) societies and suggests the necessary preconditions for the introduction of what have come to be termed 'zero-tolerance' policing strategies. Significantly, this is a policing philosophy that has been subsequently adopted in several constituencies in the UK and enthusiastically advocated by its supporters as a successful strategy for dealing with those found begging on our streets. Second, there is a critical consideration of the origins, prescriptions and implications of that policing philosophy in the USA. Third, there is an examination of the findings of a small study of beggars in the UK – the Leicester Study – that addresses the issues introduced for discussion. Finally, and in conclusion, it is argued that there is need for a policing strategy that provides a balance of intervention between the interests of those involved in begging and those of the wider general public.

Begging in contemporary North America

Hagan and McCarthy (1997) inform us that approximately 100 million children and adolescents live on the streets and are involved in begging worldwide. This is a stunning statistic but for this author substantially less so than the later revelation that there are between 10,000 and 20,000 street youth in Toronto alone, and that these are involved in a range of street-level economic activities of which begging is central. Poverty, starvation, sweated labour, hawking, begging and child prostitution are for many of us – raised and educated in the developed societies of industrial modernity – acknowledged characteristics of underdeveloped societies. We have tended to perceive Canada rather differently.

Canada is usually considered to be in the vanguard of the developed world. It has been perceived as a dynamic society – distinguished in popular discourse by the 1970s' whiskey advertisement as 'the young country' – to where many, including this author's mother, have aspired to emigrate. In a more academic language it can be seen as a society where the modernist project of the application of science and rational calculation had created a socially engineered world of opportunities and access to the good life for all. The recognition that homelessness and begging is now so widespread in that society provides devastating evidence of the failure of that project.

Hagan and McCarthy (1997) conducted an extensive field study of young people who had left home and school to live and beg on the streets of two of the biggest cities in Canada: Toronto and Vancouver. Examining the social worlds and subjective perspective of more than 400 young people encountered begging, the study also considers the very different responses of the authorities in the two cities. Toronto, we are informed, provides a more welfare-oriented framework of support services and shelters; Vancouver substantially rejects that approach, favouring a rigorous criminal justice crime control model. Perhaps not surprisingly, the authors found that young people living on the streets in Vancouver have both a considerably more traumatic experience and, at the same time, are similarly inclined to involvement in more serious criminal activity than their contemporaries in Toronto. The crime control model has also become the dominant orthodoxy for responding to begging and other street activities south of the border in the USA.

Kelling and Coles (1996) provide a detailed account of begging and other street activities that had come to dominate the major cities of the USA. For example, we are told that Golden Gate Park in San Francisco had been turned into a squatter camp by the homeless and was considered a 'no-go' area by other citizens. The New York City Subway had also become home to hordes of apparently 'homeless' people, who, among their various scams, charged legitimate passengers for the right to use the transportation system. Kelling and Coles provide a meticulous and scholarly account of attempts by the authorities to confront these groups and their various civil liberties apologists both on the streets and in the courts. The American Civil Liberties Union (ACLU) has defended the right of US citizens to beg by citing the First Amendment to the US Constitution, which purports to guarantee the right to free speech. Those city authorities that have sought to restrict the activities of street beggars have had to locate often complex enabling legislation in the context of the constitutional amendment or find their policing initiatives declared illegal by the courts. The New York Subway system was finally cleared of people aggressively begging following the appointment of William J. Bratton, Commissioner of the New York Transportation Police, and a myriad courtroom confrontations (Bratton, 1997; Kelling and Coles, 1997; Hopkins Burke, 1998b). These are significant individuals. Bratton was later appointed Commissioner of the New York Police Department and was responsible for introducing a policing strategy later termed 'zero-tolerance'. George Kelling was responsible – in association with the eminent Right-Wing political scientist, criminologist and special adviser on crime to President Reagan, James Q. Wilson – for giving that style of policing theoretical validity (Kelling and Coles, 1996). That approach to policing will now be considered.

Zero-tolerance policing

'Zero-tolerance' is a generic expression used to describe a variety of what I have elsewhere termed "proactive, confident, assertive policing strategies" (Hopkins Burke, 1998b, 1998c). There are variations in these strategies but, in general, they are theoretically informed by the 'broken windows' thesis, developed in the USA in the early 1980s by Wilson and Kelling (1982). In short, this thesis asserts that just as an unrepaired broken window is a sign that nobody cares and leads to more damage, minor incivilities – such as, begging, public drunkenness, vandalism and graffiti – if unchecked and uncontrolled, produce an atmosphere in a community in which more serious crime will flourish. Over time individuals may feel that they can get away with minor offences which leads them to commit more serious offences.

Proponents of zero-tolerance style policing, such as Bratton (1997), have adapted the 'broken windows' thesis to argue that a positive police presence targeting petty offenders on the streets can lead to substantial reductions in the level of crime, and they point to the success of experiments in their own constituencies to support these assertions. During the period 1994 to 1996 the official statistics purport to show the crime rate in New York City to have decreased by 37% – the homicide rate alone by 50% (Bratton, 1997, p 29). Opponents observe not only a lack of evidence supporting a direct causal link between these initiatives and any apparent decline in the crime figures (see Morgan, 1997; Pollard, 1997; Read, 1997; Currie, 1997; Taylor, 1997; Crowther, 1998), but – in particular, those of them living and working in the UK – also consider these tactics a return to the failed military-style policing tactics pursued by metropolitan forces in inner-city neighbourhoods in the UK during the 1970s and early 1980s (see Lea and Young, 1984). The Scarman Report (1981) into the associated disorders that had occurred in Brixton, in South London, had stressed that all aspects of police work should be premised upon *active* community *consent, trust* and *participation*. Society needed to recognise that the police working on their own could not make a significant impact on local crime problems. Effective crime prevention was the responsibility of the whole community. Community policing subsequently became the official orthodoxy in the UK (Hopkins Burke, 1998b).

For supporters of the community policing model the introduction of zero-tolerance policing strategies are simply a backward step to military-style policing with the same inherent risk of inciting widespread public disorder (Morgan, 1997; Read, 1997; Crowther, 1998; Wadham, 1998). From this point of view, there is an unspoken implication and assumption that the police have a tolerant attitude to minor criminal activity in order to avoid further alienation and potential serious social unrest (see Morgan and Newburn, 1997). It is a perspective that nonetheless – as the evidence of numerous crime surveys show – carries little favour with widespread sections of the population who demand a visible and active police presence on the streets (Hopkins Burke, 1998b). Evidence suggests that the introduction in New York City of an assertive style of community policing – later termed 'zero tolerance' – has been favourably received by a widespread public constituency embracing all ethnic groups (see Silverman,

1998). Central to this initiative was the election in 1994 of Mayor Rudolph Giuliani.

Giuliani is an intriguing figure who was the first Republican Mayor of New York City for over 60 years. Previously a federal district attorney, he was elected after campaigning on the issue of crime and disorder; specifically on the issue of dealing with aggressive 'squeegemen' – youths who extort money from stationary car drivers by 'washing' their windows – and panhandlers (beggars) (see Kelling and Coles, 1996). Now Giuliani appears, at first sight, to be a straightforward, fundamental Right-wing Republican with an agenda based on a fusion of authoritarian social policies and free market economics, epitomised by his welfare budget slashing policies and his 'get tough' approach to policing. Indeed, Bratton firmly locates this policing revolution in terms of a reaction to the post-Vietnam liberal/libertarian discourse that had come to dominate US public life (Bratton, 1997). Closer examination reveals a more complex picture.

New York City is an intensely populated metropolis of fragmented and diverse communities that could best be described – to use the language of contemporary social science – as post-modern in nature. The evidence can also be interpreted to suggest that Mayor Giuliani should be conceptualised as a new style – post-modern – politician who is alert to at least some of the implications of trying to govern such a society (see Hopkins Burke, 1998b, 1998c, 1998d). A summarised account suggests the following.

Modern societies are mass societies that aspire to full employment, demand management and public investment in health education and welfare (Harvey, 1989). They are essentially characterised by moral certainty and confidence in the explanatory power of grand social and political theories to solve the problems of humanity. There are competing ways of seeing and dealing with the world – for example, liberalism, socialism and conservatism – but the adherents to these different perspectives believe in the capacity of *their* particular doctrine to solve all problems in society.

In recent years there have been increasing doubts about the endurance of the modernist project in an increasingly fragmented and diverse social world that some social scientists and philosophers have termed the post-modern condition (see Lyotard, 1984; Baudrillard, 1981, 1988; Bauman, 1989, 1991, 1993). Politically, the traditional parties of the 'left' and 'right' – and, for that matter, the centre, for this is no mere centrist manifesto – have proved incapable of representing multiple interest groups as disparate as major industrialists and financiers, small business proprietors, the unemployed and dispossessed, wide-ranging gender and sexual preference interests, environmentalists, the homeless and the socially excluded (see Giddens, 1994). Post-modern politics are consequently complex and characterised by moral ambiguity with the recognition of a range of different discourses that can be legitimate and hence right for different people, at different times, in different contexts. It is a perspective founded on cultural relativism, the notion that there is a series of legitimate discourses on a particular issue and that it is difficult, if not impossible, objectively to choose between them. The objective truth – or competing objective realities – of modernity, are replaced by a recognition of the multiple realities or moral ambiguities of post-modernity. These realities are invariably complex, highly susceptible to inconsistent interpretation and are contested by individuals – politicians and members of the general public – who often make short-term, pragmatic and inconsistent judgements without reference to any coherent body of knowledge.

Essentially, the aspiring electorally successful post-modern politician needs to identify crucial political issues that concern the widest possible range of interest groups in order to build successful electoral coalitions. The issue identified by Giuliani was that of crime. New York City was widely recognised as the crime capital of the world, its people were scared and they wanted something doing about the crime problem (Bratton, 1997). Mayor Giuliani was elected with an unambiguous determination to do something about it (Pearce and Harrison, 1997).

It was in this sociopolitical context that Giuliani – supporting his determination with a willingness to provide funds for additional officers, initiatives, and equipment – appointed William J. Bratton Police Commissioner with a mandate to target crime. Bratton enacted this mandate by introducing a computerised managerial system (known as 'CompStat') that was most noticeably used to target 'quality of life' crimes. This so-called 'zero-tolerance' policing strategy was used as the means of recovering the streets of New York City for the 'law-abiding citizen' (Kelling and Coles, 1996; Bratton, 1997; Silverman, 1998). Significantly, it is a style of policing that has remained politically popular with an extremely large cross-cultural section of the population of New York City. Its apparent success was to encourage similar experiments in the UK.

The first 'zero-tolerance' policing initiative in the UK was introduced by the Cleveland Constabulary in 1994 but this targeted burglars not beggars (see Dennis and Mallon, 1997; Romeanes, 1998); a more pertinent example was instigated two years later in London. In November 1996 the Metropolitan Police implemented a six-week experiment 'Operation

Zero-Tolerance', in collaboration with the City of London Police and the British Transport Police, in King's Cross. The purpose of this partnership between the police, public sector, private and voluntary agencies, as well as the general public was "to target and prevent crimes which are a particular local problem, including drug-related criminality" (Metropolitan Police, 1995). 'Operation Zero-Tolerance' included elements of the New York approach of targeting minor crimes such as dropping litter, graffiti, aggressive begging, and low-level disorder (Bratton, 1996) adapted to deal with specific problems found in some locales in London. Appraisals of the initiative suggest an improvement in the quality of life of residents and workers in the targeted areas (Johnston, 1997).

Politicians in the UK have undoubtedly responded to widespread public support for zero-tolerance-style initiatives. Notwithstanding this public support, there has been considerable resistance to the concept from some very respected sources. Key members of the Association of Chief Police Officers (ACPO) have expressed scepticism about its utility (Crowther, 1998). Charles Pollard, the highly respected Chief Constable of the Thames Valley Constabulary, has described it has a "short-term fix and long-term liability" (Pollard, 1997, p 139). A key main concern from this viewpoint is that insensitive policing could lead to an escalation of conflict between the police and the communities they are charged with policing (Crowther, 1998). A further major misgiving is that such initiatives are simply discriminatory in targeting and criminalising economically excluded groups living on the streets (Wadham, 1998). The evidence of the Leicester Study reported below supports the assertion that, overwhelmingly, those found begging on our streets can be legitimately considered legitimate members of an excluded 'class' or social group but, at the same time, it is found that they are worthy of police attention and regulation of their activities.

The Leicester Study

It was the purpose of the Leicester Study to investigate the life-styles and motivations of people found to be engaged in begging in that city. It is the intention here briefly to reconsider data that informs the conundrum posed at the outset of this paper, for if, on the one hand, those engaged in begging on our streets provide an often intimidatory presence to be negotiated by ordinary people, then their activities merit close police attention; if, on the other hand, they can be considered an excluded group unjustly treated by society, they are indeed worthy of humanitarian consideration.

Interviews were conducted from the first week in May 1996 to the first week in June 1996. A total of 40 beggars were encountered at different times during that period and they were all invited for interview. None refused (Hopkins Burke, 1998a). All but two were males and three quarters of these were over 25 years of age. The great majority (32) were long-term homeless and this was the case regardless of age. Younger people were more likely to be sleeping on the floors of their friends or living in squats while older people were far more likely to be 'living rough'. Involvement in begging was a long-term and regular reality for the majority (25 had been begging for more than a year). Furthermore, those who had been begging the longest were far more likely to be sleeping rough and to be begging for longer periods (16 had been begging for more than a year and were sleeping rough).

It was possible to distinguish between two ideal types of beggars. Those with 'somewhere to go', whether it be their own home, a squat or a friend's flat, were far more likely to beg for a short period until they acquired sufficient funds to satisfy a specific need, for example, something to eat, while those who were sleeping rough were likely to focus virtually all the conscious part of their lives begging. It is certainly the case that this latter group were far more likely to have alcohol-related problems than the former. However, both groups can be objectively classified as homeless. Without doubt, the people encountered begging on the streets of Leicester were by any objective criteria seriously economically disadvantaged and worthy of sympathetic consideration. On the other hand, however, a strong case for the regulation of their activities can be made.

Most people interviewed during the course of the Leicester Study chose to go begging when and where they thought they were most likely to receive money. The most popular times were those, such as the morning and evening rush hours and the lunch period, when more people were out and about, and the most popular places were those crowded city areas with narrow access where people were unable to easily avoid beggars. This invariably involves some degree of tacit – and on occasion more explicit – intimidation.

There is competition among beggars for the best 'pitches' and there appears to be self-regulating mechanisms by which these are 'allocated'. There is evidence that intra-group violence is an essential aspect of the vagrant way of life and it is extremely likely that physical coercion underpins much activity in the begging underworld. The vast majority of beggars encountered also claimed to have been the victims of both verbal and physical abuse from members of the public. There is clearly a case for the regulation of the activities of beggars both in the interests of the general public and in order to offer some protection to those involved in this way of life.

The research evidence suggests that the police in Leicester have managed to maintain a reasonable balance between maintaining order and providing some protection to beggars without engaging in overtly zero-tolerance-style policing initiatives. Less than a half of those interviewed during the course of the study had been warned by the police for begging on the street while less than a third had been arrested for this offence. Nearly two thirds had been arrested for offences other than begging, with the most common offence being 'assault' and 'drunk and disorderly'. The evidence of the Leicester Study suggests that the police in the city are fairly tolerant of beggars, unless they are 'in breach of the peace' and behaving in an aggressive fashion. Some of those interviewed suggested that some police officers actually 'look out' for the safety of the more vulnerable beggars. These findings might help to explain the generally positive attitude of beggars towards the police in Leicester. They will now be considered in the wider context of the arguments presented in this chapter.

Discussion and conclusion

It has been observed in this chapter that street begging has been a central focus of zero-tolerance policing strategies introduced both in the USA and the UK. Furthermore, it has been recognised that these activities are now widely considered – by the public and politicians – as a legitimate target for a vigorous police intervention. The evidence suggests, nonetheless, that those found begging on our streets can be considered, in the main, an economically excluded group. There are undoubtedly those who make false claims to their status, for example, those who claim to be homeless when in reality they have accommodation. Nevertheless, there appears to be little evidence to suggest that begging is a particularly lucrative way of life and indeed the literature suggests that virtually all beggars have one thing in common – their poverty – although this is a relative concept. Beggars are members of a class of people ('underclass' or workless class) who are *excluded* from the normal basic standards of living most of us would consider acceptable – they can be simply characterised as an *excluded* class.

In terms of one part of the conundrum introduced at the outset of this chapter, the message appears unambiguously clear; people begging on our streets have legitimate rights and are worthy of humanitarian consideration. On the other hand, there is evidence that large numbers of beggars and vagrants on our streets can provide a somewhat intimidatory presence to be negotiated by ordinary people going about their legitimate activities in the business areas and shopping centres of our cities and towns. These are the venues in which members of the excluded social classes come into contact with members of the included social classes (those of us with the good fortune to have access to jobs and/or legitimate opportunities). Members of the former group can appear frightening to some of the latter – particularly when beggars have a self-conscious awareness of their own intimidatory presence.

The Leicester Study uncovered little evidence of *overt* 'aggressive begging'; nevertheless, intimidation was found to take on more subtle forms. Many of those interviewed admitted to seeking out those areas of town with the highest congregations of relatively affluent people – choosing those specific places where geographical space is narrowly constrained and members of included society are forced into the close proximity of the excluded. This strategy in itself – one often non-contentiously employed by charity collectors – constitutes an insignificant and usually non threatening degree of intimidation. A critical level occurs when other factors – commonly, a rough and dishevelled physical appearance allied to the visible possession and consumption of alcohol – are present. Intimidation is, nonetheless, a subjectively experienced emotion received conversely by different groups – for example, men or women, the young or old – and there is an extensive criminological literature that considers the subjective nature of the 'fear of crime' (for a critical review see Sparks, 1992).

The evidence of the Leicester Study suggests, furthermore, that intimidation is a self-defeating begging strategy. The particularly rough looking alcohol consuming beggar was usually far less successful in obtaining donations from passers-by over the longer term than their more placid conventional-looking contemporaries. Moreover, the former group were far more likely to be the target of a police intervention.

It would seem relatively easy for the police to take a particularly assertive stance with a group of people who tend to have few friends, supporters or champions. It would be relatively non-problematic to simply clear our main business precincts of those found to be begging – to introduce a policy of zero-tolerance. Furthermore, it is extremely unlikely that this disparate group would be the focus of even loosely organised social unrest. In many ways they would make an easy target for a police service seeking the support of the wider community and certainly for politicians seeking the popular vote. The real problem is what would we do next.

It is doubtful that a further criminalisation of people found begging on our streets would prove a cost-effective and long-term solution to their problems. Warnings and cautions might divert some people on the fringes of begging from these activities but it is extremely likely that the great majority – particularly the large group with identified alcohol-related problems – would simply be diverted to other geographical locations with a lesser police presence or perhaps diverted into the commission of more serious criminal acts. Systematically, throughout this chapter I have used the term 'zero-tolerance-*style*' policing. I have done this for the simple reason that a 'zero-tolerance-*in totality*' approach has proved an impossibility to implement or sustain either in the USA or the UK. In New York City an extra 7,000 police officers were employed, and sophisticated computer crime mapping techniques were used, to rationalise the police response to *target* specific areas for a limited time (see Bratton, 1997). A more accurate description of the New York initiative – and certainly all zero-tolerance-style experiments in Britain, where it should be noted extra resources have not been made available (see Pollard, 1997) – would be the *selective intolerance* of a targeted crime problem (Hopkins Burke, 1998c). Discretion is an inevitable and essential tool of a hard-pressed police service that always had to prioritise its resources (see Bayley, 1994; Morgan and Newburn, 1997). I have observed with my own eyes that even where a high profile zero-tolerance policing strategy is supposedly being pursued – for example, New York City in 1995, or King's Cross, London in 1996 – (at least some) passive, unobtrusive and extremely polite beggars have gone about their business with apparently little intervention on the part of the authorities.

We should note, moreover, that overt crime control strategies such as 'zero-tolerance' tend to favour commercial interests and are suggestive of the Los Angeles-style policing approach described by Mike Davis (1990), where modern technological surveillance, private security and public sector policing conspire to protect affluent and business areas by excluding the dispossessed from their precincts. It is a selective policing strategy that targets and criminalises the deprived and disadvantaged, the sad and mad, in order to protect business and commercial interests. It is simply *unfair*.

People have a right to be protected against aggression, intimidation and incivilities and it is appropriate that the police take action to ensure this protection. The zero-tolerance targeting of beggars is, nonetheless, fraught with dangers and there are three closely linked reasons why this is the case. First, there is the pragmatic case. The criminalisation of begging and associated activities will not provide a cost-effective and long-term solution to the problems of poverty and inequality in our society. In short, the incarceration of large sections of society would be an extremely expensive and short-term way in which to maintain social order. Second, there is the normative case. Targeting and criminalising the deprived and disadvantaged is simply *unfair*. The nature of power relations in our society means that policies tend to be directed at those who are already socially excluded and marginalised. Third, there is the threat to civil liberties. Without appropriate safeguards, there is a real danger of a slow drift to a society intolerant to those who fail to conform to a narrow definition of normality. It is that conundrum that this chapter has sought to address; the need to regulate and control those found begging on our streets while heeding the rights and liberties of some of our most disadvantaged and excluded citizens.

Possible solutions to that conundrum will need to be targeted at two distinct but closely interconnected levels of intervention. First, at a micro-(or street) level, action against those involved in begging and other street-level incivilities will only be successful in the long term if the police act in partnership with other agencies – both professional and voluntary – in dealing with all aspects of the problem. There seems absolutely no point in introducing 'zero-tolerance' policing strategies that simply remove beggars from the streets and displace their activities to other areas or that criminalise and incarcerate them at great expense to the taxpayer. Nevertheless, a micro-strategy will only work if there is a political commitment to deal with the long established societal problem of economic exclusion. Hence, at a macro-(or societal) level, there needs to be a policy commitment to ensure the reintegration of excluded groups back into the mainstream of included society.

References

Archard, P. (1979) *Vagrancy, alcoholism and social control*, London: Macmillan.

Baudrillard, J. (1981) *For a critique of the political economy of the sign*, St Louis, MO: Telos Press.

Baudrillard, J. (1988) *Selected writings*, Stanford, CA: Stanford University Press.

Bauman, Z. (1989) *Modernity and the holocaust*, Cambridge: Polity Press.

Bauman, Z. (1991) *Modernity and ambivalence*, Cambridge: Polity Press.

Bauman, Z. (1993) *Postmodern ethics*, Oxford: Blackwell.

Bayley, D. (1994) *Police for the future*, New York, NY: Oxford University Press.

Beier, A.L. (1985) *Masterless men: The vagrancy problem in England 1560–1640*, London: Methuen.

Bratton, W.J. (1996) 'How we cleared up New York', *The Sunday Times*, 24 November.

Bratton, W.J. (1997) 'Crime is down in New York City: blame the police', in N. Dennis (ed) *Zero tolerance: Policing a free society*, London: Institute for Economic Affairs.

Coldham, P. (1992) *Emigrants in chains*, Baltimore, MD: Genealogical Publishing.

Conroy, J. (1975) *Some men of our time: A study of vagrancy*, MA Dissertation, Department of Sociology, University of Leicester.

Crowther, C. (1998) 'Policing the excluded society', in R. Hopkins Burke (ed) *Zero tolerance policing*, Leicester: Perpetuity Press.

Currie, E. (1997) 'The scalpel not the chainsaw: the US experience with public order', *City: Analysis of Urban Trends, Culture, Theory, Policy, Action*, vol 1, no 8, pp 132-7.

Davis, M. (1990) *The city of quartz: Excavating the future in Los Angeles*, London: Verso.

Dennis, N. and Mallon, R. (1997) 'Confident policing in Hartlepool', in N. Dennis (ed) *Zero tolerance: Policing a free society*, London: Institute for Economic Affairs.

Giddens, A. (1994) *Beyond Left and Right*, Cambridge: Polity Press.

Hagan, J. and McCarthy, B. (1997) *Mean streets: Youth crime and homelessness*, Cambridge: Cambridge University Press.

Harvey, D. (1989) *The condition of Postmodernity: An enquiry into the origins of cultural change*, Oxford: Basil Blackwell.

Healey, J. (1988) *The grass arena*, London: Faber & Faber.

Hopkins Burke, R. (1998a) 'Begging, vagrancy and disorder', in R. Hopkins Burke (ed) *Zero tolerance policing*, Leicester: Perpetuity Press.

Hopkins Burke, R. (1998b) 'A contextualisation of zero tolerance policing strategies', in R. Hopkins Burke (ed) *Zero tolerance policing*, Leicester: Perpetuity Press.

Hopkins Burke, R. (1998c) 'The socio-political context of zero tolerance policing strategies', *Policing: An International Journal of Police Strategies and Management*, vol 21, no 4, pp 666-82.

Hopkins Burke, R. (1998d) 'An Englishman in New York City: critical reflections on zero tolerance policing', *Police Quarterly: Journal of the Police Section of the Academy of Criminal Justice Sciences (ACJS) and the Police Executive Research Forum (PERF)*.

Jessop, B. (1990) *Regulation theory and the transition to post-Fordism*, Cambridge: Polity Press.

Johnston, P. (1997) 'Mean streets where they test the zero option', *The Daily Telegraph*, 8 January.

Kelling, G.L. and Coles, C.M. (1996) *Fixing broken windows: Restoring order and reducing crime in our communities*, New York, NY: The Free Press.

Lea, J. and Young, J. (1984) *What is to be done about law and order?*, Harmondsworth: Penguin.

Lyotard, J.-F. (1984) *The postmodern condition: A report on knowledge*, Manchester: Manchester University Press.

Metropolitan Police (1995) *Policing Plan 1995/96*, Scotland Yard: Metropolitan Police.

Morgan, R. (1997) 'Swept along by zero option', *The Guardian*, 22 January.

Morgan, R. and Newburn, T. (1997) *The future of policing*, Oxford: Clarendon Press.

Murdoch, A. (1994) *We are human too: A study of people who beg*, London: Crisis.

Pearce, D. and Harrison, J. (1997) '"Broken Windows" – NYPD Blues', *Police*, December, p 11.

Pollard, C. (1997) 'Zero-tolerance: short term fix, long-term liability', in N. Dennis (ed) *Zero tolerance: Policing a free society*, London: Institute for Economic Affairs.

Postan, M. (1972) *The medieval economy and society*, Harmondsworth: Penguin.

Read, S. (1997) 'Below zero', *Police Review*, 17 January.

Reiner, R. (1997) 'Policing and the police', in M. Maguire, R. Morgan and R. Reiner (eds) *The Oxford handbook of criminology*, Oxford: Clarendon Press.

Rogers, N. (1991) 'Policing the poor in eighteenth century London: the vagrancy laws and their administration', *Histoire Sociale (Social History)*, no 24, pp 127-47.

Romeanes, T. (1998) 'A question of confidence: zero tolerance and problem oriented policing', in R. Hopkins Burke (ed) *Zero tolerance policing*, Leicester: Perpetuity Press.

Rose, L. (1988) *Rogues and vagabonds*, London: Routledge.

Scarman, Lord (1981) *The Brixton disorders 10-12 April, Report of an inquiry by the Rt Honourable Lord Scarman*, Cmnd. 8427, London: HMSO.

Silverman, E.B. (1998) 'Below zero tolerance: the New York experience', in R. Hopkins Burke (ed) *Zero tolerance policing*, Leicester: Perpetuity Press.

Slack, P. (1974) 'Vagrants and vagrancy in England, 1598–1664', *Economic History Review*, no 27, pp 360–79.

Sparks, R. (1992) 'Reason and unreason in "Left realism": some problems in the constitution of the fear of crime', in R. Matthews and J. Young (eds) *Issues in realist criminology*, London: Sage Publications.

Taylor, I. (1997) 'New York/Manchester: zero tolerance or reclaim the streets', *City: Analysis of Urban Trends, Culture, Theory, Policy, Action*, vol 1, no 8, pp 139-48.

Wadham, J. (1998) 'Zero tolerance policing: striking the balance', in R. Hopkins Burke (ed) *Zero tolerance policing*, Leicester: Perpetuity Press.

Wilson, J.Q. and Kelling, G.L. (1982) 'Broken windows', *Atlantic Monthly*, March, pp 29-38.

Index

Y

young people 53, 63–77, 189–91, 222
youth training 67–8, 69
Youth Training Bridging Allowance 69
youth transitions *see* transitions

Z

zero-tolerance policing 219, 220,
223–7
failure 99, 231–2
in UK 14, 58, 221, 224, 226–7, 231